CHALLENGING
WOMEN

To
Joe, Kate, Same and Eddy

CHALLENGING
W O M E N

*Gender, Culture
and Organization*

SU MADDOCK

SAGE Publications
London • Thousand Oaks • New Delhi

First published 1999

 SAGE Publications Ltd
6 Bonhill Street
London EC2A 4PU

SAGE Publications Inc.
2455 Teller Road
Thousand Oaks, California 91320

SAGE Publications India Pvt Ltd
32, M-Block Market
Greater Kailash – I
New Delhi 110 048

British Library Cataloguing in Publication data

A catalogue record for this book is available
from the British Library

ISBN 0 7619 5150 4
ISBN 0 7619 5151 2 (pbk)

Library of Congress catalog card number 98–61179

Typeset by Mayhew Typesetting, Rhayader, Powys
Printed and bound in Great Britain by Athenaeum Press, Gateshead

Contents

Acknowledgements

This book is the result of ten years work with women managers working in local government and in local organisations. Many of the women interviewed in the early 1990s were inspirational at a time when it was difficult to introduce new ways of working into the mainstream. I wanted to give voice to those challenging and committed women who struggled to reorganize services when it was difficult and who often suffered for their integrity. Shifting male gender cultures is not an easy process – and is not about male and female differences but establishing more open and egalitarian relationships between women, and between men and women. It is a political process not a creed.

The women in this book contributed to a significant culture shift in British society even if many avoided the term feminist, a term misappropriated many years ago. Glynis Burgoyne, Rohima Khan, Julie and Cath Joyce, Maureen Ryan who worked in community projects were exceptional in their energy and commitment. I should also mention those women who straddled the interface between local council and the community, and who worked to change internal practices and 'join-up' services long before the current government's modernization programme. A few examples being Caroline Bond, Pat Cochrane, Annie Grice, Annie Faulder, Juliet Pierce, Lily Rushton, and Jude Stoddart.

We all shift ground and interests and I would probably not have managed to complete the process of writing were it not for Di Parkin, Bronwen Holden and Simon Miller. I was also galvanized by the support of Graham Frost, Pat Gore, Marion Macalpine, Miranda Miller, Hilary Wainwright, Judith Weymont and Joyce Maddock.

At Sage Commissioning Editor Rosemary Nixon and Production Editor Vanessa Harwood have been extremely supportive, and without the administrative support of Lorna Tittle and Janet Pike I would have been lost.

Introduction

This book is concerned with the role that women play in organizational change and how male gender cultures influence the direction of public administration transformation. The influence of male gender cultures on men, women and institutions is tacitly accepted but its effect on challenging women and their creativity is little acknowledged. Gender matters are complex and the dominant gender culture influences men and women in their reactions to those who challenge common narratives and behaviours. Women are not all the same; they are as diverse as men and every woman has her own particular way of handling the male cultures in which we live. The accounts in this book demonstrate how challenging women managers are extremely innovative and should be in demand within any changing global economy in which people are struggling to adapt and survive. Yet the voice of radical women is suppressed and rarely heard because, in spite of the logic of economics, the patriarchal attitudes remain powerful throughout the world, in the west as anywhere else.

The women most irritated by male cultures are those who are vilified precisely because they are radical managers. Gender debate within business and organizations focuses on senior women and on women's distinctive management style, but there is little public recognition of challenging women nor of the role they play in organizational change and especially within public sector transformation.

Those innovators who can shift the pendulum swings between the market and bureaucratic, rule-bound behaviour are in demand. Equality programmes continue to focus on women as victims and the potential of women as transforming innovators is hidden behind a smokescreen of rhetoric about 'gender differences'. Organizational theorists and management gurus talk of 'dismantling structures', 'virtual organizations', the retro-organization and taking down the Berlin Walls which continue to separate employees. The language has changed from one of competition to one of partnership, network and collaboration. Within the British public sector the market is no longer considered a satisfactory motor for change – yet market mechanisms and managerialism have colonized thinking on the 'Left', the 'Right' and in administrations. The way in which New Public Management has taken root in many public administrations is through a systems approach and through structural change – in spite of the renewed interest in 'individual agents'. There is a need for sustaining organizational cultures, but the reality in many public authorities is an intensification of work and the blame culture. The top-down systems approach to change gave rise to a huge interest in senior executives and women high-flyers – but it is clear that the vision of senior managers is important only as a gate through which creativity can flow from many others below them. Even senior individuals can only act as innovative catalysts. They can never be substitutes for healthy work environments which sustain staff and their relationships with those inside and outside the organization.

Organizations cannot deliver quality services if their staff are unwilling to participate in change and are not motivated to work collectively. The spirit of competition has become redundant within the 'global market' and in service organizations where those with the confidence to seek out new partners and 'know-how' to develop trusting and collaborative relationships are to be nurtured. Notions such as 'partnership' and 'collaboration' are hardly new or revolutionary – but valuing the ideas of co-operation and collaboration is very different from knowing how to get hostile parties to co-operate.

Managers are searching for ways to improve servicing and to motivate staff, recognizing that both were difficult under the command–control management regime. There is an interest in new organizational forms which will encourage partnerships, learning and change. The concept of innovation is not usually connected with social relationships but with high-tech research. However, it is precisely the lack of collaboration and motivation in all sectors which focuses attention on what conditions and factors facilitate positive people relationships and partnership in organizations. Critical to new forms of partnerships, alliance and networking are 'trusting relationships' which release the social capital in any community of its people and their resources. Yet these new forms and collaborative cultures are hard to find.

The search for new forms and partnerships in a climate of competivity is also hampered by the tendency of the male academic establishment to seek new models in the mainstream when the creative process is developed in the margins. A synergy between 'innovative individuals' and 'structures' is required if social innovators are to be given the space, opportunity and encouragement to kick-start the transformation processes. This is no easier in a competitive environment than it was within the rigidity of corporatism and bureaucracy; the obstacles to partnership and social change are not so neatly packaged as previously presented by various forms of Marxism or liberal economic theory. Both bureaucratic and competitive purchasing systems create suspicion rather than openness and while there is a desire for change, there is also a mismatch of systems. For instance, companies spend huge sums of money on training and career development while at the same time 'downsizing' and 'restructuring' – thereby creating insecurity and hostility. Executives may declare a commitment to partnership but then rely on reductionist performance measurement which is insensitive to emergent relationships. Within the global market few feel safe from redundancy; most are fearful of not meeting unrealistic goals or are unable both to develop practices and fulfil existing workloads. The resultant increase in employee stress, sickness rates and reduction in morale makes learning new ways of working less rather than more likely.

There is a desperate need for strategic management frameworks and change processes that will motivate rather than demoralize staff and which will encourage and support partnership and innovation. Policymakers are seeking partnership and collaboration and need to know the following:

- What type of organizational framework can generate a sustaining culture and encourage staff to work collaboratively?
- What are the critical conditions for a collaborative culture?
- What structures, if any, will allow staff to forge new relationships inside and outside the organization in order to respond to local conditions flexibly while endorsing corporate principles?
- How to support collaborative working relationships and to kick-start a process of change?
- How to identify resistance to social innovators and overcome it?

Answers to the above questions presuppose a social value framework that supports social transformation and staff relationships which are capable of developing more inclusive forms of measurement. A paradigm shift in thinking about change is needed which focuses on a people perspective rather than technical systems, in order to facilitate a meeting of minds between leaders and those engaged in grassroots activity. At a time when corporations are searching for a new business ethic and public sector transformation is at a turning point, those who have experience of developing social alternatives are vital to the organizational transformation. The experience of those in the sociale economie makes them trailblazers in terms of networking and new ways of working. Although evidence of networking is often absent in mainstream research and organizations, it is thriving in the margins where people are struggling to develop new organizational forms. It is these innovators who are the most likely to demonstrate pathways for social change, in organizations and across apparently deep cultural divides.

Public sector transformation

The UK political climate in the 1970s was a time of radical change, with local activists stimulating debates around local democracy, diversity and decentralization. Issues concerning community involvement, local accountability, service responsiveness and the need for more integrated services were debated in many community consultation meetings and in some council chambers. More radical decentralization policies led many radical women to believe that there were possibilities for them within local government, especially in metropolitan authorities and the Greater London Council. Thousands of women became managers in local government during the 1980s. Many had been active in the women's movement, including those in northern cities such as Leeds, Sheffield and Manchester. The changing nature of local government and the fact that so many women had a strong commitment to public sector provision created an ideal opportunity to analyse their distinctive contribution to management and organizations.

Those women managers chosen for interview were innovative and passionate about the public services and their desire to transform management practices. They were innovators, leaders and confident of alternatives; they were accustomed to discussion and supported each other. Their views were not merely representative of women's experience but demonstrated the extent to which these particular women were innovators capable of thinking through many of the obstacles to partnership, collaboration and new organizational agencies. Although frustrated and thwarted by male gender cultures, these women were far from being victims, but were innovative and daring in their efforts to challenge institutional practice in order to transform public sector management and to develop more equitable and better local services.

Findings

What emerged from the research was that women managers appeared to have a strategic approach to change both inside and outside organizations. These women were challenging structures and the management frameworks; they were less concerned with style and more with social objectives and inclusive management. Those with experience of the sociale economie sector and community organizations were experienced at juggling social objectives within finite finances, at negotiation and in developing contacts and networks staff. Those with previous experience in innovative projects appeared to have the advantage of a knowledge of how to resolve tension conflict and handle ambiguity. These women also had a sense of 'connectedness' and were confident of the possibility of collaborative working partnerships. This was particularly true of those who had worked on the margins of local government in the community or radical community projects. They had learnt how to build bridges between users and mainstream services and were well suited to co-ordinate inter-agency work and partnership. Radical women with diverse and varied experience had observed the tensions between policy and real lives, management formalities and local diversity, which made them astute and good judges of realistic strategies and other potential managers. This ability to make judgements on the basis of a breadth of experience enabled some women to be able to assess which type of change programmes would work and which would not.

This is a significant skill, given that the major problem in almost all organizations is how to create cultures which will sustain collaboration. This is something which those institutionalized in bureaucratic departments find difficult, whereas those on the margins have had the experience of developing new ways of interacting and working and have less fear of change.

Women managers did have a strong 'user' focus, which influences their everyday judgements and decision-making, and a people approach to change. Themes emerged that reinforced some fundamental thinking which many of the women shared. These factors, experiences and attitudes made them innovators in organizational change. They tended to have a principled but hands-off approach which stimulated motivation among some and hostility among those opposed to change and their ideas. Characteristics of these radical women included:

- a process approach to change and new relationships;
- a people approach, not a systems approach;
- confidence in the social values of the organization;
- a local connectedness or social awareness;
- confidence that those who are on the margins or challengers were instrumental in social transformation;
- a confidence in the community and the workforce that inspired trusting relationships.

Although cultures vary from company to company, many of the frustrations and experiences recounted by the women in this book in their struggle for social change are not confined to those in local government or in the UK but appear to be common to organizations in all sectors. The most radical women who were insistent about the need for a change in public sector management if services were to improve showed:

- confidence in alternatives based on social values;
- ability to handle diversity, ambiguity and change;
- experience in developing organizations where social objectives determined work – plans, programmes and indicators;
- an awareness of diversity and gender cultures;
- a capacity to be critically aware and capable of trusting others;
- a desire to develop a collaborative culture.

Challenging women are shown to have a significant role to play in the transformation processes – and exhibit the very skills required to manage change programmes. The problem remains that the gender cultures within organizations thwart such women. In the 1980s it was difficult for women to deviate from the civil servant role and traditional practices and radical women were ridiculed for being outspoken. These women were thwarted, ridiculed and sometimes 'sacked' or penalized, often for management innovation. Although most women are struggling to shed the male definitions of them, those women who challenge the criteria and frameworks are most vilified. Questioning women were often said to be a nuisance and when they voiced their opinions and attempted to initiate change they were bypassed or sidetracked. The women interviewed were largely committed to social change not personal career development, yet were penalized for their leadership qualities. Women have been developing new ways to manage for many years but their potential and skills were not recognized in middle management unless they adopted 'caring' or 'coping' responses. The male preferences which underpinned acceptable manager qualities and practices continue to undervalue those women who do not conform to female roles. It was precisely because so many women felt constrained that they were zealous in their efforts to transform management.

Those most political in their outlook labelled themselves 'challengers'. They rarely used the term 'innovator' and the majority thought that their perspective on management was really just 'commonsense'. Those women who were confident of new possibilities were able to transcend the pressures because they had the vision in alternative practices which many of their colleagues lacked. Their decisions and managing style were rooted in their political perspectives and social values. They were concerned to influence change or inject social values into the work culture and they recognized that without an agreed (corporate) social-value base within management, partnership would be difficult between workers and managers, community and officers, men and women. Women's own experience, thinking and politics make an enormous difference to their confidence in alternative forms and ways of working.

Those who questioned traditional practices recognized that promotion was unlikely to be offered to them. Senior women were well aware that had they been innovative in the middle grades they would have been less likely ever to have been promoted; they were often politicized by the boys' room banter in the board room. Quite unconsciously gender management strategies divide women and there is a growing tension between those who are committed to change and those who are more energetic in 'making the systems work'. Women who are personally ambiguous often have to be very skilled at management in order to overcome the pressures to conform. The macho climate of the 1980s resulted in a growing tension between those who challenged performance management and those who were intent upon improving their managerial skills and making the systems work. It is difficult to remain confident of social change during periods of restructuring when parameters are constantly shifting around narrow financial objectives unless reinforced by experience and active engagement with the realities of the processes of change. It is both an opportune and difficult time for managers who have to grapple with structural change while also being 'open' in their leadership style in order to steer staff in the direction of 'collaboration' within the combative environment of market contracting.

Many women wanted managers to develop a greater responsibility for services and respect for users. Decentralization policies in the UK were largely ineffective because they did not dismantle bureaucratic practices and could not respond to the needs of various communities and local people. Local democracy requires sustenance and cannot be decreed 'overnight' from 'the top' by politicians. Managers need to develop organizational parameters that can encourage the community and their staff to engage with each other more openly. Since the 1980s government public sector reforms and managerialism have been tempered by public service staff, managers and practitioners and the public; who demonstrated the limitations of the market and fought for various forms of 'quasi market' by active transformations, partnerships and alliances. This is not merely because of a change of government, although that provides some cultural change, but is dependent on collaboration between agencies and individuals at all levels of service with organizations and institutions which measure what matters as well as money.

The conflicts between women usually concerned their gender management strategies. There is a need to unpack the mindsets and thinking among women as well as traditional gendered power relations. Too often, the emphasis on 'definitive theory' has dismissed the voice of those women most engaged with change, almost because they did not fall into the convenient stereotype of the downtrodden. Radical practitioners and difficult women are apparently 'deviants', not leaders or innovators. The most frustrating experience for those demanding systems change in local government was the belief in the neutrality of management and the total separation between policy and practice. The political lack of interest in the effects of bureaucratic practices on all was then transferred to managerial methods. The question that policymakers need to ask is why are so many strong and articulate women managers underutilized during periods of transformation when all organizations are desperate for alternative practices and innovative staff.

The inability of managers and policymakers to comprehend the obstacles to change appeared to be largely due to the entrenched male gendered cultures and the dominance of 'gender narratives' that ridicule radical and challenging women – a fact given force by the cases of Professor Wendy Savage, Dr Daly and Alison Halford. Overcoming traditional divides and working beyond 'role' with colleagues in other agencies and departments in the public sector is fraught with difficulties and innovators frequently make enemies rather than allies when they tentatively suggest changes or challenge tradition. The irony of the situation is that those senior managers and theorists who claim that the collaborative culture is the key to transforming public service practices do not acknowledge or accept challenging women and continue to characterize them as 'difficult'.

Many women were aware that to be too direct about the operation of gender dynamics was a dangerous strategy. Even those conscious of the deep gendered underpinning of management knew it was better to focus on specific projects rather than to challenge irritating, patronizing behaviour or object to personal slights. There was a tacit acknowledgement to remain 'silent' about gender dynamics, however frustrating that proved to be. Many men realized the extent of the power of male attitudes and culture and appeared to be just as 'cowed' by them. Masculinity and male codes do need unpacking but the spate of press articles (1996) suggesting that 'men are misunderstood victims' is disingenuous. Women manipulate because they cannot be straightforward within a male culture; men remain silent about masculinity because of its confining nature. Articles presenting men as victims are unhelpful for the male gender cultures oppress men as well as women; but this is a much narrower oppression than that experienced by women who have to survive within an alien male public world. If gender analysis were more seriously focused on the dynamic within gender cultures and its influence on organizational practices, then men and women may be less threatened by women's capacity to transform practices and relationships. An openness about male gender identities and masculinities is needed. Traditional masculinities undoubtedly inhibit possibility and confidence in alternative relationships – would benefit both men and women and certainly allow communication to be both freer and more open.

However, although gender cultures play a dominant role in the continuation of blocking tactics in organizations, so too do the professions, economic and management systems. The polarized thinking of the market and state, biology and the environment, public and private, or male and female is far too limiting and makes the articulation of the transforming processes difficult. The language is missing and those who are cognisant of the key process relationships are unnoticed, undervalued and unrewarded. While the centralizing role of national governments results in people feeling powerless within the modern world, there is also strong evidence in the UK public sector of how collective and individual agency can have a transforming effect on even the economic and management mechanisms; although they appear immutable, they are in fact malleable. These transforming relationships are not ineffectual and do play a role in resisting change and socializing work cultures. Although employees are weak as individuals and people are colonized by overpowering economic and management narratives, challenging innovators can generate sea change in thinking as well as structural revolutions and work towards new structures, new ways of working and the introduction of social value to management decisions. Out of the old divides is emerging a new nexus of power relationships, especially between agencies, staff and consumers; but to be effective and sustaining they need political support and financial and regulatory frameworks.

There needs to be a synergy between the 'social realities of individuals' and 'conceptual paradigms'. New paradigms for organizations and thinking are developed on the margins, not by the establishments. Change agents are on the margins of the western world, corporations and the formal and male establishments. Yet, the search for the individual innovators and identification of their leadership skills continues in the mainstream, using traditional measures and techniques. Making sense of gender relations is part of the process of change. Individuals can overcome the confines of material, social and intellectual mindsets more easily when the reality of an alternative is articulated or experienced. The following chapters show that, in spite of the obstacles, women are never so passive or so trapped that they cannot create new realities and relationships – even if only within their own department.

Challenging and creative women

From talking to creative women managers a powerful conclusion emerges that they cannot be contained within one category; neither do they conform to one model, refer to one philosophy, nor maintain one strategy. But they do share a holistic and analytical approach. They appraise their work cultures, environments and colleagues and make informed judgements, which are not merely rational (in the narrow sense) but the result of an intellectual feeling and experience. They talk of moving between having a sense of optimism for change and a deep pessimism. They are tactical and strategic, thoughtful and reflective, sometimes passive and sometimes very determining. Their sense of possibility is dependent not just on themselves, their thinking and experience, but on their work environments and support from colleagues – especially that of the chief executive. They demonstrate the potency of agency, but also its tendency to sleep and hide when oppressed or overwhelmed by alienating social surroundings. Each woman has her own personal (political) philosophy which is not insignificant in her attitude to her own role as a change agent. It is the conceptualizations of individual agency and potency within a framework of institutional con-straints which is difficult, especially if individuals are thought of as isolated beings, either trapped or empowered, depending on the particular (political) perspective of the observer.

Gender culture oppresses not just women but anyone wanting to break free from professional or managerial formalities. If policymakers and politicians desire an egalitarian infrastructure for service and its manage-ment, then management needs to be anchored by local connection, social values and a people-oriented approach to change. Women are breaking through the barriers of gendered institutional and professional traditions and challenging the motor of globalization and authoritarian relationships. They are capable of steering public sector management on a course which brings synergy between fair industrial relations and staff development and closer to 'quality' service provision. However, a lack of seriousness about the gender imbalance in politics and economic life has resulted in a distorted colonization of New Public Management that monitors perform-ance by reductionist measures of efficiency which inhibit evolving and emergent relationships upon which partnership is dependent. Depressingly, those who have most experience of managing social change and developing new organizational forms and practice are not those who are determining either policy or the public sector restructuring process.

1   Management innovation

> Downsizing has resulted in increasing levels of stress, insecurity, lack of trust and
> decreasing motivation, fun and career opportunities. Survivors are less prepared
> to initiate new ideas and participate whole heartedly for the good of the
> company as their own futures are uncertain. This suffest a conflicting scenario
> from the perspective of generating creativity and innovation in the workplace,
> this confirming the motivational paradox. (Sahdev and Vinnicombe 1977: 15)

The concept of globalization and the realities of international trade have
had a deadening effect on politicians and organizations. However, while
there has been vigorous opposition in the UK to the 'free market', there is
much less debate about the colonized thinking about management systems
which appears to be working against the forms of collaborative practices
desperately sought by public sector policymakers. The author suggests that
those developing collaborative practices are innovative and innovators.

The concept of management 'innovation' in this book refers to approaches
to managing and change which could facilitate shared practices and collaborative cultures, and improve working relationships. In the global
marketplace organizations require innovative thinking about management
itself, how to manage staff in a manner which is supportive and developmental rather than commanding and dictatorial. New ways of managing
people and systems are required by organizations in the public, private and
independent sectors. No organization, however small, is immune from the
effects of the international financial markets and the constant flux of
changing markets. Cosmopolitan customers demand both style and quality,
or so the advertisers would have us believe. Business organizations and
public bodies have been through constant and massive restructuring in
search of efficiency and greater competitiveness. Within global markets
competition drives the squeezing of public sector investment, the delayering
of management hierarchies and demands for greater worker flexibility, open
markets and revised tax and welfare systems. The Labour government
(1997–) appears intent upon riding the waves of international capital rather
than attempting to quieten the sea, and the minister responsible for European financial and market integration appears ready to pressurize other
European countries in the same direction.

The term globalization is used and abused, mostly as a blanket term to
describe the domination of international financial markets, and tends to
infer that there is only one global market economy which is set on an
unstoppable trajectory. Undoubtedly the influence of international market

forces can be seen throughout the world. However, globalization is also fuelled by its own terminology and used as a concept to persuade people of the futility of challenging the motor of liberalization. Whole governments appear undermined by this narrative, as do those who seek to socialize international trade; there is, in fact, no dominant system which cannot be tempered within the human sphere. Collective action and social judgements can have an effect on even the most deeply ingrained market and finance systems which are confirmed and operated by conscious people, not robots.

The dominance of one international financial system has the effect of persuading politicians that their role has become managerial rather than political. Yet all systems have a social-value base, some more limited and oppressive than others. The introduction of managerialism into politics and public sector management was intended to create more effective systems which analyse impact and cost as well as activities, but systems themselves have an impact. There is more to politics than law enforcement; there are also socially just rules and systems which are inclusive rather than exclusive–perfecting efficiency is not enough and in politics it is dangerous.

Management and management innovation are not neutral concepts; they can be adapted and changed not only by politicians and leaders but also by collective action from the bottom up. Too often 'management techniques' are assumed to be good or bad. Although the dominant managerial models have serviced capital and have been developed in the private sector, there is no reason why management innovation cannot be articulated and utilized by those wanting to socialize the markets and management – but this requires a critical analysis of the impact of management systems and the development of new approaches to managing staff. Management innovations that support emergent practice are highly significant in a context where competitiveness and quality depend on staff motivation, and where new organizational forms and partnerships are business and political objectives but are thwarted by market conditions. Management approaches and strategies that provide a synergy between standards and diversity and individual judgement and reduce the conflict between workforce and managers in a context of change are much needed.

What do we mean by innovation?

The Austrian economist, Joseph Schumpeter (1947), first distinguished between the concepts of invention and innovation. He suggested that whereas invention was about finding out about new things, innovation was about making things work better. Invention and innovation both tend to be associated with research and development (R&D), invention and products. Creative scientists and intellectuals are viewed in the UK as rather isolated, clever but socially inept people, whereas those who manage processes and put ideas into practice are generally seen as more gregarious. People who invent 'things' tend to have very different skills from those who are innovative in their efforts to get things done. Whatever the form of authority, managing people and processes requires greater interpersonal and social skills, whereas inventors tend to be wrapped up in more intellectual or artistic creativity. Chapter 3 analyses the various approaches to management and management skills.

The word innovation tends to be used in the context of scientific R&D to refer to high-tech product development, rather than the quality of people relationships, and conjures up a picture of 'boffins' at work. Invention or innovation are rarely used to describe innovative relationships. However, even the information technology industries require effective communication and positive staff relationships in order to turn innovative product ideas into real new products, increased sales and improved company performance. While individuals may be inspired to be intellectually creative, organizations require innovative environments and working contexts in order to encourage team working among all employees. Innovative management requires very different skills from those involved in product development. It concerns the creation of sustaining environments in which partnerships can develop and employees can work beyond their allocated roles and job functions. A creative environment is one which allows individuals to break from tradition and force new processes and interpersonal relationships. Edith Penrose (1959) was the first to apply the term 'innovation' to organizations and, in particular, to small businesses. For her, business growth depended on a manager's desire for fulfilment, usually by pursuing financial objectives; she considered that business organizations required an open system approach if they were to be innovative. The most significant feature of innovation was not what it referred to but having the personal space or the freedom to be creative. In other words, innovation requires a climate where people are free to innovate. Penrose (1959) suggested that innovation is a creative activity based on three fundamental characteristics:

- an ability to handle ambiguity;
- an overall or total perspective into which to fit the fragmented pieces of information;
- a fresh perspective.

Having vision is not enough. Innovative managers within organizations need to be able to recognize the barriers to change. It is also important to understand how to proceed to the next state or relationship and what obstacles may be encountered on the way. Those leading change or managing within changing circumstances must be able to see past obstacles to their ultimate objective and to envisage strategies and actions to overcome blocks and barriers. This is a quite different skill from overseeing operations and dictating orders within well-established routines. Often those given the responsibility of change are not aware of what is involved in the process, nor of how much they negotiate rather than dictate orders. Sometimes managers are asked and expected to network when they are not free to do more than exchange views and have no power to initiate; they merely report to their corporate managers on contacts. In other words they are being asked to be creative within very confined boundaries and set parameters. This is very different from management innovation which is about breaking out of the existing frameworks or boundaries, whether in scientific thinking, in organizations or in relationships.

The big idea or management innovation at the beginning of the twentieth century was 'scientific management', a mechanical model of organization that was seized upon as the blueprint by American industrialists such as Henry Ford. This model persisted throughout industry and administrations during the 1940s and remained all-powerful until the 1960s. Although challenged by managers and management theorists, it still permeates private industry and public institutions in both the UK and the USA. 'Taylorist' concepts continue to dominate the thinking of the western world on how to organize labour in the production process. Until the 1980s, the organization of corporations and public bodies alike was seen as fixed, unassailable and fragmented. Personnel managers were responsible for matching staff to organizational functions and moulding employees to the job and the company culture. Rationalization and efficiency were important themes of organizational analysis from the 1940s until the 1980s, when the overwhelming objective was to make operational systems work faster and more efficiently. Large organizations developed a high degree of vertical compartmentalization and a separation between the managers who managed staff and those who dealt with finance, strategy and sales. Instruction tended to be in the form of commands and bottom-up communication was often nonexistent. The changing nature of the markets and increased competition forced many companies in the 1980s to think more seriously about the 'quality' of their products or services, while also increasing productivity. Peters and Waterman (1982) had a massive success with *In Search of Excellence*, which became the manager's bible for many years. Other American consultants and academics such as Moss Kanter, Porter and Drucker made fortunes by writing popular management recipes on how companies could deliver 'excellence' and profits at the same time. Organizations became aware of the competitive potential of 'quality': 'Excellent quality is not longer a competitive advantage for suppliers . . . without it suppliers are out of the game' (Kanter 1995: 99).

In the service sector the need for sustaining work environments is even more imperative, for staff relationships are the key to quality services. Management innovation within this sector is therefore essentially about developing new ways of working and organizing, with more open communication. Unfortunately, managers are too often obsessed by systems and technologies and confined by hierarchical structures and conformist behaviour. Bureaucratic administrations tend to reinforce negative relationships between managers who centralize, control and reinforce traditional assumptions about junior and female staff, while also generating blame cultures which degenerate into a total lack of motivation towards customers. The fear culture and suspiciousness of government motives resulted in the majority of public-sector employees viewing almost all restructuring with distaste. Managers have had the problem of delivering and improving services within a context of financial constraint, bureaucratic structures and virulent 'blame' cultures. Those who are attempting to be innovative do so within a sea of formality and rule-bound behaviour and meet blocking tactics and hostility. The traditional organization that relied on line management and central control came under threat as the market speeded up. Line management systems were too cumbersome and repetitive habits among workers and managers were inadequate. The changing market demands competitiveness, efficiency, speed and motivated staff who can deliver greater productivity but with less management control. These changes presented difficulties for the large unwieldy organizations. Corporations had to change and the personality cult of the business guru also grew. Drucker, Moss Kanter, Peters and Waterman spoke as if their global perspective was relevant to their audiences anywhere in the world: 'In future, success will come to those companies, large and small, that can meet global standards and tap into global networks. And it will come to those cities, states and regions that do the best job of linking businesses that operate with them in the global economy' (Kanter 1995: 163).

In order to meet these new pressures, the very form and structure of the large corporation and public administration came under threat. Multinationals such as IBM dramatically restructured in an attempt to devolve responsibility to smaller and more motivated work teams.

New organizations

A new discourse emerged on the New Organizations (Peters and Waterman 1982; Drucker 1989) which represented a shift away from the competitive monocorporations towards flatter, decentralized units co-ordinated by a central corporate body. Paul Thompson suggests that there are three alternative modes of organization: the hierarchical bureaucracy; the competitive trading firm; the networking group of companies which collaborates (Thompson and McHugh 1990). There is reported to be a move towards the networking form (N-form) which relies on partnership and collaboration away from both the market and the bureaucracy which is neither a bureaucratic organization nor a 'cowboy firm'. The network form is a more permeable or osmotic organization and reflects the desire among executives and theorists for organizational arrangements which can deliver a management focus on the following:

- achieving synergy across the organization;
- ensuring all activities add value;
- adding value to the organization as a whole;

- establishing partnerships and alliances with other parts of the same organization and external stakeholders;
- promoting new streams of product or service while maintaining old streams of delivery.

Ferlie and Pettigrew (1996) assume that the network type of agency and flatter organizations are more commercially viable and capable of much greater responsiveness than either the bureaucratic administration or the isolated competing company. As Vince and Booth (1996) note great things are claimed for the network organizations: 'Felicitous properties, flexibility, responsiveness, adaptability, extensive cross-functional collaborations, rapid and effective decision making, highly committed employees, and so on – not found to the same degree in alternative organisational forms' (Kanter and Eccles 1992: 525).

Unfortunately, there was relatively little evidence of new organizational forms in the early 1990s, either in the public or private sectors (Nohria and Eccles 1992). Few managers appeared to be actively working at any type of transformation process. Executives sought these ideal forms and theorists started to engage with alternative modelling of organizations. Ferlie and Pettigrew (1996) reported that there was some evidence of a shift in international company structures and their interconnection and collaboration, demonstrating a move towards a network-type or N-type organization: 'The network perspective redirects our attention away from formal structure and policy . . . it conceptualises market processes in highly relational and socially embedded terms. Concepts of trust, reciprocity and reputation move centre stage within a network framework (Ferlie and Pettigrew 1996: 82).

Miles and Snow (1995) identified the various types of network organization, including the stable form where a few large firms form partnerships, dynamic networks operating in uncertain environments and the internal networks which flow between the centre and periphery of large multinationals such as Kodak, Hewlett Packard and IBM. Later Miles and Snow (1995) suggested a fourth form, a central organization which connects many mini-networks of companies across a particular sector or industry. According to Baker (1992), the network form is dynamic and can adapt to the pressures of change and accommodate new environments. Responsiveness is at the heart of the network form and is dependent on the quality of the network team and staff relationships. Teamwork, motivation and shared practice are the basis of the network form and distinguish it from traditional organizations and their associated management hierarchies. The N-form is only possible when the focus is on people management, what Miles and Snow (1995) term a 'human investment philosophy' (HIP). This management approach, based on trust and mutual respect rather than command and control, provides the agency with the capacity to evolve and to change. Networks and partnerships only function with managers who take risks and are capable of moving beyond both habit and the immediate towards new unknown relationships. Managers in the N-form have to be able to readjust their attitudes and be open to possibilities, which they cannot do if their efforts are not reinforced and rewarded.

The big question is how to move managers and oceanliner-type corporation or bureaucracy towards being more like the N-form. It is not merely a question of new definitions but of developing mechanisms and processes which reward managers and staff for new relationships, new partnerships and people approaches to management. There has been an assumption in the UK that massive restructuring and macro-economic levers will directly result in new organizational forms – aided and abetted by the market processes of globalization. One of the reasons why effective or real network forms are slow to emerge in the public and private sector (Nophria and Eccles 1992) is because conditions for partnership are missing both in the bureaucratic public administrations and the market environment.

However, networking, inter-agency working and partnerships are common within the sociale economie, the voluntary sector and in community organizations, although hidden away on the marginal sectors of the economy. There is in fact a blossoming of social agencies and forms of social ownership, but this remains under-researched which may account for why a serious discussion about reorganization and management practices was so slow to seep into local government. Le Grand and other academics appear to be uncertain where to fit non-government organizations (NGOs) and social enterprise agencies into their schemata – thinking that the aims of NGOs are either unknown, confused or unclear (Le Grand and Bartlett 1993). This is a little strange given that the objectives in independent organizations are constantly debated and, although difficult to implement, they are certainly not unclear. This uncertainty about NGOs reveals more that researchers have tended to ignore the sociale economie and its role within the UK economy. Since the research base on the sociale economie is weak, then so is the appreciation of the extent of new organizational forms, networking and partnership within the radical end of the sociale economie or not-for-profit sector. By contrast, those involved in social development in the south are well aware of the significance of local enterprise and the voluntary sector in sustaining communities and economies.

Those organizations directed at social gain or social capital can provide examples of both alternative organizational models and new approaches to management through shared interests of workers and board members that have been achieved through local connectedness, social values and personal commitment. Organizations seeking to provide local services, employment or support to disadvantaged communities include a wide range of agencies which within the European context is known as the 'sociale economie'. These can include voluntary organizations, mutual societies, co-operatives, community enterprise and local projects. The significance of the sociale economie sector is that it demonstrates how enterprising organizations can develop trading activity in partnerships with staff and local communities.

The sociale economie also includes various types of community enterprise, credit unions and co-operatives. There is huge diversity ranging from large established charities to small, innovative community projects and businesses, including both profit and non-profit making organizations. Some are well-established voluntary organizations and friendly societies with a rather hierarchical structure while others are local and very innovative.

There is a wealth of voluntary initiatives in the UK. Many, such as the mutual societies, co-operatives and charities, created during the nineteenth century. The Conservative Party turned this tradition to their own advantage in the 1980s and set up new quangos on health in order to undermine local authorities and local elected bodies. The Tory preference for the quango as a substitute for state providers has made the more traditional 'Old Left' suspicious of the not-for-profit sector. However, in spite of the fact that many of the large quangos were and are unaccountable because they operate in an established nexus of social relationships, according to some they often remain as focused on social priorities as other public sector agencies.

One conclusion that could be drawn is that whereas local government and the civil service are subject to constant scrutiny and are tightly regulated and controlled, local non-elected bodies have a much freer hand to operate as they wish. The evidence, however, does not support this assumption. Whilst there have been some well publicised instances of bad practice within non-elected bodies the recent report of the Public Accounts Committee shows the extent to which the majority of instance of failure far from occurring in quangos or agencies were found in the 'old style' government departments. (Stewart et al. 1995)

This managerial form of accountability dominant in British quangos has its roots in the public sector ethic among managers and board members. The power nexus surrounding the way in which quangos operate is complex and owes much to regional commitment. Even those sponsored by central government can, with local involvement, develop locally accountable forms which are more independent than many in the more rigid bodies or financially driven private corporations.

The problem with private sector legal frameworks is that they often totally exclude even the possibility of introducing social relationships and values into trading. By contrast, those in the sociale economie, although focused on trade, training or service provision, are distinctive in terms of their values and social objectives and in the way that staff and volunteers work together. In the sociale economie collaboration and networking are not only desirable but a necessity. Their main asset is social capital and they depend on emerging networks and the ability to form partnerships. Flexible management is the key to innovative NGOs especially in disadvantaged areas where managers have to be able to handle community disputes and complex financial balance sheets. The significance of the independent organization is that it provides a range of organizational

frameworks which embrace diversity, staff flexibility and local accountability is undeniable.

The difference between organizations within the sociale economie and
those driven by the market is their prioritization of social values, reinvest-
ment of surplus income and attitudes to the broader community. They seek
social rather than financial gain. Those organizations in the local and
developing sociale economie are very different from the large corporation
mutual societies, charities and quangos in that they are not merely focused
on market opportunities but on local need, social priorities and conser-
vation. Many have grown out of the social movements, including the
women's movement. Local projects have developed legal frameworks and
ways of working which are just not visible in the press or in research and
are often missing in larger established organizations. These more innovative and often local projects have some common characteristics:

- local connectedness;
- social value objectives;
- rely on sound relationships/people;
- flexible in response to need;
- models of governance;
- new ways of working;
- employment for the marginal (socially excluded);
- staff managed by strategy rather than control supervision.

The network form is essentially a learning organization and depends on
more confident social relationships from which alternative models of
organization emerge; modelling does not change realities, people do. Social
relationships and social networks have to be developed as well as con-
ceptualised and they require nurture and support. A commitment to individual learning is key to network success in any sector. The shared value
base is the strength of the sociale economie but organizations in this sector
do not generate immediate or interim financial returns and often reflect a
loss on the balance sheet – yet their social return is great. Measuring social
gain is as huge a problem for the smaller sociale economie sector as it is for
small business. This is why social audit is critical for SMEs and non-
governmental agencies. Social audit provides accounting tools which can
relate business agendas to local need and demonstrate the value of social
capital and local connection to business development and public sector
agencies.

Innovation in small organizations: marginal to the mainstream

Interestingly, community organizations and NGOs exhibit many similarities and suffer from many of the same problems as innovative small
businesses. They are:

- marginal to mainstream business;
- a challenge to existing businesses;
- service a market niche;
- cluster together in specific locations;
- respond to specific interests.

Innovative community and local economic projects demonstrate these same characteristics; some of which public administrators can experience as a nuisance. This is not surprising since social innovators do not respect convention given that they are breaking new ground. Although respected as creative such innovators present a threat and are treated as outsiders by managers and those in the mainstream of the profession. Innovation is radical by nature and when first presented it may seem strange and mistaken, even though twenty years later the same idea becomes incorporated and accepted within the establishment as commonplace. For instance, many of the services developed by feminists in the 1970s such as battered women's refuges were at the time controversial and met with resistance. Yet within ten years these refuges had become accepted as a part of mainstream local authority housing provision.

Women are extremely active in innovation at the local level and in NGOs and community groups, but they are rarely visible as directors of the larger sociale economie negotiating agencies. Women are key to local social innovation, whether in the voluntary or trading sector. They often set up new community organizations, only to have them taken over by men when they become successful. This is true in all communities: a growing Bangladeshi women's clothing company was destroyed by jealous men and by local Labour politicians who listened to male leaders and never sought the women's views.

Although there are many similarities between NGOs and small businesses, there are also some significant differences, the major one being the legal frameworks of those in the social economie which enshrine social objectives. These organizations seek to be effective and efficient as well as democratic, which requires good communication networks and negotiation skills. The smaller radical organizations seek to be democratic as well as effective and it is these agencies which are involved in city regeneration and poverty alleviation programmes through the development of local projects and communities, providing work or local services. Interestingly, much of the American literature on the management of change was based on work by community organizations in grassroots reorganizations in poor areas; for example, Alinksy, the development worker who set up local projects with the Polish community in Chicago. Within the community context it is possible for employees and the community to collaborate because they desire social change and each party has some degree of shared commitment and values.

Peter Drucker (1989) has drawn attention to the role of the not-for-profit sector in the USA and to the fact that often those leading innovation within the community were women. Women develop and work in community-based projects because within them they can find the space and opportunity to develop their own ways of working; this is true of black, Asian and working-class women as well as white women. Those who have had experience within NGOs tend to have a corporate view and a grasp of local detail. Social enterprise and many NGOs provide models for public sector agencies. They are accountable, but small enough to be flexible, and staff are more likely to be motivated because they are committed to the agency. Those countries which lack small businesses and local involvement in any forms of the sociale economie are not just poorer in services and work, but are likely to have weaker democratic structures.

Pressures and weaknesses within the sociale economie sector

A major problem for many NGOs and local enterprise is that they are pushed to become more like mainstream organizations and businesses in order to gain credit, credibility and grants. There is a danger that too many innovative organizations will cease to be innovative because they are forced into forms of management, accounting and structures which work against their strengths of informal networking, responsiveness and social auditing. Like the private sector, independent social enterprise and NGOs are subject to market pressures; they have to meet deadlines, fulfil contracts and evaluate returns on investment. The difficulties of how to develop volunteers and workers as managers, to place social gain within traditional accounting and to adopt the language of business, efficiency and managerialism have distorted many of the innovative practices in the larger voluntary organizations and the viability of new ventures. The strength of NGOs is their flexibility, but this disappears when grants and contracts start to become too closely tied to administrative structures and numerical targets. During the 1980s many workers were demoralized by the demand from local government that each voluntary organization should be able to match and mirror the local authority's bureaucratic and administrative systems. They had neither the resources nor the administrative back-up to deliver innovation on this basis. Donors, banks and funders pressurize social enterprise to become more businesslike in its management practices. For large organizations such as Age Concern or Citizens' Advice Bureaus this may create efficiency which is not to the detriment of their core work but in newer, smaller and less well financed agencies this pressure can divert workers from the community, cutting them off from the local people with whom and for whom they are building the agency. Investment in administration systems before they are necessary merely takes employees or volunteers away from the important activity of building relationships which is the key to the social agency. Similar tensions are frequently mentioned by those working on development projects and where funders give preference to those local agencies with management systems and practices which mirror their own.

This has a negative impact on local projects which cannot meet short deadlines, do not have the resources for endless reports and presentations and do not know how to formulate elevations before the development process has even begun.

The significant strength of the sociale economie sector is in the relationships between users, staff and managers. Staff are usually committed and motivated, although only recently have such relationships been reflected in contracts. Shared corporate objectives are the key to the level of motivation among board members and staff. However, internal staff dynamics can be autocratic rather than democratic. In many NGOs one person who is the driving force often dominates the organization, usually a founding member and a zealous worker. The more established societies and charities are also extremely bureaucratic. There of course many difficulties involved in managing small organizations: roles are often confused; volunteers are frequently exploited; very strong leaders can dominate meetings, especially when these are too informal and ad hoc. Many voluntary organizations can be chaotic and do give preferential treatment to particular groups. Each worker (paid or unpaid) is expected to act in accordance with the principles and values of the group; the values of the agency unite and drive it. Many agencies have a management body that is resented by the workers. As the people who do the work and have an equal commitment to the organization, they may feel that they should also be running it. Such tensions are common when the employees feel that they are more committed than the management or board members. In larger NGOs the non-executive board members tend to be selected for their fund-raising capacity and status whereas in small organizations they may have local and campaigning experience and want to interfere more with the management agendas.

The downside of innovative people working on innovative projects is that employees and board members can be too passionate and too partial in their work; both employees and management committees can be prejudiced against outsiders. Local connectedness, which is a valuable asset in development and partnerships, can also descend into clan loyalties. Nepotism is as common in local enterprise initiatives as it is in large and small businesses. For instance, many of the unemployed centres and community enterprises developed in Scotland during the 1980s were dominated by men from a particular section of the estates. They were reluctant to help others from different areas and women and younger people tended to avoid these centres. Many of these enterprises were corrupt, but they did provide work and jobs for 400 men – none of whom would not have got work elsewhere. However, the connection between the sociale economie and jobs has narrowed the understanding of these agencies. They are not only concerned with providing jobs but also and more importantly with social development, social gain and social capital. Some transaction schemes do not trade in money or pay their staff.

Clearly many NGOs are neither accountable nor very effective, but their frameworks and commitment to social values allows the possibility of a synergy of interests between board members, staff and community – precisely because of the loose consensus around social values and objectives. In spite of local difficulties, there are lessons to be learnt from the locally based sociale economie sector which provide examples of people actively working at partnerships between local communities, employees and managers in order to develop social capital and social gain. The significant relationships are based on:

- social or local connectedness;
- informality;
- networking;
- strategy skills;
- the importance of juggling personal values with the organization's values.

In spite of the wealth of experience of innovation in the sociale economie and its significance to mainstream management innovation, this sector continues to remain largely unobserved. The significance of the non-government organizations and the radical sociale economies is that they are grappling with how to build organizations which can cope with diversity and be flexible in a manner which balances the interests of community, staff and organizational effectiveness. Although diversity is desired and sought by those in larger organizations, their management systems and criteria often work against change and exclude the marginal and the different from the workforce; they continue to treat staff as unthinking cogs in the machine.

Management innovation in larger organizations

The Japanese are currently experiencing a downturn in the financial sector and are suffering from increased competition from other South East Asian countries. But throughout the 1980s the Japanese dominated both performance and the thinking about how to deliver quality and quantity. Deming, the total quality guru, was ignored for many years in the USA until the Japanese took up his ideas and adopted his systems and philosophy. Deming (1983) developed critical management guidelines which identified faults in the operational systems. He argued that people were motivated to work for improvements as part of their job satisfaction. He sought to ensure 'quality' of services by reinforcing staff involvement in the operational processes. Deming recognized that to achieve quality improvements employees had to have commitment and involvement in the company. Many of the management benchmarks he developed are really guidelines for good management practices, as well as protocols for recognizing operational faults. Deming's philosophy for successful enterprise was based on three basic precepts:

- customer satisfaction;
- continuous improvement;
- quality determined by the system.

The adoption of a continuous or total quality approach resulted in a constant readjustment to changing circumstances, made possible by the vigilance and commitment of employees. This responsiveness was said to:

- reduce waste;
- increase productivity;
- increase turnover.

Deming understood that the morale of the employees was critical to quality service delivery. He recognized the value of frontline staff; their commitment was an essential ingredient for success. Managers had to listen to their staff because they were the people who talked to customers and clients. Deming believed that quality workplaces were the key to motivation and employee involvement, wherein lay the effectiveness of continuous improvements or total quality initiatives. Senior management's role was to provide stability and trusting relationships in order that continual improvement could evolve as a system. Deming's often quoted phrase, 'drive out fear', was misinterpreted by managers as a command that 'fear must disappear'. What he actually meant to suggest was that blame cultures were counter to total quality cultures. Unfortunately, his message did not tell managers how to drive out fear, how to eliminate the old command and rule systems.

Deming (1983) recognized the significance of leadership and the need for agreed shared values but he was opposed to quotas, numerical goals, slogans and targets. His management principles were based on breaking down staff barriers, encouraging pride in work, planning to create constancy and consistency, on-the-job training and a vigorous programme of education and self-improvement. This ran counter to the way in which many UK managers have been interpreting total quality thinking and its programmes. The techniques of total quality management, quality circles and standards and re-engineering have largely been adopted as methods to be bolted onto traditional management practices and cultures. Unfortunately, the British interpretation of 'quality' tended to focus on the mechanistic operations of management and to ignore the so-called 'softer' side of management and the impact of working culture and corporate ethics on morale. The focus has been on the development of quality standards (BS 5750, now known as ISO 9000), controls, target setting, and over-specification of tasks. Deming resisted over-specification, targets, short-term contracts and performance-related pay because he recognized that these would limit potential, restrict creativity and inhibit teamwork.

In the USA the total quality movement was attached to the personal growth movement and change and connected to structural and planning mechanisms. The aftermath of the Vietnam War brought economic decline, race riots and a loss of confidence in politics and organizations. This was accompanied by a growth in personal therapies and 'you can do it' philosophies, which were adopted and extended within corporate thinking. Organizational development (OD) became a huge growth industry from the late 1970s onwards, based on West Coast personal therapies which glorified the notion that with determination anything is possible.

Edgar Schein (1987) sees organizational development as a psychological area of interest concerning changing individuals rather than changing organizations. He put forward a model of the 'staged' changes through which individuals go when confronted with change programmes and proposed changes in their companies:

- unfreezing of old thinking;
- identification with new roles and relationships;
- integration of new roles.

The first stage is likely to produce resistance, stress and anxiety in all staff. The second stage is never reached by those who cannot move out of stage one. The last stage easily becomes stage one in a new political climate.

Motivation was an unfashionable concept during the 1980s. 'Empowerment' became the buzz word for management techniques which would galvanize or motivate staff to work harder and more collectively in teams. The concept of empowerment was used to express the need to energize employees. They were encouraged to adopt fresh initiatives, see change as positive and engage with quality and improvement. Bryman and Howard (1994) observed that empowerment programmes reflected management's interests and rarely resulted in employees having greater control over working conditions. They concluded that empowerment was conceived as a gift from managers to employees which they could withdraw at any moment. Individual employees were the 'recipients of power' rather than the 'sharers of power' (Alimo-Metcalfe 1995). Empowerment was merely another mechanism whereby 'individualism' was encouraged and individual achievement rewarded, rather than by sharing or transforming activities; another avenue to reinforce conventional (male) manager tendencies at the expense of interpersonal relationships and a collaborative approach. Alimo-Metcalfe (1995) observed that what was being encouraged within many training programmes was the development of those same male values of self-assertion, separation, independence, control and competition. Empowerment workshops encouraged employees to have more responsibility without having any more control over their working environment. This version of empowerment, taught in most business schools, is an extension of Maslow's self-actualizing principle (1970), which is again a glorification of American individualism:

> It is here that gender bias in Maslow's hierarchy becomes most apparent. The self-actualising self is an autonomous self, one that denies relatedness and thinks

in terms of hierarchy. The self-in-relation which informs feminist theory (Gilligan 1982) is a self that thinks in terms of connections with others. Whether it reflects gender, class, racial or cultural differences (Harding 1986), the self-in-relation is one that does not see itself as separate from, or superior to, other selves. (Cullen 1992)

An enormous mythology has spread about management innovation and its magical ability to transform organizations. Managers were inundated with a battery of techniques developed by expensive consultants, sometimes called 'snake oil merchants', in order to acquire the necessary market edge over their competitors. In fact management consultants, like organizations, vary between those working in large accountancy firms and freelance operators. Many of the more radical management consultants have become less interested in models, functions and on–off management fixes and now seek to develop learning, shared values and shared practices. Both managers and management writers tended to ignore the impact of social conditions and corporate values on the motivation of the workforce. Instead they have continued to concentrate on external incentives such as pay and empower-ment strategies, conceptualizing the employee as an individualistic, self-motivating decision-maker, who can be tempted by therapy, pay and bonuses. Fortunately, although the empowerment model is individualistic, in reality many trainers do encourage quite different skills of listening and team-building, as well as encouraging assertiveness. However, much asser-tiveness training in UK institutions proved to be counter-productive because senior managers wanted employees to be efficient but not critical. These courses sometimes led to an even greater disillusionment among women who were already analytical and frustrated. Clearly some empower-ment initiatives did benefit some employees, especially those on the pro-duction or front line who had never had perks or even praise before the introduction of quality circles or focus groups; for these workers any attention made them feel valued. However, those in slightly more senior positions were sceptical and the mere fact of attending a quality circle did little for them; younger, graduate project managers in Britain wanted to know how their ideas and suggestions for improvements were going to affect their status, pay and corporate thinking.

The prevalance of authoritarian cultures within British organizations is acknowledged as a problem, but perhaps the degree of conformity within American companies is less well known. The American company culture is friendly but one where conflict is avoided. IT companies provide examples of the American corporate ethos, where informal chat is encouraged across grades but critical debate is avoided. These companies give staff open access to senior management but rarely to discuss hard realities, and trade unions are actively discouraged. Workers who are accustomed to the controlling behaviour of British managers find this environment refreshing and liberating, but it soon wears thin for those wanting information on corporate strategy and future plans. Employees have to work very long hours to demonstrate their commitment to the company if they are to be accepted and promoted. In fact two project managers in a site in Bristol reported that the over-friendly atmosphere served the company well, for it made any argument and dispute difficult. Those who were openly critical were marginalized and made to feel outsiders.

There can be little doubt that the motivation of public sector staff is in part due to their commitment to the public services, which they and their families use. American companies such as Sears are envious of the commitment of public sector staff in the UK, realizing the connection between corporate public sector values, motivation and low staff turnover. Americans report poor customer services from many US companies which runs counter to both management jargon and public relations hype. Anita Roddick of the Body Shop is also clearly aware of the significance of corporate values in motivating staff. There is no reason to be cynical about the connection between staff values and sales, for staff are more likely to be able to differentiate between superficial pronouncements and serious claims if they are closer to production. In fact this connection is an important one in rebalancing the power relations between workers and management, without a degree of sympathy from staff, companies are unlikely to be successful within democratic countries. Staff value and staff motivation are interrelated.

Staff can be sceptical about change and organizational development (OD) processes which appear to advocate teamworking or quality circles in a manner which is completely detached from corporate or business agendas. The narrowness of organizational approaches within American companies is perhaps why they have been slower to establish themselves in Britain. There are two explanations for this: one is that the UK culture was too authoritarian for personal change amongst employees to be tackled in this manner; the other is that the approach is superficial and does not address the real issues of who owns and controls the company. While it may be a positive step to empower staff, if this only takes place through minimal measures such as training programmes which place all the responsibility and onus to change on the individual employee, then the power relations between employees and corporate managers remain unbalanced, the company remains undemocratic and the impact of OD is limited.

The culture of planning and social infrastructures has led European managers to put more trust in organizational restructuring and the impact of Taylorism has been much more significant than OD in British companies. This preference for structural change and distinct worker–manager relations reflects the cultural differences between the UK and USA. The distinction between labour and capital divided the functions of employees and managers and this was endorsed by most trade unions. This division in the UK has left employees excluded from decision-making and a wide lack of interest in corporate plans and values. International companies and public administrations have been restructuring almost continually for the past fifteen to twenty years and most change programmes have been led from the 'top' with little staff involvement, utilizing a battery of management techniques and information models. The obsession with the role of executives and senior managers has led to a neglect of more junior staff, overlooking the fact that the inertia and prejudice of middle managers often inhibit new relationships and block the initiatives of senior staff.

This focus on senior managers is also reflected in women's management development, where potential is viewed through the prism of high flyers and those not interested in executive positions are considered second rate. Although the role of senior managers is critical during periods of change, how they manage staff, how they organize and their sensitivity to power relationships and cultures are also important. Senior managers can exercise radical and innovative thinking in seminars and appointments committees and yet be totally unaware of what is happening within their own organizations and incapable of linking change with existing structures and practices. Often they are out of touch with customers, frontline staff and the community, resulting in their falling prey to any new management fad and information system when they lack specific knowledge relevant to their own organizations. It is only human and predictable that in hierarchical large organizations those in senior positions will desire and seek standard uniformity – especially if they are out of touch with the frontline employees who could inform of how practices should change in order to meet local needs. Standard practices and crude control measures have a devastating effect on staff and performance within those agencies which impose rigid standards. Control systems that are set without staff agreement only erode morale and trust. Coercive persuasion is counterproductive in organizations which require responsive staff.

The pressure on all organizations to be efficient with fewer staff has resulted in business process re-engineering (BPR) as a way of streamlining processes. BPR determines change from a whole systems approach. Senior managers analyse the necessary operational processes in their organizations and break down old departments which work against new desired pathways. BPR represents a total overhaul of the organization. A steering group guides the process of matching skills to tasks and functions in order to achieve improvements in cost, efficiency and quality. British managers have taken to BPR in a way that they never took to the more people-focused organizational development; precisely because it concern system's change rather than employee learning. BPR could result in greater collaboration if a more people approach is adopted with implementing the process.

Thousands of businesses have re-engineered work in order to focus employees on processes that clearly provide value to customers. They have done sway with their functional silos and created new organisational structures – process-complete departments – each able to perform all the cross-functional steps or tasks required to meet customers' needs. Although many of these efforts have paid off in the form of lower costs, shorter cycles times, and greater customer satisfaction, many others have resulted in disappointment: companies have endured the trauma of re-engineering only to discover that their performance is no better – and in some cases actually worse – than before.

What caused things to go wrong? There certainly are a variety of possibilities, among them a failure to focus on parts of the business that were significant to customers and a failure to integrate autonomous, functionally-focused information systems into a shared, process-focused database and network. But something else that is often overlooked is the tendency of managers and re-engineering teams to underestimate the actions required to transform the way employees behave and work with one another. (Majchrzak and Wang 1996: 93)

If the drive for change is 'efficiency' rather than service improvement, the pace of change is too fast for new staff relationships to develop. This is a problem given that it is the level of staff involvement which determines the success or failure of the process. Although BPR has been adopted as the process which will result in more efficient operations and shorter throughput cycles, many initiatives fail because managers continue to ignore cultural barriers to change, and the fact that demoralized staff make unwilling partners in the process.

The dominant attitude among managers that performance will improve from a change in the system is misguided. Without the good will of staff and a collaborative culture, BPR can actually damage working relationships. Re-engineering may be introduced to improve efficiency but it can lead to less effective operations than those that previously existed in the original functional and vertically organized departments. They observe that managers continue to believe that structural change will naturally create a common sense of purpose when in fact the very opposite is true. Staff resent major restructuring and although they remain silent because they are insecure this does not make them willing parties to change. If BPR is introduced as yet another form of mechanical restructuring, although brilliant on paper it is probably doomed if it is yet another way of avoiding the development of work contracts, relationships and communication with employees. Staff resistance has to be addressed if managers are serious about developing a collaborative culture. Employees have to be involved and motivated if any change programme is to be successful in the longer term. This requires a learning context for managers as well as other employees.

The learning organization

Ferlie and Pettigrew (1996) have been critical of the narrowness of organizational development, which has remained divorced from external and internal political forces and has focused on the capacity of employees to change. The traditional approaches to management change have tended to ignore both the need to readjust power relationships and the need for a processual approach. The concept of a learning organization was developed in order to provide a conceptual framework in which to generate a synergy between employees' learning and sustaining organizational conditions. Management can be regarded as a learning process rather than one of direction and control. The learning organization (Garrett 1987) provided a conceptual framework in which active and transforming employees shift the organizational structure away from the command and control model of vertical hierarchies and formal communication towards fewer management levels, informal communication and decentralized units (Dorward et al. 1992). Within a learning organization the pace of change has to match the time needed for employee relationships to improve. New practices and emergent relationships need space and time for discussion and require sensitive corporate responses not ad hoc top-down directives. Learning is not a solitary activity, it requires positive interactions with others during the course of which teambuilding, partnership and collaboration develop. Whereas traditional management thinking demands that employees conform to routines and cultures, the learning organization aims to create a collaborative culture. Its corporate values and practices need to work in harmony with employees. The willingness of employees to learn is fundamental to change in any organization. If employees are inhibited and cannot learn, then the organization cannot develop. The concept of the learning organization assumes a dynamic relationship between organizational change and the ability of employees to learn and improve relationships. The problem for managers is how to achieve this dynamic relationship, what are the conditions for collaboration and how to transform large institutional companies or administrations. In reality few learning organizations exist because the balance of power in most makes employees suspicious of change.

Social contracts at work

The so-called neutral language of management has for too long lulled politicians into thinking that management and managing is not their concern. This lack of reflection on what conditions are likely to lead to transformation has resulted in an almost universal adoption of corporate restructuring as the lever of change. Yet, such an approach rarely produces responsive employees, or learning organizations. Employees will continue to be sceptical of restructuring, management hype and market logic until they can see the benefits of change for themselves or for their communities. This is especially true within countries where there is a tradition of oppressive practices, and where employees are unsure about company or government motives for restructuring.

Although the UK government promotes the 'Third Way' as an alternative to both the market and state mechanisms, it would appear to be a limited alternative which favours feeding the markets rather than promoting the value of social capital. Those in NGOs have for some years used the term the 'Third Way' to describe the balancing of social and business interests. Within this third sector many recognize that staff commitment and motivation are the key to any organization's success; also that the need for employee flexibility is very different from flexible work schedules. One does not result from the other.

There are many forms of flexibility, but importantly there is a huge difference between flexible work practices and flexible staff. The concept of flexibility is not neutral and its acceptance within a staff group depends on how it is introduced and whose interests it serves. Young unskilled workers in the retail industries often have no idea when they will work or whether they will work the next day or the next week. This instability means that they have no control over their time or income. For managers flexibility can result in greater control over work and leisure time. Flexibility can also provide women managers, professionals and consultants with more control over their time, but more often it involves further erosion of the rights of weaker unskilled employees.

Organizations need employees with positive attitudes, not employees with 'attitude'. A willingness to engage in partnerships and changes in practices requires good morale and high levels of motivation, which are hardly likely to be achieved through one-sided forms of flexibility. Companies and public bodies are desperate to understand the dynamics of motivation in order to move beyond old habits and repetitive tasks towards innovation and partnerships, but positive and new relationships do not result from coercion and command structures. Authoritarian regimes do not generate creativity. If companies and public administrations do not recognize 'that democracy is inevitable' (Slater and Bennis 1990) they may find that they are sabotaging their own corporate strategies. For many years there has been a powerful belief that the 'downsizing' and restructuring of organizations would lead to a greater competitiveness and that management practices would automatically become more open and responsive. Short-sighted executives saw no need to invest in human resources because it was costly and/or unnecessary. However, even the most hard-nosed Wall Street economists are beginning to see the error in these assumptions and to recognize that staff are their main asset and that good employment practices are essential. Slater and Bennis (1990) wrote that within American corporations 'internal democracy was inevitable'. Their logic was that because competitive markets demand better and better quality products, the only companies to survive will be those that develop new types of contractual relationships and in effect develop forms of internal democracy.

The upward spiral of senior managers' pay in the UK public utilities after privatization was one of the many reasons for the general public's rejection of Thatcherism in the 1997 general election. There continues to be a public distaste for huge perks and excessive payments to directors, while many staff earn less than £4.00 per hour. Company directors continue to receive average pay increases that are many times higher than their employees (Labour Research 1997). Labour Research found that over 120 executive directors in the UK receive golden handshakes of over £100,000 and that two directors had received more than £1 million per annum. There is a similar backlash from working people in the USA. This was demonstrated when in the same year AT&T cut 40,000 jobs the chairman received an extra £16,000:

> With many angry employees venting their rage by turning to extreme politicians, it is time to share the gain, as well as the pain, of global competitiveness. Corporations exist in a social and political context where a sense of equity, as in fairness, is a key value that can be ignored only at their own peril. Fortunately, equity, as in stocks, is a tool that can be used to restore fairer balance to corporate America's skewed compensation. (*Business Week* 22 April 1996: 68)

In the USA executive pay jumped by 27% while factory worker pay fell by 2% in 1995 (*Business Week* 1996). Why should the community believe the public utilities when they say that they care about public services if their executives earn a thousand times more than their employees? Why should employees engage with change programmes if they can see no change in the company (contracts, ethics), in managers (communication and respect), or indeed any advantages (satisfaction and pay). Without staff confidence in the company, all directives calling for empowerment are worthless. Unless employees think that they can benefit as well as the company from restructuring, why should they bother to engage with change?

Far-sighted businesses appreciate the new social contracts reflect a readjustment in management. Positive and balanced manager/employee relations are necessary for company survival. Social employment contracts have to change if the relationships between managers and staff are to improve and to provide the basis for new, more collaborative and creative working practices. This shift from employee suspicion to trust at work is dependent on the growth of new relationships and communication between parties which have been separated historically by power struggles.

Paradigm shifts in thinking are a first step, but social realities must also change and be evident. An MIT study showed that workers only respond to new initiatives when they sense that reciprocal obligations will result from the mergers or reorganization (Fukuyama 1995: 260). The transformation of organizations is dependent not only on narrative change or mental paradigm shifts, but also on the difficult renegotiation of business ethics, internal democracy and politically inclusive policy frameworks. Those who are socially excluded or out of work are hardly likely to believe in management and political rhetoric which does not provide hope for the future. To date none of the varieties of social democracy and capitalism has managed to free agencies to develop while also protecting staff; unbridled market activity has created greater divisions rather than building bridges between diverse and unequal communities. The current challenge within the western world is to develop organizational forms and ways of managing that combine and encourage dynamic agency rather than obstruct it. The problem, however, is not merely one of finding new models but of finding ways of engaging with employees and the local communities within change initiatives. Social and organizational change is dependent on agreed values, trust and new relationships. The separation between public and private values is no longer useful and social transformations are dependent on individuals transcending the public–private divide. Fukuyama (1997) is astute about employee–manager power relationships and the need for company obligations, but he appears to ignore the fact that the public role of women is critical to social transformation precisely because of their socialization and emotional work within relationships. He recognizes that the process of developing collaborative work relationships is dependent on a feminization of the public world of trade, politics and organizations which is connected to the transference of social concerns and ethics from the private to the public realm. But apparently he believes that this will happen without women and that they should return to the home to protect society from the damage done by men. This appears to be a strange conclusion but, unfortunately, although illogical is all too common.

The following chapters suggest how gender balance and radical women are critical both to the process of negotiation towards socialized work contracts and in management through their roles as negotiators, leaders, innovators and bridge builders within the process of social transformation and how male gender cultures operate as a barrier to this process.

2 Management style, gender and the professions

Women managers, on average, were judged more effective and satisfying to work for as well as more likely to generate extra effort from their people. Women were also rated higher than men on three of the four components comprising transformational leadership. Such female leaders were rated as having more idealised influence or charisma, being inspirational and individually considerate than their male counterparts. Although rated higher on intellectual stimulation, this difference was not large enough to be considered reliable. (Bass and Avolio 1993: 10)

Management is not a neutral concept. Managing within the private sector reflects the corporate interest in finance gain, but management can also be based on social principles. Management practices, techniques and procedures are tools which are either appropriate or inappropriate given the aims and objectives of the organization. Managers play a crucial role in determining organizational forms and business success and have a pivotal role in supporting transformation. Leadership skills are said to be key to successful management and change (Kanter 1989; Pettigrew and Whipp 1991; Kotter 1995). For many years the Left assumed managers to be agents of capital or the state. Many labour process theorists categorized managers as bosses and willing parties in ruthless restructurings, but as any other group of employees they vary in their political and social affiliations. To dismiss managers as being only motivated by corporate objectives is to ignore the role of managers within the public sector. To counter this view and unpack management power relationships Landry et al. (1985) distinguish between management and those people in managerial positions:

There is a vital distinction to be made between 'management' and those people holding managerial positions, and 'management' as an assortment of integrative functions, which are necessary in any complex organisation – planning, harmonising related processes, ensuring appropriate flows of information, matching resources to production (service) needs, marketing, financial control, linking out to demand etc. . . . these skills were seen as capitalist and reactionary by nature. (Landry et al. 1985: 61)

The role of a manager has changed dramatically over the last fifty years, while managers can help transform organizations, most adapt and conform to traditional expectations and ways of managing.

Changing model of perfection

During the inter-war period organizational theorists described the agreed functions of managers as planning, co-ordination, organizing and controlling staff and budgets. Managers during the 1950s and 1960s were the carriers of plans and knowledge, troubleshooters and committee people. Up until the late 1960s business leaders were said to possess particular personality traits, this approach corresponded to the prevailing personality theory when beliefs about leadership were influenced by historical and cultural factors. By the mid-1970s the private sector was demanding more creative and competitive behaviour from its managers, they were still expected to be solo operators but also team players who could deal with staff. Mintzberg's managerial roles of the time included: figurehead, leader, monitor, spokesperson, troubleshooter, entrepreneur, and negotiator (Mintzberg 1979). Manager qualities began to be matched to different and particular types of organization. For example, Charles Handy (1978), who was critical of rigid trait theory, linked particular manager typologies to the various types of western organization. His typology was based on four Greek gods: Zeus, Apollo, Athena and Dionysus. Zeus is a leader and a likely entrepreneur; Apollo prefers a routine and role culture (bureaucracy); Athena has a more female persona and feels at home in a task culture and Dionysus is the free thinker and a lone worker, who networks but avoids institutions. Maccoby (1978) classifies managers in a similar manner as: the jungle fighter, the company man, the gamesman and the craftsman. Each manager type is associated with a particular organizational structure.

There are limits to the usefulness of stereotypes and typologies. However, they do draw attention to the influence of particular organizational forms on manager behaviour and the fact that particular types of people are drawn to particular ways of managing. Modern management theorists (Drucker 1955, 1989; Kotter 1995) continue to describe the features of successful managers.

There continues to be a common, rationalist view that assumes that management is a neutral function and that managers act on the basis of 'knowledge' with no reference to their emotional responses or prejudices. Drucker (1955) disagreed with this trend and the tendency to sanitize management and divorce it from cultural influences, conflicts and power relationships. The prevalent rationalist view assumed that managers could be detached and act in accordance with agreed plans and corporate interests. Management functions were viewed as technical, rational and divorced from value judgements. Management language or jargon also reinforced the technical rational position. Managers stopped talking about 'capital and labour' many years ago and instead refer to managers and employees. The neutralization of the management role has had the effect of hiding conflictual relationships and detached management from the turbulent political world in which organizations exist.

However, policymakers and the public apparently prefer to think of management as a separate and neutral domain free from prejudice with predictable and fixed functions, untainted by politics. This version of management, free of political ideology, reinforced the belief that management theory and manager behaviour could be defined and idealized. Management functions and competence are assumed to be standard across agencies, whether in the public or private sectors. This view made the discussion of appropriate and inappropriate responses more difficult. A manager may learn the ropes and old habits but these may not be the appropriate or the most effective. Drucker (1988) suggested that whereas an imaginative manager would respond to specifics and act appropriately within a command-control organization s/he could be penalised for acting so.

Leadership and vision

Within the traditional public administrations, management involved the supervision of standard procedures. The current climate requires more imaginative skills as well as the capacity to manage existing operations. The changes in markets, organizational change and need for on-going strategy work has placed a greater emphasis on more flexible forms of management (Du Gay 1993) in order to overcome the inertia of the large corporations and public administrations. Globalization has demanded that managers move from being supervisors and transform into strategists and change agents. Managing change requires leadership qualities, particularly in service organizations where management largely concerns managing of staff. A new consensus emerged that leaders had to be charismatic rather than tough (Peters and Waterman 1982; Drucker 1989; Handy 1994).

Burns (1978) wrote that leaders may be power leading or power wielding, where the latter order and the former encourage. He thought that many in leadership positions in Britain were not leaders, but bullies or tyrants. Leadership in the UK was associated with dominance not vision. The legacy of the British Empire had a profound effect on what type of person and which qualities were valued in leaders, but it was assumed that they should be preferably: white, ex-public school, stiff-upper-lipped and emotionally detached men. There was a huge shift in thinking about management and managers in the 1970s although this was not evident in most public administrations. The 1980s brought a renewed interest in the qualities of leaders and in particular whether women were capable of being executives. There was beginning to be a recognition that people would no longer tolerate tight control and dictatorship at work, employees had to be encouraged to work. Leaders could no longer get away with just being decisive bosses; they must have vision and be able to relate to people. Goldsmith and Clutterbuck (1985) noticed that this shift is more pronounced in the USA than it is in Britain. By the 1990s there appeared also to be a cultural shift in the UK, employees are now much less deferential and expect respect from managers as well as pay. Charismatic leadership is the most frequently mentioned quality when recording key variables in transformation and change processes. Multinationals, hungry for customers and new markets need charismatic managers who are capable of motivating the workforce through demonstration of the following attributes:

- give employees credit when they do good work;
- delegation;
- being clear about tasks and functions;
- being fair;
- thinking about the overall company's interests.

Globalization demands that executives can inspire, be able personally to transcend cultural boundaries and have an ability to communicate vision with clarity. This takes confidence, astuteness and openness. In the past, the autocratic leader and the authoritarian manager dominated both public and private organizations in the western world (Handy 1989). Economic, social and political changes demand a greater responsiveness from large corporations and public administrations and a shift away from the traditional hierarchies to decentralized agencies and teamworking. Managers must have vision and an understanding of change and people. The 'solo player', 'heroic leader' and 'privileged mandarin' are all redundant in organizations operating within the global context. The most successful executives in the 1990s listen, inspire and support staff (Kotter 1995), which suggests that, in theory at least, the macho style has lost its credibility. According to Handy (1989) leaders must be able to:

- listen;
- communicate;
- have vision;
- encourage and inspire staff;
- reinforce and confirm others;
- identify skills and problems;
- team build.

Gone are the days when women could succeed by learning to play men's games. Instead the time has come for men on the move to adopt a more feminized approach to management games. According to the management gurus successful change is dependent on managing on the basis of long-term organizational objectives and strong personal values. These leadership skills and qualities appertain to organizations in all sectors.

However, public sector managers operate in a much more complex political environment than do their colleagues employed in private companies. They have to be able to juggle social objectives and work with multiple stakeholders within limited budgets and sometimes changing financial priorities. Public sector managers must manage daily operations in the knowledge that the next day dramatic changes could occur in service configurations, which may affect their staff and departments. Public sector bodies have many customers or stakeholders who can influence and affect policy and change strategies, consequently managers need to be able to:

- lead and develop employees to take over managerial functions;
- be autonomous and self-regulating;
- break down departmentalism and hierarchies;
- negotiate and facilitate change with other agencies;
- secure and procure funds;
- be a public figurehead.

In order to fulfil these varied functions Brown (1994) of the Office of Public Management says that the essential qualities for public sector executives are:

- self-knowledge;
- balance not conflict;
- a passion for the work;
- recognizing and affirming social values;
- learning what to avoid;
- being able to empower others;
- valuing relationships.

The strategic approach towards operational processes and employees indicates a very changed role for public sector managers. They have the responsibility for shaping behaviour at work and creating a positive environment in which employees can engage with change (Ghoshal and Bartlett 1995). They envisage the management function to contain a portfolio of processes that are understood and endorsed by the employees who are trained in all the necessary competencies. Maruta (1995) says that it is 'values' that drive this process in his company in Japan, Kao. As chief executive he reports that he has personally imbued staff with social values which are the bedrock of the business. Each Kao employee is encouraged, he says, to challenge existing processes and to question whether company products are socially useful. Maruta (1995) believes, as do many in NGOs, that top managers are responsible for the social values which drive the organization and that these values should also reflect those of the local community in which the company is based, even though the company's core values remain:

- individual ability;
- innovation;
- entrepreneurship.

Within Kao every manager is held responsible for the renewal process and each must be involved in challenging the status quo and existing procedures if innovative new processes are to emerge from the in-house team. According to Maruta (1995) and Ghoshal and Bartlett (1995), managers are necessarily the 'agents of disturbance' or challengers. This is an interesting idea and one which few UK managers would recognize as desirable. Past wisdom must not be a constant, but something to be challenged. Yesterday's success formula is often today's obsolete dogma' (Maruta 1995). This approach could be said to be female; it certainly mirrors the style and approach many women express as desirable and the qualities they value.

What managers are really like

Unfortunately, although the logic for change is powerful the realities inside organizations can work against change. In spite of the calls for more transformative styles of management, the disparity between the realities of management practice and the fantasy of the strategic and visionary leadership could not be greater. While management theorists are constantly drawing attention to the need for diverse talents, whether these new and sharing skills are actually exhibited by managers is a moot point. Many doubt that even a small percentage of managers exhibit either visionary or transforming skills (Thompson and McHugh 1990). Restructuring is very real, but the creative and challenging management is illusory, if it exists at all.

There is a real problem in transforming managers. The thinking that everyone is able to take initiative ignores the impact caused by the oppressive work environments on staff and the habits they have acquired. It is very difficult for managers to change when they have worked in administrations and companies which encouraged compliance and responses diametrically opposite to those currently desired. Added to this, the contract culture exaggerates combative rather than collaborative behaviour, increasing the mental stress induced by the fear of constant restructuring. People revert to old habits in stressful situations. A huge gap exists between rhetoric and reality in management. Managers continue to cling to top-down change levers and technical management systems which oppress staff and staff responsiveness.

Studies by Mintzberg (1987) and Kotter (1990) showed that strategic managers were extremely rare; the creative and challenging manager is a figment of the guru imagination. Manager behaviour is most often reactive, emotional and unstrategic. Yet, management thinking continues to assume rational responses and managers continue to refer to technical systems which rely on rational manager responses. In fact, most managers react to changing environments and pressures in the following ways:

● crisis management;
● ad hoc and opportunistic judgements;

- exhibit habitual and rigid behaviour;
- reduce networks and talk only to 'like' colleagues;
- stress and pressures result in greater domestic trauma;
- a lack of energy and commitment;
- lack of originality, creativity and confidence.

Few managers are likely to change if they are not nurtured, retrained and motivated. This is particularly the case within the service sector and within public administrations which are totally reliant on staff motivation and their relationships. Within the public sector the role of manager is becoming more and more difficult. Politicians often use managers as the convenient 'whipping boy' for their own failures. The disparity between what organizations require and how managers should behave is the cause of much frustration, and has been for many years for those managers who want to humanize organizations and prioritize service.

Transforming style

While women managers often mimic male behaviour in management, most also express a desire for change. Alimo-Metcalfe's (1992, 1995) work shows that women managers are motivated by organizational goals rather than by the promise of promotion; they are tempted by posts which are interesting and involve their personal development. This tendency to seek self and organizational improvements indicates that many women are focused on change and transformation as well as career development.

Many have noted over the years that men and women differ in their approaches to managing people. Susan Vinnicombe (1987) demonstrated how women managers appear to approach managing differently from their male colleagues. She used the Myers Briggs Type Indicator (MBTI) and differentiated between those who are traditional, catalyst and visionary managers (see Table 2.1). She found a preponderance of traditionalists among men (60% men compared to 29% of the women), while women managers were spread across all groups with a preference for the visionary and catalyst approaches. Visionaries she suggested were natural strategic managers, whereas catalysts excelled at public relations work.

Matching manager responses to new environments

In the past, acceptable managerial responses involved adhering to set procedures within a static management framework. Transactions took place between people who knew their function and roles because they rarely changed. This was called transactional management. Transactional managers reinforced the performance of subordinates through known

TABLE 2.1   *Approaches to managing*

Strengths	Weaknesses
Traditionalist	
practical common sense	makes snap decisions
attentive to facts	lacks responsibility for change
systems focus	poor at relationships
steady worker	concerned with difficulties
super dependable	
realistic about time scales	
Catalyst	
charisma and commitment to staff	can be drawn into pleasing others
communicates well	has difficulties with rules and conventions
comfortable with changing environments	may spend too long on issues
comfortable with diversity	takes over problems and responsibilities
Visionary	
strong on intellectual vision	may be insensitive to others
creative and progressive	devalues others who are not intellectual
enjoys problem solving	expects too much of people
outspoken	restless and easily bored

(Vinnicombe 1987)

rewards and punishments, they relied on their status and formal authority and a pecking order through which paper transactions moved.

By contrast, transformational leadership involves moving beyond role and developing new relationships rather than conforming with established hierarchies: 'vision, planning, communication and creative action which has a positive unifying effect on a group of people set around clear values and beliefs, to accomplish simultaneously impacts on the personal development and corporate productivity of all involved' (Anderson 1992: 37). Bass and Avolio (1989) were interested in what qualities are essential components for transformational leadership. They concluded the key skills were the ability to inspire, be charismatic, to intellectually stimulate and to listen. They were not interested in gender analysis at the start of their study but were drawn into a comparison between men and women because women scored higher in every category bar one. Their work was supported by Kalabadse (1986) who concluded that women tended towards team-coaches and visionaries rather than traditionalists or company barons (autocrats).

A core component of transformational leadership according to Bass and Avolio (1989) is an ability to empower staff. This ability is not the type of empowerment described by Maslow (1970) which referred to individual achievement. Transforming managers could empower staff because they were empowered themselves by high self-esteem and personal control which provided a bedrock to their visions and change strategies. Transformational leaders use their skills to facilitate change and change through collaboration rather than competition. This is not easy. Although there has always been a tendency to believe that women are socialized into transforming roles, many women do not bring their transforming approaches to management, perhaps because they are not encouraged to do so or because they do not possess the skills.

Rosener's (1990) study with American women executives uncovered many unexpected similarities between the men and women. They earned the same money and suffered the same conflicts over children. However, where they differed significantly was in relation to their style of leadership and management. Rosener (1990) found that women were more likely than men to use transforming approaches because they want to escape the constraints of female gender roles, to motivate others and to achieve shared objectives. They also believed that their personal contacts were as important as their formal status at work. They believed in the softer side of management because they thought people performed best when they were valued and when they felt good about themselves.

Many continue to doubt that gender differences are real. In order to assess how far women managers have transforming skills the National Health Service Women's Unit commissioned an event for senior managers called 'Managing Beyond Gender'. Two groups attended, one male and one female, both were given the task of role playing the parts of senior managers setting up a new television station. They had to devise programmes, secure budgets and negotiate with politicians. Eight regional groups were involved in the simulation. Most of the women did demonstrate a preference for 'relational' rather than role aspects of work, while men preferred to stick to formal structures and roles. A striking difference was that the women involved everyone in decision-making and provided each member with new opportunities. The men tended to reinforce existing skills, for example, a finance director would be given the finance director's role in the simulation. The men also chose their leader immediately, who then allocated other group members to the various other functions. The women allowed a process to take place whereby individual members became attached to particular roles. The male group saw the mission statement (social values) as something which was required by politicians and therefore essential for public relations work; the women paid more attention to discussing the mission statement as a route to establishing shared values which would underpin programming. The women were rather poor in communicating their values to politicians and other outsiders. Although these training sessions highlighted regional differences there were significant gender tendencies and most of the regions confirmed distinct gender differences. However, the north west group bucked the trend, men were more facilitative than the women. Brown (1994) suggests that there are lessons to be learnt from these simulations, in particular that gender balance is needed in organizations. 'The internal application of mission to strategy and the external presentation of that link is required. Neither "bullshitting" nor internal managerial correctness worked in the simulation' (Brown 1994: 43).

The evidence suggests that women pay greater attention to the relational aspects of their work, but find it difficult to communicate their importance and relevance in a task-oriented culture. The simulations reinforced the work of Bass and Avolio (1993) and their distinction between transactional and transformational approaches to managing and management:

> For women, the world is a network of connections in which support and consensus are sought and confirmed. For men, the world is made up of individuals in a hierarchical social order in which life is a competitive struggle for success, the gaining of advantage over others and avoiding a loss of power. Male leaders will pay attention to the fairness of rules, and are attuned to paying attention to the failings of their followers, rather than caring about them as individuals as women appear to be more likely to do. (Bass and Avolio 1993: 13)

Women's life experiences suggest that they desire a different approach to organizing people, leadership and management. Their approach relates closely to the notion of transformational leadership (Bass and Avolio 1989; Posener 1990). Arroba and James (1987) also note that while many women dislike organizational politics they tended to be good at 'reading' organizational culture and personal dynamics. Women tend to be aware of processes and of the likely problems involved in the implementation of changes. Those women who were visionary could be innovative precisely because they were aware of the resistance to change and understood the need to persuade and develop staff if this resistance was to be overcome.

The literature on women in management suggests that women's negotiating style of communication is critical to facilitating transformation. Many in management circles have started to talk about the need for learning and adjustment within organizations undergoing or in need of transformation. Mintzberg (1987) talks of the crafting strategies necessary if people are to make mutual adjustments to one another; others of the need for a personal readiness to collaborate (Poxton 1995), and calculative compliance (Willmott 1993). Thus emphasizing the need for a willingness to listen and negotiate when managing change. Many women managers are actively:

- collaborating with colleagues and other agencies;
- breaking boundaries and making readjustments;
- thinking strategically about how to achieve improvements;
- thinking holistically;
- wanting social changes and egalitarian relations within management.

These findings are not now considered unusual and are well founded across many countries. Women are more likely to make personal adjustments within relationships and appear to be more interested in collaborative ways of working (Bass and Avolio 1993). Women are more likely to want to redefine the boundaries and the meaning of concepts such as authority and legitimacy in order to develop social relationships. Those actively engaged in transformation stretch ideas and relationships in order that the various parties move closer to understanding each other, often to more original and richer ideas than those achieved by individual effort (Berenky 1986: 119). A more feminized version of authority is said to be developing in some organizations which seeks to engage and inspire rather than deliver ultimatums, which emerges as a consequence of personal readjustments and collaboration. The observation of women's potential as transformational managers should direct executives towards their role as change agents within public sector transformation, but too often it does not. Women may be visible in management and in senior positions but their creative energy is too often lost within the stresses and strains of working and living within still dominant male cultures.

Women's responses in male cultures

While gurus (Peter, Handy and Drucker) may think that a paradigm shift of feminization in managing is crucial to organizational transformation; in reality it would appear that in Britain managers continue to confirm traditional practices and reinforce male behavioural responses. Unfortunately, women's preference for relational processes and organizational development is rarely valued or formally acknowledged within recruitment, appraisal and performance measurement.

Virginia Schein (1975) showed that women managers were selected and appraised against male characteristics. Fourteen years later, Schein (1989) repeated her work on sex stereotyping and the results remained the same. Another study by Schein and Mueller (1992) showed that in the 1990s the very same characteristics were sought by managers. Both men and women continue to think that men tend to be better managers because they demonstrate male responses and qualities. Men and women continue to be rewarded for being decisive, competitive and playing-by-the-rules (transactional in style).

Beverley Alimo-Metcalfe (1992a) argues that there are key stages in the assessment process where gender bias is rife: in selection, at interview and in promotion. The elements involved include the criteria used to select candidates which reflects the gender bias of selectors, but also male qualities which were seen as characteristic of successful managers. Although the bias of selection criteria and recruitment practices generally has been much researched and is the subject of much personnel training, the ongoing judgements and appraisals during the course of a woman's career are largely of an informal nature but are just as significant.

Cultural attitudes determine the values required by leaders and influence the dominant management style in organizations. Understanding of this cultural backdrop is critical to understanding how women managers fare at work. Women are judged against the accepted definitions of what is a 'good manager' and what are 'acceptable leadership qualities'.

Alban Metcalfe (1987) showed that men and women managers saw themselves in very similar ways. She observed that women perceived themselves to be more confident at work than in their social lives; that female managers were better qualified academically than men, but less professionally qualified. Many were concerned with juggling families and work, whereas no man in her research mentioned this as an issue. In spite of the fact women reported being confident at work, they are often less relaxed, because they feel under a greater pressure to prove their capacities. She found that many male assessors were so surprised by the intelligence and capability of individual female candidates that they selected them as brilliant or unusual. Abramson et al. (1978) called this the 'platypus effect'. 'It matters little what the platypus says, the wonder is that it can speak at all'. Women frequently observe that older men are so surprised when a woman can read accounts they mistake this for excellence and appoint them.

However, within traditional cultures it is women as well as men who appraise women as having lesser competence, so it is unsurprising that studies continue to demonstrate a preference for male candidates over equally experienced and more qualified women for managerial, professional and academic posts (Gutek and Stevens 1979; Alban Metcalfe 1987). Clearly gender stereotypes permeate all organizations and levels of management. Studies in the 1970s (Schein 1973; Broverman et al. 1975) showed how men rationalize their images of women by assuming them to be less interested in responsibility, challenge and career advancement.

Women do avoid promotion in organizations which appear to them as culturally blind to their talents and ideas. A major frustration for women managers (Maddock 1993a) is their inability to discuss or articulate what they felt was a better way to manage. The want to find a style of managing and a set of measures which would endorse those relationships they valued. They felt that they were not understood; their words were heard but did not make sense to their colleagues. When they voiced something that sounded vague and confused they knew that this merely reinforced their managers' views that women were indecisive, woolly and vague. A huge frustration for women managers was that when they attempted to develop new relationships and ways of working more collaboratively they were either unnoticed or ridiculed (Maddock 1993a and b).

Pressure to conform in male cultures

Women managers are likely to be a much greater force for change if they are not pressurized into modelling themselves on men. White et al. (1988) conclude that women high-flyers should be less concerned with abiding by rules and found that this was exactly what successful women executives did do. Successful women were said to be free of such conformity but they paid for this deviation from the female role and were subject to much hostility and criticism.

Interestingly, women in the USA were more inclined to model themselves on men than women in Europe. This is perhaps because male role models in American companies are more exaggerated than in Europe and that pushy women are more accepted within the US. The North American political context makes it difficult for any employee to proclaim differences as a way of improving the work environment as the labour movement is weak, all employees including women have had to assert 'sameness' rather than 'difference' in order to win arguments. Rosener (1990) and Gordon (1991), both American, suggest that women managers were far too conforming to male models and that this disadvantages other women.

What should be of concern to senior management is that the strategies adopted by many successful women, such as keeping public and personal roles totally separate, playing the game, and being hard-nosed are disliked as behaviours by women. Women disliked the feeling that this mimicking behaviour afforded them. Unfortunately, women also believe that masculine behaviours are necessary in business and in the boardroom and that more feminine responses such as intuition, co-operation and emotional openness are thought to be a disadvantage in public life. Those women who want to avoid the male culture are unlikely to choose to become executives or public figures. Women have a choice whether to conform to these pressures or rail against them; both are equally exhausting and stressful.

The female experience does appear to have given many women powerful insights into personal relationships, but it does not persuade them to enter male cultures or to integrate their perspective into management. Many women realize that resorting to more open and conciliatory responses when others remained competitive and closed can be counterproductive. Women have been so deeply affected by male cultures, they are so humble or conciliatory in personal interactions that they lack credibility when they argue for change or new ideas.

The psychological impact of male cultures on women is evident in all work relationships and is visible in women's coping behaviours which underpin why so many women are unconvincing leaders within establishment organizations. Rotter's (1972) concept of a 'focus of control' is one explanation of women's lack of success when arguing for change in conventional organizations. Women low locus of control and lack of focus diffuse their efforts, they lack the necessary focus for achievement. Many women are proud of being able to handle multiple pieces of information at any one time and of being holistic. However, within the work environment focused on very narrow targets, a scatter approach can be ineffective and viewed as indicating a lack of confidence.

Women have every reason to be underconfident when working in very male cultures and they are also afraid of breaking ranks with women and appearing too pushy. Many traditional cultures have socialized women to be humble and deferential. What have in the past appeared as female wiles or feminine 'traits' are in fact learned responses, many of which have been the only appropriate response for women given their powerlessness. Seligman (1975) observed that women learn a form of helplessness in many societies and organizations. Humility or helplessness are both ways of avoiding direct confrontation. A lack of control and appearing helpless can become advantages for those who want to avoid responsibility. Avoiding responsibility is much harder for men who suffer from the opposite problem and are thought to be in control even when they clearly have no power. The male socialization process develops a sense in men that they must be in control, and consequently many men find accepting situations where they are powerless extremely difficult. Women by contrast, accept their vulnerability much more easily. While men may react in anger at any conscious reference to their weaknesses (Miller 1974). Some women find helplessness an escape from difficult realities. Helplessness may have been appropriate in traditional cultures it is totally inappropriate in management.

Unfortunately, the legacy of patriarchal relationships affects men and women, damaging both, but rendering women weaker, if more aware. The legacy of centuries of male cultures have resulted in psychological dynamics which many would wish to escape but lurk beneath the surface of all relationships. Within this context women are unsurprising change agents, they have every reason to seek change, even though many women are adept at informal influence and personal forms of power. Clearly not all women have learnt the same responses. Many women managers are not passive or good conciliators, some are bullies. There are huge differences between classes and races (bell hooks 1989). The post-60s generation of women have completely different expectations of sex, personal relationships and work than their mothers. But many of the old stereotypes persist, even if access to jobs is easier and younger people live in egalitarian social environments.

Alimo Metcalfe (1995) observes that women continue to have a tendency to talk down their talents and to defer to others in discussion. Women ascribe their successes to luck or to others, but when things go badly they blame themselves, whereas many male managers have a 'high locus of control' and attribute their success to their own ability and their failure to bad luck. Unfortunately, many of the desired qualities of modern managers such as leadership, negotiation skills, appear to be exhibited by those with focus and control – men (Alimo Metcalfe 1995). The assumption that women will be negotiators and conciliators remains powerful and is reinforced by daily realities. The gender cultures influence the manner in which women are judged, selected, assessed and appraised. Women themselves collude with these assessments. It is a rather schizophrenic world where women feel unable to be themselves, yet also unable to object to the stereotypic definitions of them as a group.

A report on relationships in the UK (Wilkinson 1994) showed that young people under 25 had less conforming gender strategies and were moving towards a more androgynous ideal. There are likely to be dramatic regional variations to these changes and although the working environment may encourage more open gender relations among younger people, this may also be true only of younger people in junior positions who have not yet been tested by the power that status beings. For example, male registrar doctors are egalitarian until they become consultants, when according to their female colleagues they revert to patronizing gender stereotypes when dealing with women (Maddock and Parkin 1994). In general, as men gain seniority they lose contact with women as equals and become surrounded by male colleagues and the pressure to conform to male traditions grows stronger. According to Handy (1991), most male executives have much more power in their executive castle suites than they do at home and it is their daughters who can be instrumental in changing their views.

More recent gender studies show men are equally trapped within narrow visions of masculinity. Some men are unhappy with the narrow definitions of masculinity (Hearn 1984) but most are content with the status quo. Everyone continues to endorse male cultures in covert and subtle ways, although women have more interest in changing gendered relations, many collude with the stereotypes as much as men. The apparent permanence of gender cultures and gender roles within traditional cultures makes it difficult for individuals to have any confidence in personal or social change. The stereotyping of men and women by class, race and other social tags is reinforced in reality by the belief that the tag is the person and defines them. Versions of masculinity and femininity ossify within romantic versions of particular groups. For example, the brawn of working-class men or the caring nature of mothers. These one-sided realities result in men and women becoming trapped in their own gender role definitions.

However, gender dynamics can and do change. Too often, people are trapped in old definitions assimilated in their youth, gender relations are ever a snapshot, never a fixed frame for life; they are constantly being negotiated and re-negotiated (Townley 1994). The problem is that people are typecast for earlier episodes in their life, but no person is always a hero, a victim or a villain. Some have more interest than others in clinging on to old stereotypes, women with most to gain from change need to negotiate strategies and tactics in a more open way.

A recent study by Alimo-Metcalfe (1995) with local authority housing officers showed that the women were becoming more confident of their transforming skills. She suggests that women managers have started to become more open and to refer to desired qualities and alternative ways of working rather than continuing to rely on traditional responses. However, women in the USA remain fearful of claiming special female qualities: 'Beware the danger that lies in attaching male and female labels to the two leadership styles; hasn't the time come when we can accept a people-oriented, fair, and co-operative way of dealing with our staff and colleagues?' (Segal 1990: 1).

Siegel suggests women should hang on to their transformational style of leadership because it is going to be in great demand in the future, but in dominant male cultures this is difficult. It is not within many individual women's power to overcome male responses by sheer acts of will. Social change requires more than rational and individual effort, it also requires an engagement with the change process by those who share views and tactics. A change in gender stereotypes is dependent on renegotiated relationships among many people and which is discussed and debated.

Although organizations are changing in the UK, managers still control staff rather than encourage them and continue to endorse male models of behaviour. While Bass and Avolio (1993) insist that organizations would benefit from recruiting women managers and feminizing male managers, there remains active resistance to this process and women continue to repress their own skills. Alimo-Metcalfe (1995) says transformational leadership may be desirable, but:

> Will it be interpreted as a shared process or as a gift of favoured managers – where managers learn new tricks to manage employees . . . can we realistically expect patriarchy to be dismantled in organisations as those in positions of power experience conversion, or will the manager become a chameleon? (Alimo-Metcalfe 1995)

Although management 'gurus' might think that women's transformational style of management is critical in organizations attempting to survive globalization, many managers continue to think otherwise. It is not so much that many officials, managers and bureaucrats do not have a social value framework it is that they do not bring them to work.

3   Working at the paradigm shift
Personal agency, having a mind for change

The challenge for feminism is to find a form of politics which celebrates individual difference and allows it to flower in all its wayward eccentricity. It must appeal to women, not as victims but as intelligent, creative people who are already in control of their lives but would like the chance to make a louder noise, to appear in a brighter light, to multiply their roles in society and to be recognised simply as themselves. Such politics involves a move away from the simple dualistic certainties of models which takes gender, for that matter class or ethnicity, as overriding systems of oppression, towards a closer look at the complex and multifaceted nature of the barriers to individual self-expression and fulfilment.
(Ursula Huws 1998)

No western country has yet solved the problems of late industrialization, the growing impact of globalization, the inequitable access to work and wealth and the destruction of local communities particularly in the South. The trading markets and accounting systems need to be socialized, but this is not likely to occur without a huge shift in thinking about the role of government and business ethics. The problem is no longer of a need for ideal utopias but of involving the public and politicians in a paradigm shift from money to people. Those involved in people development would say that social capital is as much of a public asset as finance capital. A country's people are its social capital. Economics and social life are inseparably intertwined but the separation of business, trade and economics from social value, connectedness and social relationships reinforces the notion that the driving forces of the financial world are immutable and beyond political judgement. Within the global economy the overwhelming power of trading and money markets overshadows social actions and interests. Often human agency is understood only insofar as it corresponds to the market model.

The market model discourse tends to ascribe 'selfish' motives to individuals and assumes people to be rational, well informed and driven solely by their own competitive and individualistic motives. In spite of the fact no one is completely rational in everyday life, we are assumed by market economists to be ambitious and single minded in our drive to achieve in business and that this energy will somehow stimulate the market, jobs will be created and unemployment reduced. The idea that increased flexibility and the 'trickle-down' effect will ultimately benefit the poor and the unemployed has been shown to be bogus. Communities in the UK are even more divided in the 1990s than in the 1970s and even the World Bank doubts that the 'trickle-down' effect is working. A recent Oxfam report (1997), *Growth and Equity*, concluded that those countries with the largest gaps between rich and poor are also those with poor economic growth rates, while those with better records of wealth redistribution are demonstrating improvements in growth: 'The message which emerges is clear. A high degree of inequality tends to be bad not only for poverty reduction but also for growth. It follows that governments serious about growth should get serious about equity and redistribution' (Elliott 1997).

The British government's economic programme is based on a 'growth' policy. Low inflation is supposed to lead to stability, and stability to higher growth. Inequality stands in the way of 'growth', the rich want cheap service labour, childcare, cleaners and restaurants. A market driven by the interests of the 'rich' or the 'niche markets' of the rich undermines the social infrastructure which supports the wider community. Elliott (1997) suggests that 'smart' redistribution would involve significant investment in the social fabric of societies, in Britain this would mean the NHS, in education and in public transport. Yet, countries around the world find that structural adjustments have been driven by detailed financial returns that undermine local and social capital.

Structural adjustment and liberalization programmes continue to hit public sector services in the west as well as poorer countries, in spite of a growing concern for the widening gap between rich and poor. As women are dependent on public services and generally poorer than men, they have become poorer through structured adjustment programmes. Unfortunately, these gender inequalities persist and remain invisible because they go largely unrecorded. Inequalities are reinforced by international accounting systems which are gender insensitive. According to a recent UN report (UNCTAD 1997) the gap between countries is also widening. Developing countries should open their economies more gradually to world trade in order to reduce the social calamities and social costs of structural adjustment. Governments should return to some form of control over employment policies in order to prevent localized, international reaction against open markets and globalization. Without more energy invested in developing appropriate forms of control over international trade even those companies with more ethical policies will undermine the fabric of social and civic institutions in less developed countries. If the west were to be as impoverished by such enforced actions as are those countries in the south, the notion of trickle-down would be abandoned.

Women find it difficult to make sense of liberalization policies which appear to bear no resemblance to their lived experience or realities. Unfortunately, liberal economics and the need for universal and rapid structural change has colonized the thinking of western governments and become the accepted form of economic discourse. This discourse has at its root a belief that people are basically selfish and people need galvanizing into work. In fact, those economic systems based on the assumption that people are 'selfish and competitive by nature' actually reinforce people acting in their individual interests. Social policies and structures can either reinforce individualist behaviour or a sense of collectivity. For example, if local services are inadequate, people will need more disposable income to buy what the state is not providing. They are also likely to be opposed to tax increases because they can see no local benefits from paying tax. By contrast, if the social infrastructure and services are good, the public are more likely to be persuaded of the benefits of paying more tax. In the UK the consensus view is that investment in public transport is needed, yet without good local transport services people need more cars and therefore cheaper fuel; a contradiction which many environmentalists face. Economic and management systems can be self-fulfilling. Most people make decisions appropriate to their own lives and circumstances which may appear irrational to economists and policymakers. Even education, which is viewed by most people as a desirable commodity, is seen by many youths as 'alien' and not something they want. State provision and structures do not alone convince people from various communities of why they should engage with those programmes that are devised for their advantage.

Multinationals are eager to enter the 'business ethics' debate in order to improve their companies' public credibility and reputations, although trading activity appears to have changed very little and continues to undermine local economies and increase unemployment. Developing democracy and organizational success is no longer dependent only on individual achievement, tradition and habit, but on the growth of social and egalitarian relationships. Such relationships are not engendered by narrow economic models which assume people to be selfish and the Protestant work ethic to be paramount, but by the active work of those working in the community building confidence and trust. The problem is that those working long hours do not have the time for running youth clubs, crèches or football teams.

Nurturing social capital

The concept of social capital has become accepted in recent years as the key to development precisely because the changing world of politics and organizational life demand adaptable people who are willing to learn. Confidence in the future and in change, a willingness to listen and to learn cannot be decreed, it has to be nurtured. It is not surprising that for women and those living in poorer communities local social relationships are the bedrock of their lives, nor that various western donors prioritize women's development. This is because it is assumed that women will bring social values and networking skills to organizations and politicians:

> People born with the habit of co-operating do not lose it easily, even if the basis for trust has started to disappear. The art of association may thus appear quite

healthy today, with new groups, associations and communities springing up all the time. But, interest groups in the political arena or virtual communities in cyberspace are not likely to replace older moral communities with shared values in their impact on ethical habits. And as the cases of low trust and the societies that we have examined indicate, once social capital has been spent it may take centuries to replenish. (Fukuyama 1995: 321)

Many have noticed the role that women play in cementing social relationships and thereby holding communities together, but, like Fukuyama (1997), they also blame the fragmentation and loss of communities on 'feminism': women are the cause of social disintegration, they have abandoned their caring relationships. This thinking which identifies social problems and then seeks to solve them by a return to traditional relationships is at the expense of women. Fukuyama values social relationships but then expects only women to cultivate them. His deeply sexist analysis ignores women as thinking people and romanticizes them as caring mothers. Like many other men he desires a world where men are free to be irresponsible and women struggle without political power to hold families, communities and marriages together. Within a male world women are responsible for social care and when they reject this role and unequal partnerships they are accused of failing in their responsibilities and for not ensuring that men behave themselves. Polly Toynbee (1997) is right to accuse Fukuyama of wanting easy solutions, by assuming that the western society could return to a former age where women were the moral guardians of society, but powerless to determine their lives. Societies and social transformation are in fact dependent on women gaining the political and public authority that they need in order to radically change political agendas. Women are critical to ethical trading is gaining ground and the feminisation process.

> I am sure he is right, women's striving for equality caused this revolution. He writes of women in society as if they were 'other' – perhaps – even the enemy. Keep them out of the labour market, give them no welfare or contraceptives and they will go back to the kitchen and cook and mother. . . . He writes as if society were constructed for the convenience of men, which of course it was. (Toynbee 1997)

Fukuyama should thank active feminists, not accuse them. Women play a significant role in partnerships. Fukuyama is wrong to suppose that women have destroyed social relationships and communities when the opposite is more often the case; oppressive regimes and capitalist trade have done a much more effective job of dismantling localized communities. The social relationships required are unlikely to emerge in authoritarian societies where all the external voices are whispering 'don't trust them'.

Authoritarian regimes create social mistrust and suspicion and leave behind them lingering personal psychologies which were nurtured in fear and oppression. The attitude is presumably just as pertinent to the modern world as it was in the 1930s. Those socialized in closed societies tend to be suspicious of 'difference' and 'diversity'. According to Orlando Figes (1996) the feudal and Tsarist traditions of Russian peasant society reappeared in almost identical forms within the totalitarian culture of the Soviet Regime. Conformists do not transform into non-conformists as if butterflies from chrysalis. Gorky's quotation 'scratch a revolutionary and you'll find a policeman' rings true in most authoritarian societies.

Developing a trust within the workplace among those who are used to a bullying culture is difficult; fear and suspicion are difficult to shift. Individuals need confidence to move from the habits of a lifetime. They also need to be given reasons why any change is going to be good for them. Stubbornness and resistance to change have their roots in years of oppression within authoritarian families or communities; they also stem from basic disagreement and misunderstanding. Those who have been bullied or were bullies find it extremely difficult to relate to other people as anything other than weak or powerful. They are likely to be loyal to those who are powerful and terrorize those who are socially weak:

> Trust is the expectation that arises within a community of regular, honest and co-operative behaviour, based on commonly shared norms, on the part of the other members of the community . . . Social capital is a capability that arises from the prevalence of trust in a society or certain parts of it. It can be embodied in the smallest and most basic social group, the family, as well as in the largest of all groups, the nation, and in all the other groups in between. (Fukuyama 1995: 26)

Loyalty within authoritarian cultures usually extends to a tight-knit male group and is generally an overrated concept. Trusting in those like yourself in warlike situations is a necessity; the Mafia, street gangs and clans defend their own but treat 'outsiders' as the enemy. Trust, like loyalty, can extend only as far as the family or the street.

The links between local male conflicts, cronyism and international trade wars result in the characterization of male disputes as of public concern, whereas the conflicts between men and women tend to be understood as domestic and personal. The significance of gender struggles is dislocated from the public arena as if only concerning individual men and women and swept aside as personal matters.

The system or thing approach

There is still a widespread belief that social change results from tinkering with structures and systems. Policy-makers continue to ignore how change processes and structural change impacts on people and why employees are resistant to their perfect modelling. The separation of gender cultures from public cultures has also resulted in very mechanical approaches to change in the west.

There appear to be two very different approaches to change: one is focused on 'things' and the other on 'people'. The 'thing' approach (systems/structures) tends to lead to forms of organization, management and measurement that undervalue people. Such closed systems are inflexible and insensitive to diversity. The people approach is sensitive to individual and local diversity but can be partial and parochial. The Labour movement debate in Britain has tended to refer almost exclusively to the 'systems' approach. It makes use of the structural levers of privatization, market testing and contracting mechanisms and ignores the impact of management style and systems. Politicians pay considerable attention to statisticians, accountants and economists, but appear to mistake the voices of staff, users and specialists as somehow being more partial. Even when economic models are proved poor predictors, they dominate policy and political discourse and are used to undermine those who hold alternative views on the basis of little evidence. The dislocation of management from policy-making also illustrates a disjuncture between systems and managerial mechanisms, which is further reinforced by politicians who value accountants and financiers above social analysts and systems over process analysis.

This tendency to mythologize the economic models and abstractions ignores the impact of models on social relationships and on people. The separation of model from practice allows the managers and economists to avoid the social implications of their models. A similar tendency can be observed in the belief that management is a neutral subject divorced from the realm of politics. The neglect of a people approach and the disregard for personal agency in social change and decision-making is reflected in nineteenth-century individual psychology, structural sociology and western economics. The dominance of structuralism within the social sciences has done much to hide the role of agency in social change. Because empiricism has often been for so long assumed to be the handmaiden of positivism within the social sciences (Brydon-Miller 1984), academics too often do not record how models and systems impact on what people do feel and think, personal accounts, especially by women, are held in disdain by the very critics of reductionism and positivism. Those social scientists critical of reductionism are often rather disdainful of everyday realities and tend to resort to model building and theoretical contortions, devaluing those more interested in empirical study and grounded research. The philosophy underpinning social and economic sciences is highly reductionist in nature and has had an impact on social scientists who ignore or marginalize the human capacity to think, be ambiguous or to have a change of mind. The social sciences too often assume that people are either driven only by unconscious selfish urges or by powerful overwhelming social forces. Mainstream social and economic sciences endorse the view that social change results solely from the mechanical shift of various economic and social systems; the fact that the social world is being constantly readjusted by thinking active agents, people, tends to be forgotten, under-played and marginalized.

The focus on systems and models rather than on process is more, not less evident within socialist Marxist traditions rather than in the more conservative laissez-faire politics. The orthodox tradition in the philosophy of science has depended on an implicit belief in empirical realism, where the objects of scientific investigation are the objects of actual experience. Historically, practically all orthodox theories of the natural sciences presupposed closed systems, systems which relied on highly predictable internal structures and causally related to ends and means relationships. This tradition has been overturned in science and was totally inappropriate as an account of social behaviour by virtue of the fact that people have the capacity to be reflexive and innovative as well as responsive. Human behaviour may be largely predictable, but it can also be unpredictable, which is what is interesting to anyone desirous of social change. The contexts and conditions which support individuals' innovative responsives need to be developed, not confirmation of the fact that people can and often are predictable and conformist. There is enough evidence on the impact of systems on communities and individuals. The problem for many was that politicians who were interested in social change were not necessarily interested in personal change and egalitarian relationships, far from seeking creativity, they sought greater control.

> At the heart of Trotsky's plans there was a broader vision of the whole of society being run on military lines. . . . He wanted the economy to be run with military style discipline and precision. The whole population was to be conscripted into labour regiments and brigades and dispatched like soldiers to carry out production orders on the economic front. Here was the prototype of the Stalinist command economy. Both were driven by the notion that in a backward peasant country such as Russia, state coercion could be used as a short-cut to communism, . . . what Soviet Russia lacked in economic development it could make up through the coercive power of the State. It would be more effective to compel workers . . . Trotsky extolled the achievements of serf labour and siezed them to justify his economic plants. He would have no truck with the warnings of his critics that the sue of forced labour would be unproductive. "If this is so", he told the Congress of Trade Unions in April 1920 "then you can put a cross over Socialism". At the heart of this "barrack communism" was the Bolshevik fear of the working class as an independent and increasingly rebellious force. (Figes 1996: 723)

The impact of military systems within politics and organizations is still evident: the 'system' paradigm remains paramount in western thought. The consequence of this mechanical view of organizations is that often those individuals and people who could collectively be innovative in transforming relationships are marginalized and invisible.

Systems can change and they can be transformed, not only by restructurings and economic macro levers, but also through the daily personal readjustments of active agents. Agency is usually attached to social or class status and men. The rigidity of social stratification and class dimensions undermines the confidence of marginal 'individuals'. The obsession with either the vanguard or senior managers has resulted in obscurity for those social innovators who are struggling to transform their realities lower down in organizations.

The capacity of people to think and to act upon personal agency is bound up with their assumptions about their capabilities and their appraisal of what is possible within their social environment. The marginalization of agency within academic frameworks and the political mindset which tends to polarize systems and volition undermines the very process of transformation. The legacies of Durkheim, Freud and Marx also marginalize the conscious and appraising person, man or woman, within analysis and in policy-making. In contrast, the positivist framework ignores this conscious and determining capacity and assumes that behaviour and social life can be accounted for by 'objective' third-party reductionism. The Frankfurt School, the critical theorists, feminists and grounded theorists have all criticized this lack of focus on the person as a thinking, feeling and determining being and wanted their research to assist social change or to explore new ways of accounting for change and the role of individual agency.

The explanation for this lies in the desire of academic psychologists to prove their scientific credibility by imitating pure science methodologies totally inappropriate to their subject; one would assume that 'personal agency' would be central to mainstream academic psychology, but unfortunately it is not. Recently psychologists have resorted to further alienation by explaining away human capacities in computer simulations and artificial intelligence models. Even cognitive theory encapsulates the 'conscious self' in a rational model, divorced from its own reflexive volition. Students continue to enrol for psychology courses in the belief that they may discover significant realities about themselves, their relationships and the social world, only to find that they are confronted with abstract models that deny their own personal and social realities. Many feminist psychologists theorists have tried to counter this tendency to ignore 'personal agency' and dynamic change. In the 1950s Goffman (1959) had developed the notion of 'self-role' to counter this reductionist tradition, to make sense of personal autonomy and personal strategy. Unfortunately, mainstream psychology refused the offer and instead began to conceive people as computers with mechanical intelligence. Perhaps this tradition can be explained by the lack of confidence in the social sciences to develop alternative validation frameworks. It is significant that those trained in the natural sciences are at the forefront of the struggle to make better sense of human life, as conscious and social agents in the name of democracy, social justice and civic life:

> The marginalisers of consciousness deny the possibility that human beings might be able to reform human institutions in order to ensure the more efficient production of goods and a more equitable distribution of power in society. They

foreclose the future and say that, if the latter is different from the past, it will not be the result of individual's efforts or deliberate collective effort. Where there is unequivocal evidence of progress, the totalising pessimism of the marginalisers of consciousness will oblige them to deny this evidence; it was not simply a spirit of perversity that moved Foucault to maintain that penal reform was merely a change of style aimed at inserting social control deeper into the criminal's soul and that the reformed prisons of Faucher were therefore no advance on the public dismemberment of criminals. (Tallis 1997: 314)

Making sense of agency and innovation is complex and depends on a social philosophical framework that neither hides completely the role that individuals can play, nor mirrors that role to such an extent that social, institutional and political forces are ignored.

The Critical Management Network is one attempt to unite social determinants with individual agency (Alvesson and Willmott 1992), but unfortunately the debate is in danger of becoming so rarefied in the realms of theory and abstraction that it does little to facilitate change within organizations or management generally. There is a powerful tendency to abstract and rarify among academics whereby their language and conceptual approach (research confirms rather than challenges negative realities) alienates those actively struggling with social change and the realities of life.

This tendency is also evident within Critical Management where 'challenging' agents tend to be conceived as individual players, divorced from other people and the power struggles around them. The tendency to focus on the individual psychology of each person (Hazen 1994) obscures the nature of adjustment processes, which involve more than one individual and are located in the power relations of the organization. Critical Theory has yet to acknowledge the problems of those grappling with difficult realities, as well as drawing attention to the limits of institutional organizational forms and of the danger in exaggerating discourse over social realities. It would appear that often those who question dislocation within organizational studies are themselves marginalized as academics. The same dynamics operate within academic circles as in other social groups where those more oppressed by gender cultures are most conscious of the need to transform value, work patterns and cultures.

Postmodern approaches to agency

The deconstruction of modernist structures, authoritarian cultures and stereotypes during the 1960s was a liberating experience, but the total deconstruction of shared-value frameworks which provided anchors for positive action was a demolition too far. Some postmodern strands have become so absorbent of diverse views that they no longer have any value framework on which to hang their future work. The problem of much postmodernist thought is that it results in such a relativist position that no analysis can develop because no one is willing or able to make a judgement on its truth or appropriateness, afraid of being accused of arrogance. The connections between motivation and change are yet again obscured because each individual's story is verified and common realities are ignored. This position is sometimes justified on the grounds of the mistaken (politically correct) notion that to acknowledge the individual difference is radical but to analyse or criticize that divergent experience is offensive. Postmodernism is in the main idealistic and romantic, dealing with 'oughts' and 'wishes' rather than realities, histories and social constraints. Some postmodernist writers appear to want to deny the reality of history and power relations in order to 'romanticize' the diverse and incomprehensible world of social change (Epstein 1996). Although interpersonal relationships ultimately influence social change, they are left underdeveloped and uncluttered by the normal negotiations of social realities. This dislocation of personal view and experience from real rootedness, combined with a philosophy of relativism results in individuals feeling isolated and alienated. The abandonment of historical analysis and social reference points is no liberation if the realities of oppressive work and personal relationships continue to exist. The hostility to women does not disappear because you wish it to, although to ignore it may provide some solace. The idealized version of realities does not remove the actual constraints and pressures presented by a lack of money and social relationships. To understand oppression may be a liberation, but usually to ignore its reality is nothing more than a retreat into nostalgia. Some differentiate between those postmodernists struggling to define new experience in a changing world and those content with bleak pessimism. Rosenau (1992) suggests that some are attempting to affirm new ways of thinking, seeing and organizing while others are uninterested in realities or the future. The more positive and affirming postmodern approach is one which accepts some universal social anchors for humans but do not deny diversity and local specificity:

> The decentered, postmodern individual has a multiplicity of fragmented identities with no distinct reference points, dispersed not concentrated, unrehearsed, nor arranged. S/he focuses on choice, autonomy, and personal liberation and does not need ideological consistency . . . The postmodern individual is relaxed and flexible, oriented towards feeling and emotions, interonisation, and holding a "be-yourself" attitude . . . content with "live and let live" (in the present attitude) . . . staying away from collective application and personal development as a threat to privacy . . . modern community is . . . oppressive, it demands intimacy, giving, self-sacrifice, and mutual service . . . domineering and humiliating. (Rosenau 1992: 234)

Bewes (1997) suggests that postmodernity has in effect constituted a retreat from 'truth', and represents a temporary lapse from political realities and a failure to engage. Both, modernism (structuralism) and postmodernism (idealism) can oppress those seeking social change. The former negates a person's role in change and undermines their confidence; the latter generates completely unrealistic expectations. There is a need to move beyond postmodern diversity and modernist reductionism to a post post-modern perspective where human social values (even though expressed in various ways) become the anchor for more affirming analysis and therefore a confidence in the future. Human beings need a confidence in what Giddens (1995) calls 'new beginnings' as well as in 'endings' if they are to engage in new thinking and social change. Individuals need affirmation in the form of social agreement in order that the process of shifting paradigms is within human control rather than outside it. The marginalization of radical agents within organizational analysis and the polarization between social determinism and individual volition is further reinforced by the fact that transforming social philosophies are only evolving. The social sciences have been dogged for many years by dualistic controversies in philosophy that veer between an obsession with subjectivity and a denial of the human subject's agency, consciousness and ability to change realities.

Over the last century, popular, academic and political thinking about society has tended to gravitate towards one or other of the poles of a crude polarity between individualism and collectivism. Thus classical social theory has swung between the individualism and voluntarism of utilitarianism and Weberianism on the one hand and the collectivism and reification involved in organicist and Durkheimian social thought on the other. At a political level, the former found expression in liberalism and the latter in labourism (and Stalinism).

Kuhn's thesis (1970) that social and individual world views shape our unconscious and conscious thinking and our mode of scientific enquiry was revolutionary. He suggested that our minds act as windows or prisms through which we interpret the social world. What this meant in effect was that the conceptual frameworks of social sciences were necessarily incomplete because they were constantly unfolding. As the person moves with the description they are influenced and guided by the historical context in which they live. Social transformation requires a bedrock of a social philosophy that is not rooted in either social determinism or individual omnipotence. Bhaskar's (1989) 'critical realism' is an attempt to move beyond both material determinism and idealistic voluntarism and provides a view that allows for each person to hold their own traditional philosophical framework.

Practically all the theories of orthodox philosophy of science, and the methodological directives they secrete presuppose closed systems. Because of this they are totally inappropriate of the social sciences — this is not to say that attempts cannot be made to apply them, with disastrous results. . . . The only concern of social science with them (Popperian theories of scientific rationality) is as objects of substantive explanation. The real methodological import of the absence of spontaneously occurring, and the impossibility of artificially creating, closed systems is strictly limited; it is that the social sciences are denied, in principle, decisive test situations for their theories. This means that the criteria for the rational confirmation and rejection of theories in social sciences cannot be predictive, and so must be exclusively explanatory. (Bhaskar 1989: 83)

Bhaskar (1989) provides a philosophical framework for social transformation that acknowledges personal agency as well as the power of the social and economic world. He makes sense of the relationship between 'social reality' and 'individual agency' which shifts the mindset from polarization between 'the idealist' and 'the determinist'. He suggests that 'social reality' does exist independently of individuals and is not a figment of the mind or imagination as some more postmodern writers tend to suggest. All individuals have the potential and the capacity to change or transform that independent social reality. He conceptualizes a social philosophy as a formulation that accounts for the relationship between human agency and social activity, rather than merely fixating them in idealized models or schemas:

On this transformational and relational conception, society is a skilled accomplishment of active agents. But the social world may be opaque to the social agents upon whose activity it depends in four respects, in that these activities may depend on or involve (a) unacknowledged conditions, (b) unintended consequences, (c) the exercise of tacit skills, and/or (d) unconscious motivation. (Bhaskar 1989: 3)

Bhaskar's conceptualization of the social construction of reality is to locate the actual existence of social reality outside, or independent of individuals, and provides a philosophical model of the transforming interaction between people as agents and the social environment. Critical realists such as Bhaskar argue for a philosophy which can actively make sense of realities and of the role of people in changing those realities, and suggests a conception of social activity which avoids determinism and a reification of individual volition. This view is in opposition to both atomistic individualism and undifferentiated collectivism. According to the transformational understanding of social activity, the existence of social structure is a necessary condition for any human activity.

Unfortunately, often the evidence of transforming realities and the role of unusual change agents are ignored because the empirical research is undervalued by some academics who are more concerned with general theory and comparative analysis of countries, states and companies than with social change. This lack of interest in changing realities results in creating an academic vacuum on contemporary cultural change that is filled by journalists.

Individuals as determining change agents

Critical realists argue that philosophical arguments are themselves historically and socially located. Historical relationships form the basis for all philosophy and a priori truths are conditional on historical realities. This approach is not dissimilar from that of Kelly's (1955) and Schon's (1983) in making sense of agency from the individual's knowledge framework and is for them grounded in their own experience. John Dewey, George Kelly and Donald Schon believed that everyone is a thinking and determining person. They made sense of social interaction by observing that capacity of all individuals to act as reflexive practitioners. Every person has the capability (even if underutilized) to appraise and construe social realities and make judgements about their actions, responses and thinking. This practical and pragmatic approach to philosophy and individual psychology puts (social) change in the hands of thinking and appraising people. They were also aware that individuals were capable of being 'inert' and 'passive' as well as 'decisive' and 'determining'. The 'self-role' theorists tended to overplay the individual capacity to be determining and decisive when in fact most people find it impossible to break from personal, historical and social roles and constraints. American management consultants suffer from the same overconfidence that all individuals are free to act, change and learn, irrespective of their environments and relationships. Kelly (1955) recognized constraint and developed a psychology based on each individual's personal constructs. From this perspective, every person is a scientist and the ultimate explanation of human behaviour lies in examining the questions s/he asks, the inquiry s/he pursues and the strategies s/he employs. This is in contrast with those psychologists who analyse behaviour without regard for the person's own view and emotions. This is a more person-centred psychology and way of conducting social science research and is known as personal construct theory.

The significance of personal construct theory was that it accounted for each person's individual appraisal of the social world in the light of their own history, experience and socialization. A person's own framework of conceptualizations is critical to their appraisal of their world and how they learn which responses are most useful and which are not. Clearly such a process will lead people to reflect the constructs common to their gender, class, race and culture. Kelly's concern was to understand people from their own viewpoints, not necessarily gleaned from their rational comments and also from their reactions and more emotive 'construals' of the world. This notion of 'construal' denoted both cognitive and emotive reactions and could be conscious or unconscious; a person may not articulate their concept and constructs. This was a total break from previous psychological perspectives, which objectified each individual as a subject for the psychologist, or from the idea that people were either totally 'rational' or 'emotional'. This split between the emotional and rational underpins popular philosophical thinking, and then a traditional gendered separation between men's and women's capacities. Within Europe, men have historically been considered more 'rational' than women, who were thought of as intellectually weaker because of their 'emotional' natures.

Kelly's followers, Bannister and Franscella (1986) point out no one actually ever responds only to immediate stimulus, they test it against previous experience and social conventions. What they respond to are their own constructions of what that stimulus means to them. If someone receives the comment 'What a nice hat', they take it as a compliment. If they know that the speaker dislikes them then they may think it a sarcastic comment. The significance of Kelly's framework is that it connects a person's values and emotion to social conceptualizations. No construct is ever 'neutral' or detached from the social world in which the person lives. There might be huge areas of life that are so emotive for a person that they cannot be articulated or described. Schon suggests that each person has an enquiring capacity – accepting that some may enquire and appraise reality more knowingly than others:

> When someone reflects in action, s/he becomes a researcher in the practice context. S/he is not dependent on the categories of established theory and technique, but constructs a new theory of the unique case. Enquiry is not limited to a deliberation about means which depends no prior agreement about ends. S/he does not keep means and ends separate, but defines them interactively as s/he frames a problematic situation. S/he does not separate thinking from doing, ratiocinating his way to a decision which s/he must convert to action. (Schon 1983: 68)

The connection between a person's capacity to listen, learn and develop social relationships is the key to the development of 'the learning organization'. Social change is dependent not just on vision of leaders but on the individual learning and willingness of the workforce. Mintzberg (1987) suggests that leaders should focus their attention on how policies, procedures and management affects behaviour and learning. The ability to learn is dependent on open minds and a willingness to learn. Learning depends not just on self-reflection and knowledge but also for experience and relating and working with others, not just in one organization but also stimulated by exposure to diverse organizations and contexts. An employee's openness to 'learning' and new experiences can be thwarted not just by their personal histories but also by the organizational cultures they work in. Some people feel they do not have the authority to question or to innovate. They feel 'powerless'. Too often it is conveniently ignored that an individual's willingness to learn is not only a personal matter, but is dependent on there being encouragement and work conditions which stimulate an interest in the future, in change and in learning. Readjustment is not just a personal exchange, as Mintzberg (1987) suggests, but involves a readjustment in the power relations in management, and between men and women. There are similar readjustments to be made between politicians and managers and between managers and staff.

There exists an unreal world where individual citizens, employees and students are now expected to analyse their own weaknesses and failings and to engage in partnerships often with those more powerful than they. The modern manager expects personal change. But there are few people who manage to change who do not have the support of friends or colleagues and even fewer who can be creative when anxious and insecure. There is a need for sustaining conditions for new and emergent relationships and also for a greater confidence in changes which reinforce social values.

The negativity attached to many political movements is as oppressive as are beliefs that change is impossible. Lynn Segal (1990) is right to draw attention to the negative effect of so much later feminist theory which far from inspiring women that they could change the social reality of powerful gender relations, instead fixated them in a framework of the overriding and all-powerful dynamic of patriarchy.

> One contradiction informing the new pessimism is immediately apparent: two decades of resurgent feminist thought and action has benefited some women but not others . . . the peculiar vulnerability of women engaged in reproduction and childcare as their primary responsibility and work makes it hard to protect them from the depredations of capital in search of cheap labour. (Segal 1990: 298)

The women's movement has probably been one of the most effective cultural campaigns ever, for although many now deny being 'feminist', their thinking had a dramatic impact on women throughout the world. Feminism has its roots in active struggle and dialogue which gave rise to new thinking about gender relations. However, it was not feminist theory which transformed social conceptions and realities, but the action of millions of women demanding egalitarian relationships, aided and abetted by financial independence and dramatic technological change. Individuals engaged in collective everyday actions can, and do, transform people's social realities. Segal (1990) notes how wearying, tiring and exhausting the women's struggle was to make men listen to them in the 1980s, but it has had an effect both on men as partners and as colleagues in the labour movement. The language used to describe the women's struggle has also had an impact on the language, thinking and values in the labour movement. The collective arguments and activities were often painful, but they provided a context for challenging traditional thinking, ways of organization and working:

> The fact that women gave themselves the space and the legitimacy to discuss traditional codes and practices enabled them to have greater confidence in changing social conceptions and relationships. For some women the emphasis was primarily on their domestic relationships with partners, parents and children – for others the world of work, pay and social justice the stronger and more confident the pressures from women for men to change both at a personal level

> and through collective political struggle, the more men will be forced to question the unthinking presumptions and unexamined prerogatives of 'masculinity'. (Segal 1990: xiii)

Men's resistance to change is not reducible to their psychic obstinacy or incapacity. Men can and do change. Resistance to change is also bound up with the persisting gender routines which characterize most of the wider economic, social and political structures of contemporary society. But social realities are not stable.

> Future relations between women and men remain open, whether the intended outcome of emancipation, activity or the unintended consequence of other agencies is undesirable. Much of the recent feminist writing on men has seemed to suggest that nothing has changed. But it is interesting, and certainly more useful, to see how things do in fact change. (Segal 1990: xiii)

It is evident that British public expectations of personal and social relationships have changed dramatically over the past 50 years. The social or cultural movements have become the most powerful levers of change in our societies. Cultural resistance may be less noticed because it is less formally organized and outside established parties, but it is no less significant. Although the trade unions are weaker in the UK than they were in the 1970s, the evidence would suggest that many more younger people are now opting out of the system altogether. The travellers' movement is evidence of the cultural gap between the young and those brought up believing that the establishment would support them. Similarly those in work are much more likely to resign if they are humiliated or treated badly. Within fragmenting cultures the key to business success has to be a willingness to develop positive work relationships with people from diverse backgrounds. Coercion is much less likely achieved in the 1990s than in previous eras. The structures and power relationships within the work environment influence each employee's ability and motivation to learn, readjust and communicate. The questions remain how to support learning and collaboration; what conditions are needed to sustain a paradigm shift in thinking and behaving; how is the move to be made from closed to open thinking, minds and relationships, within a gendered culture where female innovators are rebuffed and ridiculed.

4   Resistance to women

I have never been quick to shout male prejudice, and yet I cannot avoid the knowledge that for many men a woman vice chancellor seems an easy target for resentment and envy. The wild stories that sometimes circulate: 'did you know she had gold plated taps and marble floors in the vice chancellor's private bathroom?' are only the trivial manifestations of a deeper feeling that the job does not belong to a woman. (Baroness Perry, *Guardian*, 17 November 1992)

Socialist feminists have strongly argued that to explain the hierarchies in the workplace we need to understand the men's desire to maintain their personal dominance at work. Cockburn (1991) has powerfully shown the extent of resistance to women that persists in British organizations, whether in public or private ownership. She recounts how women organize and resist these obstacles. Not only are women held back by well-accepted structural barriers of long working hours, inflexible working patterns and expensive or no childcare (Stone 1988; NEDO 1990;), but they are also trapped by traditional gender cultures (Maddock and Parkin 1993).

In 1975 Broverman and colleagues noticed that men held a very stereotyped view of women as workers. They were seen as dependent, passive, non-competitive, illogical, less competent and if not competent then less objective. Kanter, in her (1977) study of Insco, observed that male managers treated their female subordinates with a mixture of patronizing humour, sarcasm and indifference. She showed how women are trapped into work cultures which not only discriminate against women's entry into work positions but often confirmed them in a belief that they were second-rate. Resistance to women is complex. Structural barriers are well reported, as is the fragmentation of the labour market (Milkman 1986), but the resistance which springs from the traditional assumptions grounded in social culture is less researched. Cynthia Cockburn, a professor at the City of London University and internationally respected feminist author, analyses women's experiences from a theoretical socio-political context. The work culture is basically still a male culture in need of socialization, in need of gender balancing:

For women to escape subordination to men the relationship of home to work has to change beyond anything yet envisaged in the name of equality policy. Men have to be domesticated and in the workplace (to use Joan Acker's phrase) the rhythm and timing of work must be adapted to the rhythms of life outside. For women, getting into the workplace, becoming workers, earning their money, has proved a necessary but insufficient step towards liberation. A further necessary condition is for men to move the other way, get into the home, start nurturing, become domestics. (Cockburn 1991: 98)

The success of the 'macho' male has been and is still totally dependent on the stock of women's working knowledge. The unspoken skills of women, such as caring ego-masseurs are completely unacknowledged and, more importantly within managerialism they are undefined and therefore unmeasured. The same task can be named differently when done by men not women, for instance, typing was typesetting for men and has now become computing. Women's work is not only under-valued they are often not visible or recognized until they conform to male behaviours and become silent about their difficulties and differences. This is as true in medicine as it is in the trade unions. Cynthia Cockburn's (1987) research into women's secondary role in the trade unions and the Labour Party led her to conclude that:

> there is tightly packaged association of working-class identity, trade union membership, Labour loyalty and masculinity, which excludes or undermines women. Seeing only themselves as central, men tend to ignore women or to regard their assertiveness as aggression, 'if she wants a place on the executive then she can't be a normal woman'. (Cockburn 1987: 67)

Women cannot win in this environment. They cannot join if they are a woman and once they start to behave as a man, they cannot be a 'proper woman'. This dynamic or 'catch 22' situation is most common in professions and workplaces where women are rare except for where they work in the most junior and menial positions. The level of hostility in Britain towards women who dare to be different, have strong views and aspire to leadership bubbles up in many of the professions as well as in management. The media are still headed by men, as are almost all company boards and quangos. A senior woman working alone among men in a highly segregated culture will experience difficulties no matter how strategic she is. Managing an antagonistic culture at work can be difficult and isolated woman are especially vulnerable (Kanter 1977; Halford 1993). Women who do not conform to such a role model are penalized and frequently scrutinized for possible failings and mistakes (Kanter 1977). Senior women are subject to gossip, abuse and criticism in work environments where staff are unused to women managers (Harragan 1977; Kanter 1977) and those women leading or initiating change are especially vulnerable (Maddock 1993b). Many women avoid senior management precisely because they anticipate such treatment (Maddock 1993b).

The cases of Alison Halford (1993) and Wendy Savage are well known, but there are many other women who have been subjected to similar abuse and distortion merely because they argued for social change within male work environments. When Baroness Perry became the first vice-chancellor she was ridiculed in the local press for a luxury bath with gold taps. Alison Taylor's life was ruined in the 1980s because she drew attention to abuse in a North Wales children's home – since which time the abuse has been acknowledged (Community Care 1996).

Both Alison Halford and Wendy Savage were advocates of new practices: Halford wanted to introduce new and broader training in the Merseyside police force; Savage was a campaigner for a woman's right to choose how she gave birth. Both have been vindicated and their radical views on care and organization now adopted as mainstream. Savage's views are now enshrined in the government's guidance on 'Changing Childbirth' (DoH 1993). Outspoken, radical women continue to be attacked for dissenting from the views of the establishment. There are degrees of prejudice, ranging from outright discrimination to more subtle forms of ridicule. Often radical women are just ignored and frozen out. A workplace may appear to have an egalitarian culture until a crisis occurs and then those women with strong views find themselves attacked even though they appear to be behaving no differently from dominant male colleagues.

There has been clear evidence of overt discrimination against women in management and in most government institutions, promotions in companies are still decided on the basis of style rather than on performance (Gutek and Stephens 1979; Alimo-Metcalfe 1992 a and b, 1995; Coe 1992). Studies by authors such as Hennig and Jardim (1978), Marshall (1984), Hammond (1988), Coyle (1989a) and by the British Institute of Management (Coe 1992) have shown that there is extensive and active resistance to women in the UK.

Cockburn (1991) has shown how the dynamics of this resistance operate and are thriving within the UK. She suggests that patriarchal relations continue to dominate men's and women's behaviour and opportunities in almost all organizations:

> I have met few, and I have to say very few men who were supportive not only of women's progress in the (Civil) Service, but also of the aims of the equality policy and the women's movement. . . . Men's resentment against women surfaced in a number of different forms. Women found some of their male subordinates unwilling to accept their authority . . . or had a chip on their shoulder . . . were awkward or created undercurrents . . . very successful women are often the target of a lot of hostility and comment. (Cockburn 1991: 66–67).

There is growing recognition that this cultural resistance to women bars them from decision-making posts. Surveys of managers in the early 1990s suggested that 86% of all women saw male prejudice as the biggest barrier for them at work (Coe 1992). In Swedish institutions, where women and men had equal status as managers, the men remained hostile to female colleagues (Ressner 1987). In Britain most male executives are married and have wives who service them and are unused to decisive women in the work context. For many men, their image of women is in the home where they expect women to be powerful, such men tend to find women who deviate from the domestic role threatening and ridicule challenging women as one way of punishing them. Women who reach positions of power are frequently subjected to rumour and gossip about their personal lives, especially if they are childless, single and attractive:

> Men, however, have a repertoire of negative representation of women, and significantly, they were critical of women only in relation to authority. It hinges on two themes, a 'belt and braces' pair. Women are not capable of authority. And they turn into nasty people when in authority. Thus, on the first count, women 'lack a bit of judgement', and 'get a bit emotional', 'are not cut out for it', 'find it difficult to be ruthless enough' and so on. On the second count, women in top jobs are 'bossy', 'pushy', 'absolute bastards', trampling on others in their ambitions. (Cockburn 1991: 67)

Kanter (1977), some years earlier, had drawn particular attention to the vulnerability of women in senior positions. The recent cases of Dr Daly (Cuff 1993) and Alison Halford (1993) illustrate graphically how behaviour quite normal in a male colleague can be ruled totally unacceptable in a woman, irrespective of talent or rank. Within traditional gender cultures, an acceptance of job segregation remains, which is sustained by women and men, who are particularly critical of challenging women.

Women entering uncharted workplaces are a challenge merely because of their sex. In fact, it is surprising that so many women have reached middle management; without equal opportunities policies women would not now be waiting to breaking through the 'glass ceiling' into the boardroom. Resistance to women in male cultures propels them into contradictory positions and conflicts. This becomes obvious as women are promoted. The woman executive has a powerful management role, but also the weaker role of being a woman. The more traditional the culture, the more difficult it is for women to balance work roles and gender identities, and the less likely that women are able to be themselves, as women and as managers.

Women in management

Women are more likely to work as managers in the public sector and in 'caring' or personnel services. It is often the case that women executives are responsible for support or marginal services, have social or welfare functions and work in areas such as personnel or training (Kanter 1977). More recently Val Hammond (1988), research director at Roffey Park Management Centre and formerly at Ashridge Management Centre has shown that women in the UK are also branching out into new fields of banking, insurance and manufacturing management and have set up women's professional associations. Of all national voluntary organizations 38% are now run by women. Although this is a higher percentage compared with other sectors, it does not reflect the fact that women overwhelmingly dominate the workforce in non-government and voluntary organizations.

A Hansard Commission in 1990 found that only 6.7% of senior managers in top CBI firms in Britain were women. According to NEDO (1990) there were three million managers in Britain of which 27% were women and only 4% of these were senior managers; in industry the figure was even lower where only 1–2% of senior executives were women. This is in a country where 45% of its 22 million workers are women. The same NEDO report showed that around 5% of all women in employment were professionals or senior managers (NEDO 1990). The Institute of Directors in the UK has 35,000 members, but only 6% of them are women. Even where women are employed in significant numbers, such as in local government, the NHS and education, women are grossly under-represented in senior management. Spencer and Welchman (1991) in their study of local government women managers reported that 'there is a near absence of women at the top'. Coe's (1992) study of women in business management reinforced this view. Even government reports acknowledge that merely naming inequality is ineffective. Recruiting women into top jobs demands strategic planning; it will not just happen (Hansard 1990).

Schein and Mueller (1992) pointed out that, although women in the USA are said to be more assertive and more ambitious than their British counterparts, the number of women holding senior managerial positions is significantly lower and amounts to only 2% of the women in employment. The situation in Germany is even worse with no more than 1% of working women holding senior positions (Anatal and Krebsbach-Gnath 1988). In addition, over 50% of male managers in Germany said that they would not even consider a female candidate for a senior management position (Schein and Mueller 1992). Schein's (1975) original statement 'think management, think male' still appears to apply. The question posed by many was that given that a greater number of women had become managers in the public sector, why were there so few in decision-making positions?

The status of women in Denmark and Sweden is higher than in any other country. Both childcare and parental leave are generous and women's representation in parliament is the highest in the world. Yet women still only occupy 28% of all seats, whereas in the UK the figure is only 4% and in the USA 5% (Segal 1990). Feminists in Denmark and Sweden are worried that even with generous childcare provision and well-developed equality policies which have been in place for twenty years, women account for only 50% of senior managers in the public sector. There can be no doubt that men are changed by a greater involvement in childcare and domestic work and a main complaint of Swedish women is that men did not take up the paternity leave available to them (Segal 1990).

There have been a number of studies highlighting the barriers which women face if they want to reach more senior grades. Jackson and Hirsh (1991) concluded from a survey of UK research literature that women have a series of obstacles and expectations to overcome if they are to enter senior management. These include: getting on the right career track; working hard at all times and making themselves available (long hours, no career breaks, being geographically mobile), qualifying themselves for promotion.

> Potential women managers compete in a hurdle race with their male peers in which they are handicapped by having to jump additional hurdles of childcare and domestic work – it is not surprising that under these conditions more women than men drop out of the race. (Jackson and Hirsh 1991: 10)

Studies on women managers in the UK (Davidson 1989) indicate that women are more likely to bear the burden of domestic caring and domestic life. The number of women political representatives in local government is also low. Marshall (1984) in her book, *Women Managers: Travellers in a Male World*, provided a British account of how the male culture of work organizations influenced not just the treatment of women as individuals but also their career decisions and choices.

However, many of these surveys continue to assume that women aspire to senior positions when in fact there is some evidence that they are hesitant about promotion in the British public sector. Women's reluctance to put themselves forward for promotion has always been interpreted as their lacking ambition. White et al. (1993) show how women's refusal and reluctance to get involved in social networks has important implications for their career development. Hennig and Jardim (1978) found that women's focus on self and organizational development led them to be less career orientated; they failed to let more senior managers know what they wanted in terms of career development. They also tended to think that people were promoted on the basis of competence and failed to recognize that even excellence was not necessarily going to secure advancement (White et al. 1993).

Other research shows women to be more ambitious in their careers than had previously been noted (Hirsh and Jackson 1990), but indicated that they were interested in promotion at different times of their lives, before having children and after they have matured. The majority of women are not just making a decision about their careers, they also have to consider other personal and domestic commitments.

Jackson and Hirsh (1991) suggest that the solution to the dearth of senior women is to be found either by employers providing flexible working arrangements and childcare or by organizations becoming more 'women friendly'. However, either of these solutions acknowledges women as active parties, who have the capacity to transform work cultures. Women are frustrated because their organizational talents continue to go unrecognized and many are leaving large organizations to work in consultancies where they can extend themselves. Others are setting up their own businesses and agencies.

Marshall (1994) notes that the senior women she had interviewed were older than their white, male colleagues who had little experience of working with senior women. This resulted in a sense of isolation and exclusion. Without in-depth studies on women's own reasons for their choices, it is difficult to establish which are the most effective strategies for managers to adopt in order to establish gender-balanced teams. It appears that a woman's ambition depends somewhat on her own circumstances and how she evaluates her workplace and its possibilities. Often the more innovative women are not those interviewed in management research and who work in non-government organizations and consultancies are evident in the literature.

Miller and Wheeler (1992) attempted to unravel the evidence for gender differences in manager turnover, suggesting that women were more likely to leave their jobs if they felt that the organization did not offer opportunities for them. Schwartz (1989) was more assertive reporting that top women managers were two and half times more likely to leave their employment than men. The author suspects that many women leave careers for a number of reasons and not all to do with domestic commitments and children; seeking more conductive environments, more interesting work and more stimulating colleagues. Too often there is an assumption that women leave management positions to have children. Rosin and Korabik (1990) found that while two-thirds of women managers had reached middle to senior management, the other third were dissatisfied with office politics, the organization and career prospects. Marshall (1994) notes that commentators are often surprised that women were leaving not to become mothers, but because they were disenchanted with the male environment of work. Marshall's (1994) research on why women resigned from quite senior management positions reported that women were: tired and exhausted; felt undermined and under-utilized; experienced conflict at work or wanted to re-evaluate their lives and recoup their sense of value and worth. This is also the author's own experience and that of women friends working in management. They became tired of managing gender relations and a highly gendered culture. According to Marshall (1994), women managers became more aware of 'gender' as they gained more senior positions. This reflects the author's own experience that women are disappointed and bored by the male bonding culture and its schoolboy sporting banter. Marshall (1994) interviewed women managers in depth from many professions, including senior managers from local government who had resigned. Common themes emerged which reinforced the belief in both male bonding in senior management and the capacity for women to be excluded and bypassed. She was surprised by the number of women change agents in her group who, she said, were either self-appointed or given difficult management of change roles. This made women vulnerable.

A recurrent theme to be found was that after spearheading restructurings, senior women were often left stranded and liable to attack from those who disagreed with them. Those in opposition to change proposals often remain silent during the changes and wait to attack those leading the changes, when the political context has swung back in their favour.

Women in local government

Since the 1950s the growth of women's employment in local authorities has been steadily increasing, from 44.4% in 1954 to 60.9% in 1984 (Stone 1988). Women are more likely to be promoted in fields such as personnel where 53% of the profession's membership is female and women hold 20% of available management posts; this is especially true in local government and other public sector areas (Davidson 1989). In spite of strong resistance, the numbers of women in middle management continues to rise, particularly within the public sector. While much of this growth has been of part-time workers, 42.5% of local authority full-time employees were women in 1984, compared with 35% in 1954. Women in the 1980s were concentrated in jobs in education, social services and libraries and concentrated in low grades and low status jobs. The majority were low-paid workers and the vast majority were part-time. While some were head-hunted for senior posts, the number of women gaining executive and senior positions was still small, even in departments where the vast majority of employees were women, such as in social services and education. By the 1990s more women managers had moved up the career ladder and were struggling to become senior managers and chief officers. The Local Government Chronicle survey reported the below figures:

TABLE 4.1   *High flyers in local government*

	1991 %	1991 %
Chief executives	1.3	4.9
Directors	4.9	6.9
Deputies	6.8	11.4

Local Government Chronicle 1996. Per cent of women in top local government jobs, England and Wales 1996

This increase may have been due to a number of factors: demographic change; male managers leaving for the private sector; government attack and restructuring; equality policies and more flexible working practices; a critical mass already working in management.

Equality policies throughout the 1980s focused on recruitment and getting women into management. However, in spite of the number of women working in local government management and their ascendancy through to more senior positions, the internal culture in most authorities had changed very little in the 1990s. This was reflected in the feelings of those interviewed, who reported that what was of concern to them was 'being heard', and a desire to democratize management structures. The author noticed an exodus of dissatisfied female managers from local government in the late 1980s before 1990s' recession. This loss of talented personnel was noticed by some managers, but the significance of the loss was understood as a cost only in terms of replacement. Senior management continued to ignore or be oblivious to women's creative potential, their contribution to working practices, organizational culture and the management of change. It did appear that by the end of 1993 many middle managers were feeling very insecure about their futures and in general had become more nervous about giving up work. The situation in local government changes by the day. Management is constantly under pressure to change, resulting in either rethinking or entrenchment. Each local authority is guided by a different political complexity and varies in the openings it creates for women and in the resistance it presents.

A study by the West Midlands Women's Sub-committee in 1985 showed that only 19.4% of elected counsellors were women, and only 3.6% of local authorities had women leaders. By the late 1980s many women had gained significant experience in management and were more secure in their jobs and in government procedures and had started to be more concerned about organizational practices and culture. Women managers working in the metropolitan authorities started to articulate a sense of the conflict, both between the pressure of work and other commitments and between themselves and the bureaucracy.

Resistance to senior women

Given the paucity of women chief officers, it did appear as a surprise in 1992 to find that four out of the five West Yorkshire education chiefs were women; all were appointed to lead the restructuring of their authority. These women were headhunted for their vision, management skills and strategic thinking; only two had traditional career paths in education. They were responsible for introducing the local management of schools and for persuading head teachers to continue purchasing central strategic services from the education authority, which was an extremely difficult task. By 1992 three had been sacked and the fourth was seeking alternative employment. All were indirectly accused of incompetence, which was never proved, or attacked in the press as unsuitable in some way. All had their personal lives made public. The women were subjected to a torrent of abuse in the local papers, most of which was untrue or distorted. One was accused of 'racism', in spite of the fact that Asian parents supported her. The resistance to senior women in the UK continues, but it has become more personal and pernicious when the woman appears to be criticizing the status quo, upsetting the male culture and introducing new management practices and a change in style. There also continues to be an atmosphere of traditional sexism within particular departments. For example, a trainer in a northern direct service organization described the work environment as:

> one where any woman who complains about sexist remarks is seen as a self-indulgent whiner; our manager is aggressive in his flirting, he relates to everyone in a very sexual way (mostly women in cleaning and catering). He takes ten minutes to get to the point. He wants to stamp his foot on everything – his head of service has said he 'wouldn't have a woman above grade five in the department' – when I met him he said to me, 'the last trainer was a lesbian and I had her sacked', his secretary is also his partner and she informs on anyone who gets out of line. (Trainer in local government: Yorkshire 1991)

Departments within one authority can vary enormously. The corporate team can be very open and gender neutral and the housing or direct labour organization can be similar to the one as experienced by the trainer above. Many of the smaller authorities recruited women from the larger metropolitan authorities such as the GLC, Manchester and Sheffield. The old guard tended to feel very threatened by this intrusion and often smeared newer managers by gossiping about them as 'looney lefties' or 'lesbians'. The sense of contradiction between personal integrity and working practices was further highlighted as women managers in local government led change programmes and major restructuring (Cockburn 1991).

Women in the NHS

Women constitute 78% of the NHS workforce. The NHS also has a powerful effect on national and local employment patterns and conditions. In 1994, 7.5% of the UK workforce was employed in the healthcare sector and over one million were employed by the NHS. Women play a key role in healthcare in all professions and their work satisfaction or lack of it can affect the NHS dramatically. In 1995 a review was undertaken to assess the NHS performance in relation to its Opportunity 2000 goals or targets. By 1995, 38% of all chief officer posts were held by women, compared to only 28% in 1984. Of senior manager posts 47.5% were held by women in 1994, which amounted to an increase of 16% over a five-year period. The number of women finance directors had risen dramatically between 1992 and 1994 from 23 to 61. It is significant that two-thirds of all NHS management trainees are women. The figures are rising and there has been extensive investment in the promotion of women into senior management positions, mainly through the NHS Women's Unit, which has supported training, career development, mentoring, work shadowing, as well as setting national equality targets for all NHS employers. By 1994 the number of women in senior positions had risen to 40%, although the number of women medical consultants was still around 15% across specialties (NHS Women's Unit 1994). However, the cultural changes have not been as positive as the figures would suggest and the NHS decision-making bodies are still very male by nature and composition. It has also been noticed that the women in management positions have had less effect on changing service delivery than perhaps feminists in the past would have predicted. Why this should be is debatable and there are real regional differences and local cultural traditions operating within the NHS, as well as the influences of government activity targets and restructuring.

Routes to promotion

The route to senior management is more difficult for those in those female gendered professions such as nursing. Of human resources managers 69% were women, yet only 39% held director posts. Davies and Rosser (1986) found that female nurses took longer than male nurses to find senior posts. Over 82% of NHS employees are women, of whom 50% are nurses. When female nurses are promoted they find it hard to act like managers, they continue to act deferentially to medics and other managers (Macalpine and Marsh 1995). This antagonizes more challenging senior women who are looking for allies. The deferential style is adopted within 'subordinate' professions as a way of coping with authoritarian realities and leads to many female professionals being overly impressed by status and authority. The gender composition within the public sector results in many women only ever working with other women and consequently they do not recognize the gendered nature of well-worn habits and practices. They do, however, acknowledge that their professional group has less status when it is a woman's profession.

The women who have struggled within male cultures and have become chief executives have learnt that to diverge from the establishment view is dangerous. They realized that they could be criticized for being even mildly controversial:

> I would say that it is still very difficult in this region to be women, not that there are not women chief officers there are a few but they are rather of the old type, hard in some ways but very deferential in public meetings. The culture is status ridden. It is not what you do but what meetings you sit on that's important. Everyone takes themselves very seriously including the women. Changing practices is difficult and the community sector suffer from this. (NHS chief executive 1996)

There are most definitely regional variations and most of the women chief officers who have attended leadership programmes in London report a northern culture where authoritarian practices prevail. This culture tends to act as a barrier to maverick women or those who are seen as 'outsiders' and not accepted within the regional establishment. Other women may not necessarily be barred from senior posts if they conform to and match the culture. This is not to say that the number of women executives on NHS trust boards are much higher in the South but that perhaps the more personal interaction between managers is less formal:

> For instance, I know that my committee will argue and disagree with me but I do not feel so pressurized to adopt very formal behaviour not to carry my status on my back. Dress has become much more informal here and I don't feel obliged to out-dress my managers nor to out-shout them as some of my northern women colleagues appear to think is the only strategy which gives them any power. (London chief officer of NHS Trust 1996)

At board level, 38% of non-executive posts were taken by women and the number of women chairing trusts had risen from 8% in the first wave to 28% in the fifth wave in 1995. The women chairing health authorities rose to 42% in 1996. There are considerable regional variations to these figures with those in the North, South West and Wales falling far short of London and the South. The number of women chairing NHS trusts had risen from 8% in the first wave to 28.5% in the fifth wave in 1995. The number of women chairing health authorities had risen from 26% to 42% by April 1996 (NHS Women's Unit). The number of women executives and chairpersons are growing. Women are more likely to have senior positions on community NHS trusts and are less visible on acute trust boards and within purchasing authorities. It has also been noted that the women chosen for these posts tend to be well connected to the establishment and the Conservative Party.

Women in medicine

There is a lay assumption that because women have trained as doctors for over 75 years, it is an established and easy career route for women. In fact this is not the case. Medicine and medical schools remain very male and rather medieval institutions, which actively encourage female students into community health and primary care and discourage them from entering specialties such as surgery. All surgical specialties require a very special determination from women medical students. A 'glass ceiling' phenomenon operates in almost all professions and areas of management in the UK. But probably the most powerful male cultures are to be found in medicine, law and business. A report (Maddock and Parkin 1994) showed that women doctors continue to suffer from male prejudice and are stereotyped as being suitable only for particular fields of medicine:

- Women medical students are discouraged from taking up careers in general medicine and all surgical specialities.
- Assumption that women doctors will become mothers and will not want to become consultants and will instead opt for associate posts and part-time work etc.
- Women doctors have to adapt themselves to anti-social hours and conditions.
- Women doctors either avoid the macho culture of medicine or have to struggle for promotion in difficult specialities such as those within surgery.

Within the male culture of hospital medicine, women medics face all the obstacles mentioned below:

- patronage;
- prejudice;
- lengthy training;
- long and inflexible hours which are difficult to integrate into family or social life;
- women medics encouraged into 'female' specialisms.

In the past women have been encouraged into general practice, although within general practice they have been the locums, the associates and on retainer schemes and not the principal trainers. There is currently a shortage of women principals in general practice in many inner city areas. Since the 1990s' NHS reforms, both male and female junior doctors are reluctant to become general practitioners. Isobel Allen's study (1988) found that women hospital doctors, who outnumber men at medical school, found it difficult to secure consultant posts in acute specialties such as surgery, general medicine, obstetrics and gynaecology. In spite of the fact that all patients are female in obstetrics and gynaecology. In other specialties more women have become consultants, but it is less accepted that they be medical directors and professors (Maddock and Parkin 1994).

Patronage is the practice whereby senior medics adopt and promote favoured younger doctors and actively promote them for posts through the informal club culture of medicine. The practice continues although discouraged by the British Medical Association. Allen (1988) suggests that patronage in medicine has grown stronger rather than weaker. The effect of this is that young white, male doctors are sponsored by older male doctors throughout their careers, while black men and women are not favoured for posts because they lack proactive support. Surgery was frequently the specialty where career progress without patronage was impossible (Allen 1988; Maddock and Parkin 1994). A negative sponsor or adversary can damage a young doctor's career irreparably (Allen 1988). It is the fear of negative patronage that prevents many junior doctors from complaining about working conditions and poor training. Those on the receiving end of negative reports from negative sponsors tend to be from ethnic minorities or are women. The tacit code which medical students learn fast is that you do not openly discuss professional conflicts and problems outside the profession. Many younger women junior doctors reported that while they would like to talk about improving practices they felt unable to voice their thoughts or difficulties for fear of being labelled, 'a moaner' or a 'whiner'. These young doctors knew instinctively how destructive negative sponsorship could be in terms of their careers.

Although the patronage system is being undermined by recent developments in medical training, there still exists the problem of persuading younger doctors that patronage is no longer significant. The majority of junior doctors in surgery still believe that without a 'backer' you are unlikely to succeed. As young doctors all believe this to be the case, it is unlikely that any junior doctor wanting to remain in the region would voice an opinion contrary to the prevailing view. They believe that doing so would jeopardize one's career (BMA Working Party paper, 'Patronage'). The patronage system is insidious and also influences selection and recruitment processes. This continues because senior consultants rely on their colleagues for informal evidence about a doctor's suitability for a post. While this system persists there is no motivation or interest in developing more rigorous criteria for person and function appraisal. In other words, the criteria for appraisal and selection remain vague and personal to the selector. It is essential in all medical recruitment training that consultants understand that they will only be capable of selecting the best candidates when they start to differentiate between posts and candidates by way of visible and agreed criteria – and cease to select on the basis of gossip.

Cronyism and the old boy network

The glass ceiling in medicine should have been shattered since women have been trained as doctors for many years, but it certainly exists in most teaching hospitals and in the medical schools where women professors are still a rarity. In NHS trusts where there are very few women consultants the glass ceiling operates lower down the organization. The old boy network operates through a subtle system. Women doctors tend to be associated with particular specialties and posts and women consultants with children are assumed not to want senior posts. Those women without partners and children appear to present a greater threat to the old boy network precisely because they are more likely to apply for senior positions. A women clinical director stated:

I have never experienced discrimination during the course of my career in medicine until it became known that I was on track for the post of medical director. I started to be shunned, receive abusive phone calls and even hate mail – so I've decided to withdraw. (Maddock and Parkin 1994: 60)

It is the fact that childless women are much more likely to be able to compete for senior jobs which causes some of the establishment to find other ways to discredit women; for example, by making reference to their personal behaviour, habits, relationships, clothes, manners or temperament. There is a string of prominent cases concerning women consultants who have been sacked or hounded out. More depressingly, training groups of women doctors end up becoming cathartic sessions for the majority of participants who have and are experiencing daily harassment and marginalization. Medicine is a difficult job for these women who refuse to work on the margins.

The most recent and the most gruelling cases of extreme gender discrimination and attack relate to Wendy Savage and Helena Daly, both consultants who were struggling to improve services. They were attacked for being 'difficult' and outspoken. In both cases the BMA tended to endorse the establishment view and contributed to the public abuse. A powerful traditional gender culture operates in many district hospitals and within medicine. Wendy Savage has written a book on her experiences; her case is well known so I will recount the Dr Daly case.

Dr Daly was a haematologist working as a consultant in Cornwall. She sought to improve working practices for children and attempted to speed up blood testing procedures, returning results within 24 hours instead of a week. She was informed that both she and her working methods were at odds with common practice in the Royal Cornwall NHS hospital in Treliske. Her patients were largely children with leukaemia and her support group included many whose children she had treated. In spite of their support she was victimized from the day she was appointed. A senior medic told her that the working practices in Cornwall were very different from those in a city teaching hospital: 'You're a single and come from a city, a teaching hospital – this is a quiet country hospital where staff are relaxed and don't like change – you have protocols for treatment the staff don't like that' (Daly 1994).

Dr Daly was working in a hospital where the majority of women were junior or part-time. Apart from herself, there were only four women consultants out of a total of 112 medical staff. It is evident from the comments made to her and indirectly about her by other consultants that she was not just a novelty but someone whom they viewed as not acceptable as a woman. She was told on her appointment that she might 'have problems with the consultants' wives'. The regional medical officer also pointed out to her the disadvantage of being a single woman working in a country hospital. This particular management and medical establishment continued to accept and define women as essentially 'wives' and 'mothers', irrespective of their professional roles. Within this culture an acceptable woman apparently meant being feminine but not too sexy, married with children, willing to serve or please, competent but not too intelligent. She was subject to constant undermining over a period of time and was attacked for being: too thin, too attractive, on drugs, difficult, unmarried and over-qualified. In 1994 she was asked to resign on the grounds of personal misconduct. She won an internal NHS tribunal, but instead of reinstatement was offered eighteen months to find a post on full pay. During this time she was also subject to a form of subtle defamation by her own legal counsel, the BMA. This is a hospital trust that has had a catalogue of accidents and management failures since 1994, but which continues to be managed by the same senior management team (apart from the chief officer) that sacked Dr Daly in 1994.

There are other women who have been down the same tormenting route as Dr Daly and who have resigned, left medicine or become locums. All the women listed in Table 4.2 were sacked for personal misconduct, whatever that is, and not for any incompetence, theft, fraud or abuse. Almost all were made redundant, dismissed or accused of 'personal misconduct' – a slippery category. All were seen as marginal, out-group members, challengers and whistleblowers. Most were subjected to ridicule and gossip, even after winning their cases, by fellow doctors, often nurses and managers.

Many of the women in Table 4.2 won their cases but were still left unemployed or forced to return to work because there was no resettlement package. Few who were suspended felt supported by the BMA legal department which has received numerous complaints about its attitude to women members who have conflicts with other doctors. Dr Wendy Savage had the political backing of a powerful women's lobby when she was attacked for her radical but now accepted views on childbirth. Those doctors working in hospitals outside major cities have less support and less access to the serious press and media.

Women doctors are rarely suspended for professional misconduct. The suspended doctors' group reported that in 1995 although 75% of suspended medics were male they tended to be dismissed for incidents relating to drugs, fraud, theft and alcohol; whereas women doctors were dismissed for personal misconduct which basically amounts to 'not fitting in' with other staff. Personal misconduct as a category is vague and appears to be used by personnel directors as an excuse for getting rid of 'difficult' women who have often not done anything other than challenge professional practices with which they disagree (Dr Wendy Savage). Some go public and contact the BMA and the press, or act as whistleblowers, which provokes the ire of more conservative colleagues and hospital executives. Many of the high profile cases of sacked senior women such as Savage, Halford and Daly were not supported by the majority of their peers but by the public or their patients. These women were dismissed as deviant professionals, yet they were in fact 'whistleblowers' on poor practice or practices they thought

TABLE 4.2 *Cases of suspended senior hospital doctors in career posts*

Female suspensions	Alleged	Outcome
Anaesthetist	Incompetence	Context jealousy
Gynaecologist	Poor obstetrician	Won tribunal but made redundant
Psychiatrist	Disagreement about diagnosis	Suspended, won case but bought out
Gynaecologist	Poor obstetrician	Public hearing, won, reinstated, working conditions intolerable
Public health	Whistleblower	Sacked, appealed, reinstated working conditions intolerable, resigned
Paediatrician	Poor judgement on sex abuse	Reinstated
Haematologist	Whistleblower	Made redundant, reinstated, working conditions intolerable, resigned
Paediatrician	Poor practice	Still suspended on full pay after 11 years. Awarded prestigious fellowship. Suffered gender discrimination from nurses
Gynaecologist	Conflict with consultants	Unresolved
Anaesthetist	Incompetence as senior registrar	All training blocked in the region, lost case, works as a locum

Notes: 1994: Males 64, females 11. Only one female doctor was found to be guilty of behaviour that would have led to sacking, i.e. abuse, drugs, etc.

counter to human treatment of staff or patients. It is noteworthy that in all three cases their views and the organizational or clinical practices they thought needed improving have since been implemented and have become part of good practice.

Scapegoats and whistleblowers

Whistleblowing has become much more common since Wendy Savage's case in the late 1970s. These men and women are labelled 'difficult', but it is the women who are attacked as deviant and marginalized. Male doctor whistleblowers are more likely reinstated or offered other posts. Medicine is still a 'craft' profession where autonomy and seclusion are very important to its members. To seek support and assistance from non-medical professionals is seen by many as betraying the profession. This adds to women's sense that they must not refer to the gendered nature of their situation. The number of men and women calling themselves 'whistle-blowers' and the number of senior women who have reported being used as a 'scapegoat' for organizational failures and faults have grown dramatically since the early 1990s. Both local government and NHS professionals have found themselves intimidated, sacked and harassed for reporting abuse and poor practice. Alison Taylor's life was ruined in the 1980s because she drew attention to abuse in North Wales children's homes. Public sector officials have experienced 'stonewalling', ridicule and resistance when they have reported poor practices. Men and women have suffered in this way. Graham Pink, sacked by a Greater Manchester hospital, reports that he thinks little change resulted from his speaking out about neglect on geriatric wards. Those who speak out are often harassed and suffer tremendous stress for a period of years because of the treatment received. In the main, however, colleagues give more support to men who 'blow the whistle'. Women are often left isolated both before and after their ordeal. Pink's colleagues were in full support of him. Similarly a consultant in Bolton who was sacked for speaking out was supported by other doctors and later reinstated. Women who speak and act out of turn tend to fare worse; they are offered fewer alternative work situations while also expecting more of the judicial process of law.

Although initially perceived as troublemakers, whistleblowers are most often vindicated some years later. Wendy Savage wanted to give childbirth back to women and her views have now been endorsed twenty years later in the government report 'Changing Childbirth', which suggests that doctors are the last resort in childbirth. Some obstetricians rarely see women in labour unless something out of the ordinary or difficult occurs. Alison Halford attempted to introduce a staff development and training approach into a very macho male Merseyside police force which was clearly an organization in need of a culture change. Dr Daly was respected by her patients because they trusted her judgement and commitment to her work. The practices she endorsed have now become accepted protocols in haematology.

Most recent cases of dangerous practices by doctors and abuse in children's homes demonstrate just how difficult it is for even senior professional personnel to 'whistleblow' on very poor practice. The closing of professional rank usually results in the whistleblower being ridiculed and themselves attacked. The unwillingness to acknowledge difficulties within both professions and institutions is very common in Britain. Those who dare to speak out have to be well balanced, well respected and very powerful. Isolated and challenging women because of their detachment can be astute commentators, but their observations and desire for change continues to be extremely humiliating to those comfortable in the 'inertia' of routine practice, and even when they know it is 'risky', dangerous or just 'not very good' – the instinct to close ranks and the fear of reprisal and hostility from their colleagues ensures their silence.

Both men and women who speak out are labelled as difficult. However, it is emerging from many individual cases that often even very experienced and able women who speak out about poor practices or incompetent colleagues find themselves suspended from work and are told not to speak to colleagues by management. Whereas men are likely to be found new posts or reinstated; women are offered 'ill health' or early retirement packages. Women with many years of experience are surprised when their colleagues are inert when they are attacked as being too 'difficult' or 'bullying'. Women are offered fewer alternatives and yet they continue to expect more from their colleagues and the judicial process of law.

5   Gender cultures, tactics and strategies

It would be wrong to speak of 'women' as having a philosophy of change in organisations, since many women are as conventional in their views of hierarchy, bureaucracy and management as most of the men they join. Nonetheless there is a strong voice among women that is characteristically *of* women, speaking for a different way of doing things. It may not be well articulated and it may sometimes be utopian but it embodies a vision of something new . . . Many women prioritise for instance social orientation over a narrow task orientation. . . . One said we see ourselves as agents of change, the "managers of tomorrow". (Cynthia Cockburn 1991: 71)

The term gender tends to refer to the difference between men and women, which in organizations has come to mean labour market segmentation. The focus on labour market stratification has obscured the influence which gender cultures have on organizational behaviour and on change management. Ann Oakley (1974) first distinguished between 'sex' and 'gender' in order to differentiate between the biological differences between men and women and those social roles dependent on male and female identities. Until the late 1980s gender concerns were virtually ignored in organizational analysis except by authors such as Mills (1988, 1989). Yet all social relationships are governed by cultural assumptions about how men and women should behave and this includes relationships within organizations (Deal and Kennedy 1984). In spite of this fact, organizational analysis remained focused on labour processes, usually in the manufacturing sector where men dominated the production lines (Feldberg and Glenn 1979), and was insensitive to women's work experiences. Labour process theorists appeared to be blind to the thousands of women who worked in manufacturing industries and more surprisingly ignored those who worked in the public services. The trade unions were little better, tending to listen to male grievances but accusing women workers of moaning when they demanded change (Mills 1988). The most glaring example of this is illustrated by the Hawthorne experiments which demonstrated how ergonomics influenced production performance and staff complicity. These experiments proved difficult to replicate because the original researchers were not gender sensitive and had failed to notice that. The original workers were female and first generation immigrants, eager to please and extremely vulnerable; whereas later researchers were confronted by male trade unionists who were not so easily influenced by male researchers (Mills 1988). In addition the research methodology was not gender aware. Where researchers did notice women as a group of workers, they assumed that the data were of little concern and assigned them to women's studies. When this was not the case they ignored gender analysis altogether and assumed that the dominant male narrative was adequate as an explanation for both men's and women's work experience.

For many years organizations, whether public bodies or companies, were conceived as closed systems which functioned on a rational basis where workers obeyed the bosses and did what they were told. They were run on military and authoritarian lines and cultural contexts and differences tended to be ignored. The fact that organizations did not work like clockwork, could be sabotaged and were subject to strikes began to alter this perspective. Subcultures began to develop and some researchers started to notice the impact of authoritarian work cultures on staff relations and productivity.

Culture provides a backdrop to the power relations and influences which galvanize or constrain people in their interactions and performance at work. Work cultures tend to be related to the outside world of local social communities. Many remain unaware of how far their thinking and attitudes are rooted in their own cultures until they encounter differences between themselves and other people. For this reason the concept of culture is useful to gender analysis.

Within every organization there are usually many subcultures, apart from gender relations, that involve local communities, work status, profession and personal identity. Corporate cultures are particularly encouraged by large companies, although these are usually shallow and do not reflect any real consensus among the various staff groupings (Hofstede 1980; Calas and Smircisch 1989). There are numerous studies which illustrate how groups operate in various work settings (Ouchi 1981; Peters and Waterman 1982; Kanter 1977), but less attention has been paid to how these cultural norms influence employees in their individual behaviours and relationships and to how gender identity plays a role in work culture dynamics. Merton and Crozier were the forerunners of later management theorists in recognizing the power of subcultures on the dynamic between employees and managers. In particular they noticed the impact that bureaucracies had on staff and how they encouraged a psychological dependency in employees which disposed many of them to be petty and insular (Merton 1957). Institutionalized employees were reluctant or unable to communicate with people outside their own social group. This was not seen as problematic until much later in the 1980s when it became necessary for public servants to cross departmental barriers in order to become more efficient. Merton was one of the first to notice that oppressive subcultures were both the product and the cause of conflicts within corporations and bureaucracies. He began to see that the hierarchical bureaucratic organization was not so perfect and did not operate in the supposed rational manner: 'The "esprit de corps" and informal social organisation which typically develops in such situations often leads the personnel to defend their entrenched interests rather than to assist clientele and elected higher officials' (Merton 1957: 210).

The fact that for many years bureaucracies were viewed as rational and clockwork institutions was unsurprising when were staff deferential, conformist and fearful of any deviation to the operations they knew. This deferential culture resulted in grievances being voiced only as extremes in the labour movement or privately to friends. Such conformity and regular behaviour was as common in the private sector corporations as it was in public administrations. When new recruits joined a company they acquainted themselves with the corporate culture and learned to adopt attitudes that were often in conflict with their former professional training or their peer group values. In a classic analysis of US organizations, Schein (1988 [1969]) showed that individuals joining a corporation underwent a socialization process and were inducted into the company by older members. At that time in the USA graduates were militant and had problems adapting to corporate values. New employees tended either to rebel, become creative individualists or to conform. Schein's original study was done in the late 1960s at a time when North American business schools were encouraging students to think and be creative. But the corporations were not ready for such innovation and wanted new graduates to conform, not to think. This caused conflict not merely between managers and workers, but also between managers and academics. Graduates did not fit the company ethos and were unwilling to lose themselves in company conformity. In corporate America, companies expected their staff to adopt the company way. Firms such as Hewlett-Packard have explicit company codes which they expect staff, including senior managers and technicians to endorse and abide by. The 1980s market demand for diversity and innovation created a conflict for international companies, between the desire for a strong, corporate, conforming culture and the need for creative personnel:

> It is really better to have a strong, stable organisation populated by local conformists who believe totally in the company and will work their hearts out for the company. Or is it better to have organisations that make it easy for people to enter and leave, that value diversity and dissent – and better for whom – the company or the individual? Can we imagine integrative solutions whereby what is best for the company is also best for the individual? (E.H. Schein 1988: 64)

The mixed message of conforming and being creative was just as much of a problem within public sector institutions where the cultures have been conformist and passive for many years. The pressure to change and become responsive from the Left and New Right was difficult to achieve for large corporations or public administrations with a largely deferential workforce. Those radicals active in the trade union movement or in conflict with their managers persistently presented a threat to management. The solution to this problem was to invent personnel management, a function responsible for appeasing staff and for softening the antagonism between employees and managers.

Kanter (1977) demonstrated that managers were very aware of the need to manipulate and cajole staff. Managers in corporations and bureaucratic institutions persisted in their belief that any comment or deviation was a nuisance; they expected quite submissive behaviour from workers and officers and viewed any deviation as insubordination or a challenge.

> Once latent tensions between organizational sub-cultures are activated, the character and outcome of the ensuing conflict depends on a lot of variables, including the political clout that a group can muster, the number of opportunities to exercise such clout, and the conditions that shape each group's position vis-à-vis others in the organizations. (Van Mannen and Barley 1984: 49)

There appears to be common organizational cultural divides in western organizations – those of the work force or operators, the managers and the executives. Schein (1996) identifies three cultures in multinationals: that of engineers, chief executives and the operators each with their own shared assumptions and values:

> The culture of engineering or management is often to design 'people' out of the system – for both manager and chief executive employees are too frequently a nuisance to be controlled rather than of intrinsic value. The executive culture is based on the tacit assumption that their role is to satisfy the investors and stave financial security and health for the company. Too often 'best practice' is defined by one group – or by executives and managers and the lack of negotiations between each group results in conflict, intransigence and reduced motivation. Healthy industrial relations rely on some discussion and negotiation of each group's role and contribution to the organisation. (1996: 18)

As Schein points out the dilemma of the twenty-first century is how to facilitate learning. He observes that learning is unlikely to occur where authoritarian cultures persist.

Individuals will react to such an authoritarian culture in various ways. An avoidance of conflict or tension by conciliation and deference could be said to be an appropriate response in authoritarian environments where the options for change are limited. Adaptive and conciliatory responses are said to characterize the bureaucrat or civil servant (Ferguson 1984). The bureaucratic organization can only accommodate conformers. Only senior staff are given permission to be creative and take rises, which they are unlikely to do when they have honed their skills in middle management where they were encouraged to be passive and inert. Clearly this degree of conformity is counterproductive within the contracting environment; it has a deadening effect on staff who are forced into negative or reactive responses. Paul Hoggett (1992) describes how employees react in various ways to authoritarian environments when confronted with bullying managers; they become:

- a victim, having no power they become conformist;
- a resister, who also has no power but is passively resistant and a saboteur;
- a collaborator, who is also rather powerless but attach themselves to those with power;
- a partisan or a rebel, who organizes when confronted with problems.

Hoggett's analysis suggests that employees develop personal strategies to cope with their powerlessness, rather like the gender management strategies adopted by women to overcome the confines of male gender culture. Those who are most creative in their attempts to handle the authoritarian work-place are the most likely to leave and certainly the most likely to be criticized by managers.

Post-structuralists such as Foucault, Lacan and Derrida stated that bureaucratic systems caused not just behavioural conformity but also alienated employees. Foucault (1972) observed that the power of bureaucracy was subtle. Employees became so familiar with bureaucratic rules and codes that they soon assumed them to be natural and unnoteworthy. Consequently, it is hardly surprising that civil servants within government administrations tend to think that the formalities, rules and procedures are natural and somehow preordained:

> The administrative environment arranges things in such a way that the experience of power is not added on form the outside, like a heavy rigid constraint to the functions it invests, but is so subtly present as to increase their efficiency by itself increasing its own point of contact. This panotic mechanism is not simply a hinge, a point of exchange between a mechanism of power and a function; it is a way of making power relations function in a function of making a function function through these power relations. (Foucault 1979: 206–207)

Because the individual and different experiences of men and women, employees and managers, are submerged and not acknowledged, they remain invisible. For this reason it is difficult for managers to articulate any need for change or indeed conflict within bureaucratic organizations. Bureaucracies engage managers and employees alike, immobilizing them and rendering them passive and fearful of change. Civil servants and public officers were expected to be impartial, detached and unemotional. This view of civil servant behaviour was in accordance with the common view that public bodies operated in a rational manner. The belief that public bodies were rational, put bureaucratic practices beyond criticism and reinforced not only detachment among civil servants but also hostility towards those who questioned formal procedures. The consequence of this perspective has been to make government officers very hesitant about questioning procedures, they censor their own anxieties and are critical of those who do query the red tape. This mindset has stifled debate and made it more difficult for managers to discuss organizational issues. Many were and continue to be uncertain how to handle ambiguous situations.

Women suffer a double whammy within bureaucratic environments. They are silenced as women and oppressed as government bureaucrats. Authoritarian cultures oppress and silence not just junior staff but also quite senior managers. Cathy Ferguson (1984) observed that in such an environment managers could:

- become hostile to speculative thought and action;
- become hostile to self-searching or doubt;
- rebuff social criticism and refuse to acknowledge political change.

Ferguson (1984) suggested that bureaucratic management systems affected all staff, except perhaps the corporate team who are in overall control. She includes professionals, managers, technicians, clerical workers and manual workers and concludes that each group is subordinated and therefore 'feminized' by virtue of being powerless. The bureaucratic culture is a 'feminizing' culture because it disempowers individuals (Janeway 1974; Spender 1982; Franzway et al. 1989). Employees working in public administrations quickly feel deskilled. The closed and authoritarian organization oppresses staff through a process of 'subordination'. As subordinated citizens employees come to feel as if they can only comprehend the language and nuances of the second sex (Ferguson 1984). Bureaucrats, like women, are expected to be conforming, conciliatory and passive and to exhibit responses which reflect a sense of subjugation (Ferguson 1984). Women are not powerless because they are feminine but feminine because they are powerless (Ferguson 1984). She detaches the passivity of femininity from women and instead associates it with a lack of power and authority. Civil servants are feminized because they are servants not because they are female.

There has long been a connection between 'weak' and 'female'; yet there is scant examination of how gender influences government and administrations other than by Franzway et al. (1989) and more recently by Witz and Savage (1992). Franzway et al. point to the conflictual demands made on public administrators who are expected not only to be caring and passive, but also decisive as public servants. The dual role and the personal conflicts faced by many public sector employees is described in Lipsky's *Street Level Bureaucracy* (1980). These two roles do not sit easily beside one another – especially as they express the polar opposites of masculine and feminine sides of work.

Hendricks (1992) is critical of the technocratic and rational–logical perspective dominant in public administrations throughout the western world, which she says excludes marginal groups. In addition she thinks that a woman-centred reality in organizations would empower and encourage diversity. The fact that women's sensitivities to community and to process are rarely dominant in organizations is not merely due to a lack of women in management but to the male gendering of workplace and public cultures.

Gender cultures

Joan Acker (1989, 1992) a pioneer in the subject of workplace gendering talks about the logic of gendered power relations between men and women as underpinning all organizations. She draws attention to the gendered nature of particular functions and structures, and to the stigmatization of women's reproductive functions within the work context. Deeply embedded in the cultural context of work are expectations of all employees to conform to what men do. The suppression of sexual difference is actively sought in western bureaucracies and corporations alike (Burrell 1984).

Within each organization there are many subcultures which can relate to local community, to race and gender roles and identities, to professional training and to the company itself. It is the cultural barriers between men and women, between management and worker, between managers and professions, the national and ethnic divides, which cause conflict. Running through each employee group are cultural ties, assumptions about race and class and, of course, assumptions about what men and women can do and how they should behave.

Gender relationships are heavily influenced by social status and formal power. Female professions tend to have less social status than the male professions and the experience of workers and middle managers has been expressed as 'feminized' because of their lack of power and autonomy within the organization. Employees have to learn whether it is appropriate to display masculinity or femininity in public and in general most communities teach girls to repress their sexuality and encourage boys to flaunt theirs. Fortunately or unfortunately for women, these gender social mores are at variance with the behaviours demanded by the corporate organization – but in spite of this the male and female peer groups appear to have the dominant effect on relationships.

Kanter's (1977) account of US corporations demonstrated how powerfully women's social status was reflected at work and in working relationships – management was not neutral but gendered male. Kanter also described how women's frustrations and anger may not have been public but could be seen in women's reactions. When they were ignored or had their ambitions blocked they were likely to develop a negative subculture which worked against corporate objectives. Women in their own groups at work resist these definitions and mock men in return: 'We see escape, bending rules, mucking in, laughs, biting wit. Defiance is here. What is lacking is the shop floor control and organisation' (Pollert 1981: 234–5). Even if women did not act in this way, the managers watched their work more closely (Rosen and Jerdee 1974). In spite of the fact that most women exhibited robust attitudes to conflict, they were viewed with great suspicion by male managers and trade unionists (Broverman et al. 1975). Although these studies were done in the 1970s and organizations have since changed, for example, there are more women in senior positions, these attitudes have been tempered only little.

Sexuality is also an important feature of the work culture (Schein 1975, 1978 and 1989). The interpretation of a woman's behaviour by men and women is very strongly linked to her attractiveness, age and marital status. Although sexual behaviour at work is usually actively discouraged (Burrell 1984), this does not stop the undercurrents of attitude and attraction and repulsion which operate and influence relationships. It is usually women who suffer from the extreme personal sexual stereotypes that are used to slander or malign: terms such as 'Bag Lady', 'Iron Lady', 'Dragon', 'Princess' or Virgin (Hearn and Parkin 1987). There are few public or private organizations which are not dominated by male values (Marshall 1984; Hearn et al. 1989) and where male cultures do not invade the attitudes of men and women in their judgements about women and their approach to organizing within the workplace. Gherardi (1996), in her account of Italian companies, outlined typical cultures by the way in which men view women as they enter the male working environment:

- friendly culture where the woman is the guest;
- hostile culture where the woman is on the edge;
- friendly culture where the woman is a snake;
- friendly culture where the woman is a newcomer;
- hostile culture where the woman is viewed as an intruder.

Some cultures are more women friendly than others and encourage women as 'newcomers' rather than as 'intruders'. Maddock and Parkin (1993) developed a typology of gender cultures from working in public sector organizations in the UK:

- the Gentleman's Club;
- the Locker Room;
- the Barrack Yard;
- the Gender-Blind;
- the Smart Macho;
- the Gender Neutral.

These cultures tended to rely either on the shared assumption that women and men were very different or to downplay gender differences and pretend that workplaces were gender neutral. The cultures we identified tended to reflect either a traditional view than men and women are very different or the equality at work view that there is no difference at all. Both attitudes are equally distorting of reality and both result in women being trapped in either a female world that is domestic or in a male work model.

The 'Gentleman's Club' is the patrician and traditional culture where men and women were assumed to have different and definite roles and life expectations. Although women were assumed to be different they were not necessarily undervalued. However, they were judged at work in terms of their roles as mother, wives and homekeepers as much as for their work competence. The 'Gentleman' at work remembers his secretary's birthday and gives her flowers, but does not promote her. In contrast, the 'Barrack Yard' culture is a military-type environment where women, like all junior staff, are directed and bullied. This is an authoritarian culture where all who are different are excluded from senior positions. Similarly, the 'Locker Room' culture encourages men to see women through romantic fantasies as sexual objects; their own sexual prowess is at stake in all encounters. This is not necessarily a blue-collar culture, but is to be found in medicine, the professions and in senior management, as well as among more junior staff. The significance of these cultures is that they influence women as well as men, but are determined by men.

During the 1980s the work cultures developed around equality programmes gave rise to a politically correct view that to mention any gender difference was controversial. The public sector encouraged women on paper but ignored the realities of their lives. The 'Gender-Blind' culture we found in many local government departments assumed that women have the same experiences as men and are able to compete at work on a 'level playing field'. This was a more positive culture for women who were able to work full-time; they were encouraged into senior posts if they fitted in with the dominant group. The 'Smart Macho' culture is an extension of the 'Gender-Blind' culture and is more ruthless and certainly not 'gender neutral'. This culture is prevalent in healthcare organizations and reinforces a functional approach to management. Managers are expected to be workaholics and to be ruthless in their pursuit of goals and targets at the expense of staff and social relationships. Women cannot avoid the baggage of the female gender roles and during the course of their lives, willingly and unwillingly, they become mothers or carers. Even if they have no dependants, they cannot escape, however hard they may try.

Female ambition in the 1980s proved that women could survive in the cutthroat world of finance and the City, but after a short time many decided that life was too short; they wanted more socially relevant activities than those which the macho culture could provide. Women and men do tend to inhabit different worlds and although this gulf may be narrowing the legacy of previous generations lives on in the assumptions about gender roles, especially in the minds of men.

Although the radical humanist and feminist perspectives gave a voice to women in organizations and made them more visible, they did so by reference to stories relating to individual experience which were often decontextualized and ignored the cultures in which men and women lived and worked. By focusing only on individual behaviour in the immediate, the significance and existence of the gender underpinnings of organizational cultures and management structures, values and norms were not mentioned; neither was the influence of the external world which forced men and women into traditional roles and relationships within organizations (Mills 1988). Individual stories are interesting, but they need texture. Everyone has a history. The political and economic environment has a tremendous impact on each person's possibilities. Workers are consumers, mothers, fathers, sons and daughters; they do not leave their social world at home when they go to work. Similarly, women and men bring their beliefs about the world to work and respond to peers and managers in the light of their own personal constructs.

The gender revolution that has undoubtedly taken place in Britain is only skin-deep and only half a revolution, and one which many men have not yet joined. There still exists a strong tendency among men to see women as attractive prospective partners, mothers, wives or sisters. The roles allocated to women defined by social convention remain deeply ingrained and still appear to some men as preordained, natural and invisible. Men are equally constrained by their own notions of 'masculinity' and too often men have less strong private identities and rely heavily on their public and work roles for their personal self-esteem. The lack of debate around masculinity results in many boys growing up with limited interpersonal skills and levels of awareness. Masculine identity has grown up around public displays of brain or strength and is suffering from lack of interaction skills. Although many young men are much more articulate and open to emotions, there are still swathes of men who are trapped in the 1950s' version of manhood and virility. The reluctance of men to communicate is the characteristic which is most frustrating for women at work.

Professional cultures are gender cultures

The professions are especially blatant in their attachment to gendered attitudes. Each profession tends to have its own gender tag; medicine is male and nursing is female. Joan Acker (1992) has written extensively about the gendered nature of the professions, particularly within the health professions of medicine and nursing. Just as bureaucrats can be feminized by a lack of control over their work, so the professions have 'male' and 'female' identities. The male/female tag of the professional group influences the status and confidence of its members. There is a web intermeshing professional and gender power relations. Female professions tend to those with less prestige whereas the male professions of law and medicine have status in almost all communities. Male nurses soon learn how it feels to be treated as a subordinate, although they are promoted faster into management than women. Similarly, the few primary school teachers who are men are likely to become headteachers. The same dynamic operates for those managing staff; male managers of cleaning and catering services are treated with less respect than those running finance departments.

When women change careers they sometimes find it politic to hide their backgrounds in the caring professions of nursing, counselling or teaching, whereas doctors, would probably advertise their medical training. Celia Davies (1995), trained as a health visitor, but realized that to earn credibility as an academic she needed to create a break with her former role. The gendered tag of a profession results in individual members adopting a style that is in keeping with the 'gender' identity of profession itself; status is attached not to individual members but to the profession. Nursing has a 'caring' public image because it is a female profession. The ethics of care, selflessness, passiveness and martyrdom are enshrined within nursing more than any other profession (Davies 1995). By contrast, doctors make decisions and, like academics, are not traditionally managed but guarded by professional bodies and monitored by peer review. The nurse–doctor dynamic continues to be played out in many work realities and fantasies in films; the nurse listens, soothes and organizes while the doctor, detached, decides and appears masterful.

The gender status of a profession is also reflected in the management style and the responses reinforced in members on meeting new situations, ambiguity and change. Those less confident tend to prefer predictable environments, whereas those used to change are bored by routine rules and clockwork management. In the female professions the make-do and coping responses are encouraged, which unfortunately do not generate leadership skills. Those who are expected to cope may be practical, but they are not accustomed to being reflective. This presents problems for those working within a changing environment, where often new and unknown roles and relationships are needed. Davies found that the 'coping' management style in nursing created constraints not only for individual nurses when they became managers, but also for their subordinates whom they managed:

> Looking down the hierarchy, coping management is hard on subordinates. It trades on their goodwill and commitment and generates work overloads and stress. It can also create a sense of confusion and guilt. The manager (nurse) cannot be blamed for she is clearly working just as hard as her subordinates. Ultimately there is likely to be low morale, burnout and higher turnover. Looking up the hierarchy, issues of resource allocation, or organization and reorganizations of work are not being addressed. As long as the coping manager copes, there is no incentive for others to enquire how the coping is achieved. And the coping manager herself, being so busy coping, is likely to resent and brush aside any overtures that may come from her seniors. This kind of dynamic creates a gulf between the coping management team and others, a gulf which can operate either with junior management against senior management within nursing or between nursing as a whole and other health professions. (Davies 1992: 238)

TABLE 5.1   *Cultural codes of gender*

	Masculine	Feminine
Development of self	Separation	Relation
	Boundedness	Connectedness
	Self-esteem	Selflessness
	Self-love	Self-sacrifice
	Responsible for self	Responsible for others
Cognitive orientation	Abstract thinking	Contextual thinking
	Control	Emphasis on experience
	Emphasis on skills and expertise	Skills confirmed use
Relational style	Decisive	Loyal to principles
	Interrogative	Reflective
	Loyal to superiors	Accommodative
	Agentic/instrumental	Group orientation
		Expressive/facilitative

Source: Davies 1995: 27

Davies (1995) also observed that the skills and responses within the healthcare professions tended to reinforce very different kinds of management and present different problems and possibilities. Clearly each are inadequate and the two tendencies need to merge in order that managers can become more open and strategic in their responses (see Table 5.1).

The lesson appears to be that if management wants nurses to become managers, then senior managers must change, not just nurse training but also the type of authoritarian management pressures on nurses in order that they might be less deferential to doctors and senior staff and less bullying of juniors. Macalpine and Marsh (1995) experts in nurse management training state that if nurses are to become successful managers then they must become strategic and be more confident of themselves. They note that nurses find it difficult to voice dissent because they have little credibility within the medical world. The recruitment of male nurses is helping this process, because they are not willing to accept the rigid boundaries between doctors, nurses and managers (Salvage 1991).

As nurses struggle to gain recognition so the boundaries between nursing and medicine are dissolving. However, the process is slow for many reasons, not least because nurses continue to be managed through hierarchal line management. It is therefore hardly surprising that those who have been bullied, bully others when they get the opportunity. There is evidence of this now that the health reforms have shifted the power balance between doctors and nurses. Some nurses are 'getting their own back':

Nurses said that they were no longer the handmaidens of the doctors. It is not surprising that in the nurse/doctor relationships that gender emerged as a key factor in managing change. This is so much taken for granted that nurses and doctors seldom comment on it, but to a large extent the combination of the male/female and doctor/nurse dynamics underlies the traditional perspective of the nurse's role. (Macalpine and Marsh 1995: 20)

Many female, junior doctors have commented on the way that female nurses discriminate against them but support their male colleagues:

They make tea for the young male junior doctors but ignore us totally, women house officers can go without tea or coffee for hours because the kettle is in the nursing staff room, the men get tea and toast and we get nothing. (Maddock and Parkin 1994: 25)

According to recent reports, nurses are now also refusing to support junior male doctors with tea and sympathy. This may be the fault of the doctors, but it is certainly related to a confusion over roles and responsibilities. A nurse manager says that nurses most certainly are getting their revenge and venting their anger at their powerlessness within the health system and with the medical profession in particular. She adds that since the NHS reforms nurses have become more antagonistic to all doctors and show this by their less co-operative responses to doctors in training.

While there has been a great deal of research on nurses and their coping style, less is said about women doctors and which strategies they have to adopt, often at their own expense. Women juniors are leaving medicine not only because of a dislike of the NHS reforms and the long hours, but also because medicine remains appallingly patriarchal in its responses to women and to patients. Women doctors have a real problem in voicing their approach to care and medicine and the majority collude with medieval practices in order to be accepted within the profession (Maddock and Parkin 1994). However, women doctors could play a role in bridging the professional divides in healthcare by supporting those who seek to break down professional barriers. Stacey (1992) suggests that it would be a positive step if doctors began to relinquish their focus on the one-to-one relationship with the patient in favour of general staff and patient relationships. It is more difficult for women doctors to change than it is for their male colleagues: the one-to-one relationship is the one place within the male medical and management cultures where they can be more woman friendly.

Many doctors, including women, continue to treat non-medical staff as their subordinates or even servants. Although attitudes are changing they remain deeply entrenched within the NHS and shore up the 'brick walls' between 'expert' and 'support' staff. Women doctors report that male medical trainees have become open and less arrogant in their relationships, but that this approach reverts to paternalist mode with they become consultants. Nurses report the same dynamic among female consultants (Maddock and Parkin 1994). Those women professionals and managers who were astute in their judgements and better at interface management often did not appear to be mainstream to any professional group – which was perhaps why they could cross professional boundaries more easily. The women who did not feel strongly about their profession or who rarely mentioned their academic backgrounds or professional qualifications, even if they had several degrees, were also more likely to be used to interface management; but they were also vulnerable as they were not protected by professional organizations and often marginalized in traditional institutions.

Global cultural differences

Societies vary enormously in their interpretations of social relationships and the values they place on various types of relationships. However, a common theme is that diversity for most represents 'oddity', while diversity is tolerated it is not usually valued. Diversity is a difficult concept in any society and presents problems to even the most radical and tolerant. It can refer to a difference in terms of personal identity of less commonly to a difference in approach to other people. There is a variety of views on acceptable management and manager behaviour which does not merely relate to gender but to cultural differences. Cultural differences may exist between whole continents or between two villages on either side of a mountain in the same county. Each culture has its own preferences and socio-values, which profoundly influence how people and managers behave in public, in private and how they are perceived. International trade has forced multinational companies to recognize cultural differences because they influence sales and future markets, although such differences tend to be played down in business schools. Although what is considered good management practice in the west has changed dramatically over the past fifty years, the gulf between management in the 1950s and 1990s is not so great.

Trompenaars (1993) suggests that there are distinct differences in the ways in which managers approach business relationships in the west and the south. These approaches are based on local social rules and the values that societies place on social relationships.

Universalism	versus	particularism
Rules	versus	relationships
Individualism	versus	collectivism
Neutral	versus	emotional
Diffuse	versus	specific
Achievement	versus	ascription. (Trompenaars 1993: 29)

The distinctions made by Trompenaars refer to local social values and to the cultural emphasis on the individual or the group, or focused on particular or holistic visions. In 'particularist' communities employees are loyal to others in the group, clan or firm. In such communities loyalty to the group is sacrosanct and group members are due protection no matter what other more corporate or formal rules dictate. The 'high trust' group can be as dangerous as the alienated 'low trust' group. Whereas low trust groups are alienated as individuals, high trust groups such as the Mafia are likely to be extremely hostile to outsiders or those who cross them.

The concept of individualism is highly divisive within both corporate and street cultures, but also within whole communities. A community's position on the individual–collectivist continuum will influence whether individualism is an advantage or a social misdemeanour. As women are excluded from these groups, because they are 'different' by virtue of being women and not men, they are put at a massive disadvantage in communities where individual different is anathema.

Detachment and connectedness were dimensions that differentiate the 'active campaigner' from the 'detached civil servant'; for example, to show feelings at work is frowned upon in northern Europe, whereas this is considered a sign of basic humanity in many other countries and within working-class communities in the UK. The differentiation between the 'diffuse' and 'specific' approach refers to how people confront problems and difficulties. Those who are focused on immediate tasks and objectives select very different information from social interaction than those who wait for themes to emerge and let matters unfold, allowing solutions to be revealed rather than presuming what the outcome should be. This is very different from the focus of UK management, which has had a dramatic effect on what managers value in their work relationships. The emphasis is not only more on cost but also on causal relationships and an unwillingness to allow emergent criteria and dimensions to reveal themselves. The diffuse approach is much more akin to the female style in that it is open to new and emergent relationships, although as more women adopt the managerial efficiency model the reality of gender differences becomes less visible.

Some of these differences are already obvious in organizations where there is a diverse workforce, but there are significant variations in the values placed on diversity itself; for example, attitudes to men and women managers vary not only from company to company, but also from nation to nation. A company may employ women managers because they are 'as good as men', but then give them very little support when they encounter difficulties, which they frequently do. American companies send women project managers to countries where the men have no knowledge or experience of how to communicate with women and sometimes even refuse to meet them. Gender equality is a minefield for international companies: 'Western women are baffling to Japanese men and have no idea how to talk to us – if you confront them they just don't know how to cope – women have definitely been targeted as the Japanese banks have been forced to cut staff' (*Independent on Sunday*, 19 May 1996).

Japanese business codes are complex and European managers find it difficult to learn the subtleties. Americans tend to be direct whereas

Japanese managers are extremely polite in their comments, never wanting to offend or be directly critical. It may be hard for a woman to become a sales manager in a multinational, but it is equally hard for Europeans to be promoted within a Japanese company. Japanese men and women would experience the same discrimination within Britain companies: 'Those who achieve the most success are those who learn and play by the Japanese rules. Do not demand promotion until you have a trusting relationship with your Japanese bosses' (*Independent on Sunday*, 19 May 1996). This is not unlike the women's experience as outsiders in management who are given the advice of 'be invisible and as men'. Trompenaars (1993) suggests that in the USA and Europe people are task oriented and focused on setting and meeting objectives; they make blunt comments like 'let's get down to business'. This plain speaking is considered rude by the Japanese, who prefer to spend time on 'getting a feel for relationships and people, getting to know the issues and building rapport'. They speak of *nemwashi*, literally 'binding the roots of trees', which means that you circle around issues before coming to the point.

Accepting people who are different is much easier if they adopt and conform to your culture and values, but if they continue to flaunt their difference or exaggerate them, this can antagonize. Although nationalities tend to be used to illustrate cultural differences, there exist huge variations within every country; for instance, those living in remote rural areas in Britain may have more in common with those living in South Asia than in London. In rural communities in the UK it is still considered rude to ask direct questions about someone's work or relationships, in spite of the fact that being straightforward or 'in-your-face' has become a norm for younger urban managers who are task driven and timebound. For those with little time, 'shooting the breeze' can be frustrating for stressed managers, even if it is confirming for others. In fact networking is much more useful to the contemporary company, but managers whose work schedules do not allow them time to develop relationships find themselves incapable of making the switch from 'work' to 'people'.

The social, economic and political environment has led some African managers to evolve diverse approaches to management to meet the challenge of managing different cultures and change:

> In my response to this challenge . . . I have found conventional western management practices too inadequate. I had to rely more and more heavily on instructive and indigence, tribal African wisdom and leadership techniques . . . I received extensive training in entrepreneurship in childhood through my grandmother when I learnt to herd cattle and also through hunting. According to the shoma powers 'the forest only gives to those who have endured its hastenings'. (Mbigi 1991: 1–2)

Frustrations emerge between people who have different expectations and values regarding ways of working and formal status, which may be due to differing cultural tendencies or to political differences. For some, age and status are valued, whereas those in western companies are usually only interested in outcome and financial profits. Education, managerialism and performance measurement have shifted the ladder of success away from social status being given as a birthright. In the west promotion and status are now accorded to those who have earned it through a demonstration of skill, competence and qualifications. Whereas previously age and longevity may have conveyed status and authority, this is less the case in western organizations which reinforce performance, not social status or age; although some women would question how performance is assessed and refer to its gendered assumptions.

Gender management strategies

The shifting sands of what is desirable behaviour in management have left staff in most organizations ducking and diving through the old 'as-is' practices and new management dreams. Women are especially adroit at this; they have been managing gendered contexts all their lives. Many authors have highlighted the strategies women are forced to adopt in order to cope and survive in the male world. At one time or another most women have adopted the gamut of gender-management tactics.

Some are better at tactics and streetwise, yet fail to really change their realities, having no longer term strategies; others are strategical in thinking but poor in tactical talents. There often appear to be class differences associated with these skills. The streetwise tactics are commoner among working-class women while the educated women figure out strategy, but find the realities of day-to-day gender relations more difficult. Many middle-aged and middle-class women in Britain have been socialized to be polite, to listen and to be helpful. This oppressive training has been as damaging to their sexual relationships as it has in management. Women manage their social realities by conforming and adjusting to their immediate peers, families and the social cultures in which they live. In traditional male cultures women often have to compensate for their femaleness because being visible as a woman is detrimental to their public role. This is especially true in the UK. Women adopt long-term strategies and develop tactical behaviour to cope with the male gender culture at home, in the community and at work. Some gender cultures demand more dramatic tactics than others, some demand total gender invisibility.

Equality policies and equality feminism downplayed gender differences because they were felt to undermine female credibility at work. Every woman who wants to transform organizations or society has to deliberate on tactics to handle her gender identity. She has to decide whether to conform in style or be open and challenging and expose herself to ridicule and hostility. Each woman develops her own gender management strategy and associated tactics, and it is these which divide women: 'Women in the workplace they are constantly called upon to negotiate organisational realities permeated by the above social practices and relations which reinforce stereotypes that confirm the powerful and marginalise outsiders' (Green and Cassells 1994: 19). Women have to control other people's perceptions of them as women; they have to measure reactions and ascertain whether they were being too aggressive, or too feminine. Gutek (1989) points out that, in addition, women have to deal with this stereotyping as a personal rather than an organizational problem.

Popular narratives can be just as confining as some social realities (Chapter 6). Women are silenced in their conceptualization of the changes that they would like to make by the dominance of male definition and characterization of events and relationships. The fact that women are 'outsiders' to male cultural and intellectual reference points (Marshall 1992) would explain why so many feel unable to speak or are not heard in management. Even senior women with authority, if heard, are not understood. Male cultures have the effect of silencing women – either because women silence themselves or because when they attempt to articulate their thinking they are met with disbelief or non-understanding.

Marshall (1984) states that women are as immigrants moving in a male country, they adopt deliberate behaviours to blend in. Marshall's (1993) gender analysis of communication and reference to 'high' and 'low' cultural contextual codes provides a tool to understanding how this silencing of women in male work environments operates. She presumes that male cultures have a 'high' level of informal agreement between those who hold similar views and have common assumptions. Consequently they need say very little to each other and talk in a minimalist fashion as they have no need to explain themselves. Women in the same work environment are not only outside the magic circle but are also attempting to develop emergent ideas that are not easy to formulate. They have to be explicit in a language to which they are unaccustomed. This results in a mismatch of gendered cultural codes. Since the male codes dominate and determine the very fabric of management language, women are unheard and frustrated. This situation is changing gradually. As management has to become more flexible and managers have to talk, and as more women are determining the style of interaction, there is a blurring of these formal codes.

The literature around gender and language has been well read and most women are aware of the various negotiation options open to them, but this awareness is still rather one-sided and many men remain conscious of sexuality and fear egalitarian interaction. By contrast, women are constantly searching for gender-neutral environments where they are not expected to listen, be encouraging, sympathetic and emotional. British women continue to conform to gendered expectation by asking questions instead of commenting and by ending sentences with such phrases as: 'isn't it?', 'don't you think?', 'don't you agree?', whereas men will invariably make a statement and expect the listener to agree (Tannen 1992).

In the men's group verbal contributions were often phrased as statements of individual position, for example, 'I've balanced the budget', or 'I've prepared my slot'. By contrast the women's group shows a high proportion of open-ended invitations, such as: 'Let's explore the tasks', or 'Let's create a structure', 'Do we need a management team?' (Brown 1994: 40)

The type of language used by the women's group may be useful in enabling agreement and in encouraging participation, but it can also be seen as indicating underconfidence. In the work plan it is important to note that black women have never conformed to these 'victim passive' stereotypes because they have always been required to be strong, resourceful and assertive (and perhaps not viewed by white men as women and therefore not as sexual objects). Others argue that assuming black women to be strong and resourceful is just as inaccurate (bell hooks 1987).

The strain of womanhood

Research in Sweden found that women's tactics tended to reflect their sympathies. Invariably the women identified with juniors and clients while the male managers modelled themselves on the boss (who was in most cases a man). Ressner (1979) found that while men and women public sector managers were given the same duties, they performed them in different ways and judged performance outcomes differently. This is significant because it provides an insight into why women talk and behave in a manner which many executives find unacceptable; for example, women tend to use the gestures of inferiors or clients, rather than assume the authority of boss. Women learnt to behave as subordinates and were penalized when they did not behave in a conciliatory manner: 'The continual strain of having to change yourself in a chameleon-like fashion, to "fit-in" can lead to anger, anxiety and a sense of powerlessness, feelings that typically underpin poor psychological health' (Green and Cassells 1994: 19)

Such pressure is just as strong in the professions where definitions and concepts are central to the work itself. Morley (1993) used the metaphor of the 'iron cage' to convey the feeling of women academics when they negotiate the male academic world. Even those senior women in government feel that they should remain vigilant and on their guard against colleagues. Women at ease at work can be close to colleagues for many years, but when they suggest radical changes or apply for more senior positions they experience hostility, ridicule and personal references to domestic commitments, work, age, personal and sexual relationships. Women managers use a battery of tactics to avoid being ensnared in the female domestic gender roles of wife, mother or daughter; for example, women may:

- disguise their sexuality;
- dress smartly in dark coloured suits;

- become very formal and proper in their behaviour and communications;
- make use of traditionally powerful female roles of 'mother' or 'teacher'.

Women develop tactics to hide their 'femaleness' and in many organizations they still have to work hard to persuade colleagues to respect them as managers. In the past this has often led them to be more ruthless, tougher and more aggressive than their male colleagues. Managing gender on a daily basis is tiring and stressful; it can be exhausting, requires tactical thinking and endless energy. Women's gender role is a managed status. Being a woman in a male-dominated environment demands handling one's gender in particular ways, with reference to one's interpretation of the prevailing power structure in the organization. Senior women in particular report having to avoid being treated as a woman rather than as professional or manager. Without constant vigilance women run the risk of not being taken seriously, not being heard and not receiving necessary information; in other words, of not being able to participate fully in the organizational system (Sheppard 1989: 145).

Dress presents a particular problem for women managers who tend to err on the side of conservatism to avoid visibility (Harragan 1977; Sheppard 1989). Sheppard reported that women managers do not want to be perceived as sexual beings and attempt to desexualize themselves; to reinforce this all the women interviewed who worked in central offices said that they had joined the professional gang and wore appropriate clothes. Dress was a major preoccupation in the 1980s and there are still regions of the country where women managers are expected to wear skirts with shoes and not trousers to work. Dress has become much more informal in cities, especially in London, although most women managers continue to wear dark suits. Women in senior management tend to have become more informal and feel freer to express themselves: 'I've never been one for smart clothes, in the 1980s there were lots of Thatcher clones but that has changed – women are more confident now' (Director).

While the issue of dress in London may have become less formal, a chief officer working in the North West of England reported being told by administrative staff: 'You've got no tights on, you can't come to work as a chief executive with no tights on'. Although what to wear at work is becoming less of a burden for many, only women doctors felt exempt from the 'smart' uniform codes; apparently their professional status and their middle-class backgrounds allowed them to be eccentric. However, they were still ridiculed for looking 'frumpy'.

Image and being tough

Deborah Tannen (1992) described the differences in the way men and women communicate, the subtleties of body language and of style. By the mid-1990s most people have become aware of impression management and the significance of style and appearance. Image and presentation skills are taught as part of management development; managers are assessed on their ability to appear competent as well as to be competent. Women have to create the impression of being the perfect 'manager' as a way of overcoming their 'women-ness' or female persona. Many women said that they had tried to make themselves more accepted by being more aggressive, pushy and 'cooler' at work:

> It is not what you do or what you want to do which is important, it is the way in which you manage – it's all impression management. They want immediate decisions – so you make immediate decisions, you turn small detail into decision – 'I've decided to close the door.' 'Yes, we will stop the meeting now.' It's no good women weeping and wailing. They just have to take control. It's all impression management. (Bradford, Senior)

Many women disliked themselves for mirroring male behaviours and were committed to changing practices even if they had to accept that they would have to learn some rougher tactics. Some women said that this toughening up process had just happened, while others felt that it was a conscious effort born out of necessity:

> I tried being tougher and adapt to what I saw as a characteristically male way of being in meetings. I did a bit of 'tub thumping' and hated myself for it. It was a process I had to go through, but I wouldn't do it again. It hurt me too much – it's all pretence and feels like acting out a lie all the time. (Leeds, Senior)

The tough tactic involved removing the image of victim by a change in outward behaviour and a demonstration of strength. Some were better at this than others. Several senior managers admitted that they had always been tough and did not find the competitiveness of chief officer meetings a problem, although most did:

> Someone told me that although I didn't know anything about sport I got very excited and loud about things I was putting forward. I think this made me look less like a victim, and so they felt comfortable with me – if fact I think they're frightened of me. (Corporate director, Kirklees)

In general, women found the sporty and bawdy atmosphere of board meetings oppressive or irritating, while some were more accepting than others. Several directors said that they had learned early on as directors that they had to act especially 'tough' when first appointed to a new post in order to gain credibility: 'I found that after I'd sacked some people I became more accepted. I'd proved that I was tough and one of the boys' (Bolton).

Women felt that if they could show that they are as tough and available as the men then they will have no problems. The pressure on women to hide their feelings, talents and differences operates in all professions in the UK. This situation is changing very fast in some organizations but not in others. Being passionate about anything in the civil service or local government continues to be considered unusual and strange.

Joining the club

Many women tried to infiltrate the dominant culture by getting closer to the men through joining sports clubs and going drinking. Most resented having to do this and preferred to work hard and demonstrate competence instead. Few women middle managers said that they had wanted to join in pub lunches or conversations about sport. They could see no real work or personal gain from going out on pub trips. Those women who had tried to join the men's clubs often met with little success. However, they persisted because they knew that mixing socially was the way to develop trust and confidence and to gain allies:

> I started out by being one of the boys, laughs and jokes about sport, and playing the same competitive games, but now I've decided to challenge whenever I can. The first thing I want to do is challenge the concept of competition – and also the virtue strength. There is a false confusion between strength and bullying. (Kirklees)

Those women most integrated with the men were often criticized by other women: 'Some women have been successful here, but not many. They have done so by adopting male ways – I think this is a decision you have to make – they're definitely toeing the line' (Rochdale).

Women managers knew that they had to be good to succeed and were aware of the continuous observations on their work. They tried to combat criticism by working hard, staying late at work, never saying no and attending endless training courses: 'Of course I don't mind women trainees but if they can't stand up for 24 hours or work in a male team, want children then you can't do surgery – surgery requires a special breed of person – male or female' (Male chair of surgical training). It is no surprise that few women become surgeons in any specialty. Some women worked every evening, weekends and very late at night. Some said that they were working harder and longer hours not to protect themselves from possible criticism but to get through the work, to be effective and to 'protect their backs' when they were involved in innovative projects which could be criticized by those whose territories were threatened by the initiative. Managers said that if you did not put in extra commitment your project was doomed: 'I had become very obsessed by work, planning campaigns. You have to work hard because otherwise someone will come from behind and stab you in the back and ruin the project'. Few women said that they worked hard to gain acceptance, but clearly the sense that you had to protect yourself from attack indicates that women were aware of having to work beyond the normal working week just to survive, but they were loath to admit it. Many pointed out that anyone who was attempting to change practices was bound to have to work harder – it was just commonsense.

Adopting powerful female roles

Women do have powerful roles to play and many wield power through the home, within the family and by informal means – but this is still influential, even if it does confirm traditional thinking. Wendy Hollway (1991) was one of the few feminists in the 1980s to acknowledge the way in which women make use of powerful female roles. It was a mistake to ignore female power and the way that women often brought their powerful family roles to work. Although the power of the domestic role is limited to personal interaction and is not public, it is nevertheless a significant route to influence. Hollway (1991) suggests that one of the major influences on older male business managers is their working daughters. Fathers listen to their daughters. The daughters tell their fathers how frustrating work is and the fathers listen, they are ambitious for their daughters. Directors have become more aware of gender because they are fathers of working women, with the result that 'dads' can be quite effective mentors or guardians for younger women. Some women who were generally comfortable with men said that they had brothers or affectionate fathers. One woman, described herself as an effective bureaucrat and at home with men 'in cardigans'. She was more concerned about making local government more democratic and improving services than engaging in gender battles. She used whatever female power she could muster and found that her most effective role was as a 'prime and respectable' nanny figure:

> I'm not supposed to speak in meetings, just take the minutes and prepare the agendas and reports – it's a high powered secretarial job à la the civil service. They have to have confidence in me. I say a couple of things in every meeting, usually summing up the proceedings, like a teacher. I convey my feelings by looking shocked or displeased – they used to bring in officers and give them a carpeting but I let it known that this was distasteful. I have managed to persuade them to distribute all the reports to a wider number of people, so the department knows what decisions the chief officer's group has decided, they never did this before. It's a very secretive environment.

Later she reflected that she was growing tired of this manipulating role, when she knew she could run the department better and more demo-cratically than the bosses whom she was servicing: 'But of course I feel by being so unthreatening I am colluding with the system. The more efficient I am, the better the system works – I think a lot of women are perfecting a system which oppresses them.'

Years of servicing male bosses have left many very able and competent older women extremely cynical about men. These women were the least confident about any possible change in gender relationships – they utilized the powerful female roles of mother, sister and teacher to good effect, but they would have preferred egalitarian, less role-bound interaction and were scathing about men for being so susceptible to such influence:

> I would put by desk in the corner to make people think I was harmless and soft – in fact I could be ruthless. In trade union meetings I never raised by voice and was always school mam-like. When they wouldn't negotiate I would look shocked and disappointed. They always changed their minds.

Relationships with other women

Women's political decisions often lack authority and credibility because they are understood to relate to her personal experience and are therefore political. There is a deafening silence on the impact of male cultures on women and men, but more especially on women who are forced into constant deconstruction and reconstruction of their gender management tactics and strategies at work. Gender relations is still understood to concern individual men and women and their battles, but gendered cultures influence not only the relationships of men and women but also those between women. To pretend that there have not always been huge differences and conflicts between women would be ridiculous. Common experience has not resulted in women joining the same battles or even playing on the same pitch. Some choose to deny the realities of gender culture. Some are so disillusioned that they despair of any change, while others struggle for their individual dreams and ambitions. Unfortunately collective action among women is less common than it was in the UK, although networking among individual women is strong.

Awareness of a gender culture did not appear to make women more supportive of each other. They were critical of female bosses, older and younger sisters and those with different cultural backgrounds. Women want their leaders to be leaders without being leaders; to be challenging and radical while not leaving the traditional fold. Those at home feel undervalued and those at work often feel alienated. Within an overarching women's movement, women are freed from conformity but those who challenge and seek change are liable to attack from men and women.

Much of women's stress at work is caused by other women, sometimes juniors but often colleagues who are jealous of other women's autonomy and their opportunities. The lack of interest in promotion by many administrative women can be traced to lack of support and/or mocking voices saying 'Who does she think she is?'

Women were critical of how women directors operated in meetings because they lacked confidence, were conciliatory and not aggressive enough in defence of their budgets and/or departments. Middle managers wanted these women to be tougher, less conciliatory, to win arguments and defend their budgets: 'The trouble with J is that she is too open and lets them all know what she is thinking – she gabbles, sometimes they bypass her and go to more junior officers. This is demeaning.'

Women new to management tended to behave at work as they would with friends. In the cultures of the 1980s this was perceived as inappropriate in the face of macho management causing some women to do the opposite and be more ruthless than they needed to be. Others thought that the negative stereotyping of women could be avoided if only other women would tone down their sexuality and become less visible. Those sceptical about change and seasoned within the authorities tended to be patronizing about women's failure to manipulate their surroundings and labelled women as they did men, simple fools incapable of changing their behaviour:

> I start from the position of being friendly to men rather than antagonistic or flirtatious – I think this is because I have an older brother and grew up with boys. I think a lot of women are either taming their sexuality or exploiting it – I don't think flaunting sexuality is appropriate at work.

One director was scathing about women who took on the established regime with a direct challenge, saying it always produced the wrong effect: 'Anyone who throws a brick at a greenhouse should expect revenge.' The same woman reported that women often lacked clear objectives and were unclear about what they thought important:

> Do they want organisation to change or feminist acclaim? I have seen one woman fall down all the flights of stairs because of the way she operated equal opportunities policies. In the end she was made redundant. If you want to achieve something you have to understand basic political realities and if you want political acclaim as an officer for your feminism you will fail.

Interestingly, the two women most antagonistic to feminists were also hostile to their male colleagues. Their problem was that they were doubtful that social or management change was possible or that men would relinquish their power and were even capable of relating to people. They were in fact much closer to the negative determinism of radical feminism than other feminists who are often attacked for being 'men haters': 'You have to remember men always hunt in packs. A woman has to be subtle and look at ways of quieting men who are extremely competitive. Men need the presence of a woman to quieten them down.'

These women were extremely aware of the effects of gender at work and of the need to develop their own strategies for dealing with it, but unfortunately they also thought that patriarchal relationships were so persistent and powerful as to be permanent. In many ways, these two women were more aware of gender than others. Yet it was this acute gender awareness of the power of men that made them the most cynical of managers and least confident of social change.

There is growing networking among women in senior positions and a greater sense of the need to support younger women. However, there are regional variations and certainly in the North West NHS organizations one chief officer of a community trust said:

> Those of us who have moved from London noticed the lack of solidarity between women, the older women chairs and officers are still deferential to men and rather bitchy about each other – they are also very powerful – this is changing but noticeably different for the way senior women in other areas meet more younger women, dress more casually and are more open about their mistakes and fears.

For instance, a chief officer in the NHS reported: 'It's no use us (women) organising women's networks. The most powerful women will not come they do not believe in supporting other women – they tend to be deferential to the men on committees but dragonlike in their own organisations.'

Strategies: coping, collusion or challenge

How a woman behaves in public remains problematic; she can rebel, be outrageous or be admired. Women do transform the gender cultures in which they live and work, but often they are also trapped into defensive tactics and conflicting long-term strategies while their male colleagues appear oblivious to the complex web of gender considerations which women have to grapple with on a daily basis. Clearly men and women rebel against rigid gender roles, but the women are chained to perceptions and expectations that they cannot control except by adopting duplicitous guises at work. Women do have less power and status in the public arena, no matter how much some would prefer to pretend otherwise.

Pioneering women in the nineteenth century recognized that they could have influence through the professions, but to enter the professions they had to shed their feminine mantle. This was much easier for middle-class or upper-class women who could remove themselves from childbearing and have some financial independence. This financial independence was a means to an end, not necessarily an end in itself. Clearly those women who already had some independence, whether through class, wealth or social status, were freer to rebel from their gender roles. Each generation has its own discourse, mood and political waves which influence women's ability to determine their lives and the type of gender management tactic they use. Tactics and strategies useful in one context can be disastrous in another. Women have basic choices to make in dealing with a constraining work environment. They can struggle, cope or organize, but whereas some women are free to run, others are shackled to the ground by lack of support, lack of money and the fact that they have or want to have children.

The question of what is effective gender management is constantly changing for every woman, from organization to organization, but it is the silence and lack of discussion about gender issues which disempowers women. They need to discuss tactics. Women do talk about relationships, but this is seen as a personal concern, not one which concerns management. Consequently management (male) assumptions continue to be viewed as neutral. Crisis management and selection criteria are not neutral; they tend to masculine qualities at the expense of negotiation and collaborative skills which many men lack.

Men have the same choices as women in dealing with traditional gender cultures. They cope, consider and challenge, but too often they lack the motivation to take on traditional gender cultures. Although, men are also trapped in the confines of rigid definitions of masculinity, most appear willing to pay the price in exchange for peer group loyalty and public status. The strains of this are beginning to show among young men, who are frozen in their peer group's image of male role models. The peer group demands conformity to notions of maleness which underplay sensitivity and the intellect and reinforce sexual and physical prowess. Many young men fail at school not because they are stupid but because school work is 'uncool'. Such masculine stereotypes restrict emotional development and literacy at a time when social relationships underpin almost all successful careers. Resistance to change in organizations is directly related to rigid male role models. A lack of confidence in any relationship results in many men who take risks and move beyond their roles, they are fearful of open relationships and will in retaliation attack those who appear to be acting in unpredictable ways. Traditional gender cultures breed bullies; these are not bad people, they have learnt bullying tactics. Unfortunately, a lack of confidence in alternatives, the future and in diversity continues to breed blame cultures in the UK, where few dare to speak out about poor practice and many are actively hostile towards those who do speak out.

6   Gender narratives

A New Feminism is here. Great, where is it, can I join? I wear lipstick, love clothes and even have a soft spot for boys – I gave birth to one and he taught me a lot about gender. But I also carried banners back in the 1970s, which probably makes me an old feminist and yet. . . . I really don't recognise myself or any of the women I fought alongside, in the current descriptions of my history. (Angela Phillips 1998: 6)

Cultural and intellectual discourse are filtered through a gendered framework which influences popular thinking about men, women and their relationships. Postmodernists might call this the 'gender narrative' or discourse which influences the roles of men and women as partners, employees and parents. Women continue to be viewed through the prism of the domestic roles of mother, housewife and carer, not just by men but also by women. Western journalists are far more comfortable with national conflict and war than they are with radical women, whom they persist in portraying as dangerous, mad, or, if from developing countries, as victims and helpless rather than as political leaders. Politicians, journalists and academics continue to categorize women according to how well or how badly they fit in with crude female stereotypes, which vary slightly from culture to culture but in the main characterize women as 'selfish' or 'selfless'. The media play a significant part in determining which women receive public acclaim and which women are criticized. Western women tend to be portrayed as careerist and less caring because they are no longer prepared to carry the emotional burdens of relationships. The gutter press has greatly distorted feminism in order to sell papers: 'Feminists are puritan, bullies who hate men'.

The media rarely capture the complexity of gender relations, the lives of mothers or of more radical women but reinforce female stereotypes of butch lesbians, bad mothers and radical feminists, and use these to vilify those women who do not fit in with the schizophrenic social demands placed on women who are expected to be both caring and ambitious. The fact that women are a diverse group that runs counter to the popular notions of disadvantage is rarely acknowledged and the press analysis of gender relations is glued to women's faults, their disadvantage and their individual struggles with lovers and husbands.

The problem for women and men is *how* to establish new practices within old frameworks. This is a tactical as much as an ideological problem. Most women are aware of the risks that they take when they challenge the traditional gender conventions which some women are never confident about transgressing. Feminist narratives reflect contemporary, cultural and political thinking and are often in conflict with one another. Feminism is not a creed although it is often interpreted as such and feminist narratives about gender mirror diverse political responses as do all other forms of politics. The questions to be asked are why social values remained undefined within the public, finance and management agendas, and why there is a huge disparity between the gender rhetoric and the personal realities of men and women.

The gendered thinking that permeates the press defines women as either disadvantaged, dangerous or sinners. Women's questioning is wilfully mis-interpreted by the gutter press in its portrayal of challenging women as difficult, strange or even dangerous. High-flying women attract press attention; and media stories about successful women usually confirm the image of a career woman as a ruthless or poor mother. Successful women are also assumed to represent feminists and one woman's mistakes are taken to undermine feminism itself.

The belief that gender inequalities have disappeared and that men are now the victims is currently reinforced by the media and younger women calling for softer forms of new feminism. According to the British press, equality has been achieved; women in the 1990s are not just equal, they are ahead. The fact that girls succeed at school and are more determined at work does not indicate that those deeply embedded prejudices and assump-tions about women have disappeared; if anything the success of women is adding to the resentments of men. The belief that the feminist creed has been proved wrong is endorsed within New Feminism, a perspective which takes a 'rosy view' about contemporary gender relations and promotes an ideal world of egalitarian relationships which few could take exception to. It is not suggested how we can achieve it – except as advice to working women to work harder and stay childless.

The acceptance of the narrow gender debate, which only refers to equal opportunities at work rather than social transformation, has resulted in the assumption that gender relations only concerns women and that only working women can be contented. Few feminists ever concurred with this version of feminism. Most were concerned as much with social relation-ships and values as they were with work. Unfortunately, even feminists have begun to respond to the media's version of equality feminism as if it had been propagated by themselves. There is a growing belief even among former feminists that the choices women make to work are undermining the fabric of our society. Women are attacked for the divorce rate, for refusing to carry the domestic burden of housework, uncommunicative partners and caring. Women have begun to attack other women for disrupting work patterns and undermining traditional family relationships as if men and fathers have disappeared completely from life:

> Inequality has brought about a curious synthesis of Marxism and free market ideology . . . the truth is that huge amounts of unpaid labour necessarily

underpin industrial economies . . . many take a sombre view of the way in which Modern feminism, which sees the family as a form of subordination and global capital, is now given a free rein to destroy the social fabric as the support which once sustained family and civic institutions is withdrawn. (Morgan/Prospect 1996: 18–19)

Yet most feminists have negotiated and balanced their home and work lives, which is demonstrated in the strategies and choices of women managers quoted in later chapters. Challenging women have for years been trying to transform social relationships, whereby they can work in a manner which does not destroy the fabric of society but improve it. Their strategies and actions have been determined not by callousness but by the force of patriarchy and traditional gender relations, which vary from country to country.

Patriarchy

Radical feminists define patriarchy as the unequal power relations between men and women in a society determined by the traditional social structures of family, state and community. The theory of patriarchy seeks to describe how gender inequality works within society and examines how the experience of gender roles and masculine and feminine identities underpin everyone's personal experience and social life. It analyses the way in which inequality has shaped women's history and provides some understanding of what is required if a more gender egalitarian society is to emerge. Feminist theories agree up to this point, but their epistemological perspectives vary enormously, as do their assumptions and explanations of oppressive gender relations. For example, Sylvia Walby (1990) defines patriarchy as the 'system of social structures and practices that men use to dominate, oppress and exploit women'. Others may view men as a less homogeneous group, themselves oppressed by class, race and economic factors and constrained by narrow definitions of masculinity.

Patriarchal relations tend to be strongest where men have very fixed views and ideas about what women should do and how they should behave in relation to them and within sexual relationships. The dynamics of patriarchy help to explain why the resistance to women is so persistent throughout the world. The theory presupposes fixed gender relations that from birth render women less powerful than men. Patriarchy has its roots in the feudal world where social power was passed from father to son through lineage and where women were dominated not just by structural or formal conventions but by blood and sexual ties to fathers, husbands and to men in general.

Pateman (1988) argues that, even though women have access to the public world of work and politics, they are hobbled by the fact that they continue to be subject to the subterranean gendered informal social codes that presume women to be subservient, less competent and domestic.

The history of the shift in gender relations is closely connected and intertwined with the history of suffrage and the development of trade. Rousseau and Locke heralded the end of traditional patriarchal lineage systems through the development of the concept of 'individual rights'. The advent of free trade and capitalism demanded a more sophisticated ordering of society, men travelled widely and could trade freely, irrespective of their birth lineage. The growth of capitalism needed freer men and the development of financial, legal and administrative systems necessary for trade liberated them from the burden of fixed lineage. Unfortunately for women, they were not included in these developments and remained enslaved to their lords at home unless of very royal birth. They were not free to trade and were not even legally defined as citizens in Europe until the twentieth century.

In Britain, as early as 1792 Mary Wollstonecraft wrote of the need for a new fraternity between men and women in *The Vindication of the Rights of Women*, after the struggle for universal franchise was advanced by the French Revolution in 1789. This cause was taken up in the nineteenth century by liberal feminists who demanded equal representation, property, custody and marriage rights. Women from the upper middle classes did benefit and they were slowly allowed access into political life and the professions. In 1919 the Sex Disqualification Removal Act enabled women to enter public office in Britain but it was not until February 1994 that the Church of England permitted them to become fully ordained as priests; and they remain barred from the priesthood in the Roman Catholic Church. It has taken a century since enfranchisement for women to gain access or membership into the professions, political organizations and on to decision-making bodies in Britain. Although societies in the west have developed the concept of 'individual rights', women are still constrained and moulded by patriarchal traditions which interact with more modern civil liberties and that 'fraternal' for women is really 'patriarchal' (Pateman 1988):

> The character of civil freedom cannot be understood without the missing half of the story that revels how men's patriarchal right over women is established through contract. Civil freedom is not universal, civil freedom is a masculine attribute and depends on patriarchal rights. (Pateman 1988: 2)

There have always been women writers who are not only aware of the possibilities of change but also fully cognisant of the power of patriarchal relationships. Cynthia Cockburn (1991) points out that women have very different lives from men, but this is rarely within the statutes and there is no historical recognition of gender difference in the social contracts which govern trade and employment, except in the past where women have been barred from office, wealth and inheritance. Women have been forced to appeal for equal rights on the grounds that they are surrogate men. Ignoring the reality of women's lives and experiences puts them at a disadvantage when they enter the public arena, whether in politics or employment. Pateman (1988) and Cockburn (1991) believe that feminist struggles must therefore aspire for more than mere rights: 'Women have not been incorporated into employment as workers but as women – the sexual dominates structures in the workplace as well as in the home' (Pateman 1988).

It is supposed that the manner in which patriarchal relations express themselves is constantly changing and that men are also corrupted and oppressed by this gendered system of unequal relationships. Some men might experience a conflict of interest over their natural tendency to collude with patriarchal assumptions and their rational appreciation that in order to manage efficiently they should encourage and develop talented women (Cockburn 1991).

Feminist writers in the 1980s drew attention to the closely woven connections between the bureaucratic functions and patriarchal relations (Ferguson 1984; Franzway et al. 1989), as outlined in Chapter 5. They also articulated very clearly the dilemma presented by gender relations for women managers. They can either achieve status by accepting and manipulating the bureaucratic structures and becoming known as a 'femocrats', or they can be open about their views and remain as juniors or 'oddballs' within their organizations (Franzway et al. 1989). The dilemma is whether to manage gender by remaining silent and seeking promotion, or to be open about criticisms and suffer discrimination. This is a problem for all women. Bacchi (1990) believes that we need to construct a social reality which includes women's perspective. This means giving a voice to women, which reflects the general problem of how women struggle to be heard when being distinctive and different within a male world that forces them into mimicking male language. The debate around presenting difference or confirming existing realities appears never ending.

The same or different?

All feminist theories and struggles have to grapple with how to present their case and have revolved around making sense of men's and women's apparent similarities and differences. This is particularly difficult in traditional society where patriarchal relations are strong and men are deaf to women's intellectual voice. The apparently magical world of women is a continuing source of mystery to many men. The differences between feminists have been concerned with what strategies to adopt when challenging both male power and male realities and how to handle or resolve gender 'same and difference' arguments. The problem for women activists has always been that they have had to frame political arguments in terms of male definitions in order that those in power would listen. The dilemma for women became more pronounced during the inter-war period when many were given the opportunity to enter and therefore mimic the male world.

They had to decide whether to stress their differences and their role as mothers (Bacchi 1990). Previously both men and women either viewed women as romantic and emotional figures (essentially different from men) or only intellectually capable when they were more male and masculine. Historically, there has always been a danger for women in proclaiming their different lifestyles, social and biological function. The woman's reproductive capacity and emotional attributes were used by men to reinforce the image of woman as childlike, irrational and therefore subhuman. It was therefore natural that the first feminists such as Mary Wollstonecraft (1792) and John Stuart Mill (1869) should emphasize women's intellectual and rational capacities and how like men women could be. To have adopted any other strategy at such a time would merely have reinforced existing prejudices; men needed to be persuaded that women could think. This strategy of downplaying gender differences was adopted by all those interested in western equal opportunities and suffrage.

The divisions between women campaigners have always reflected the problem of whether they should campaign for equality on the grounds that women are equal to and no different from men or to assert themselves as themselves and appeal for parity on the grounds of justice. Equal rights feminists concentrated their efforts upon getting women into the labour force, but they underestimated how hard it would be for women to engage in work when they had domestic commitments. By contrast, the social reformers were more interested in making working women's lives more bearable, which meant that they were forced to argue that women did have different lives and different experiences from men. In Britain, Eleanor Rathbone, a leading reformer and a member of the Fabians, argued for state benefits, family allowances and pensions. She saw that freedom for working-class women was totally dependent on improving the social conditions and employment prospects for the whole community, not just changes for women. The suffragist Maude-Royden agreed and said that the strategy of promoting women as if they were men was alienating when they knew that their lives were completely different. There was no way that they could compete within the workforce unless perhaps they were childless. Work for women was one way of achieving financial independence, but such independence was a means to improvement, not an end in itself.

The debate continues and is heavily determined by each country's attitude to women and to work. In the UK there is a history of labour movements and trade union struggle and it is easier for women to argue that common practice is 'bad practice' and that just because conditions suit men does not mean that they suit women. There is a British tradition of labour movements battling for employment changes and until recently a powerful trade union movement, but this is not the case in the USA.

During the 1970s and 1980s feminist strategists in the USA continued to insist that women were the same as and just as able as men. For them women's liberation was achievable by claiming that there was no difference between the sexes and that therefore there was no reason to exclude women from decision-making, management or business. This dilemma of what argument to use when battling for women's liberation still separates and frustrates women, especially in countries where women's recourse to justice is based on laws which refer to individual rights and are weak on justice for social groups. Women in the USA still persist in arguing for justice on the grounds of equality with male practice because they have no alternative. There is no labour movement tradition justifying or supporting workers' grievances; employees are expected to adapt or leave; it is a sink or swim environment. Milkman (1986) quotes the Sears case where a woman lost her claim when it was shown she could not be a good salesperson because she disliked the 'dog-eat-dog' style of sales operation. She was not a good seller because she was not a macho salesperson and was therefore unsuitable for the job. This expedient political strategy was certainly not promoted by all American feminists but it was dominant. The perspective was adopted by the press and then exported to other countries, with a distorting and devastating effect on the reporting of other women's movements, if not the direction of struggle itself. This has also undermined many women in the USA. Suzanne Gordon (1991) paints a rather bleak picture of American women whom she says have been led by the nose into accepting that to succeed they must compete with men and to do this they must accept traditional practice – in other words be highly competitive:

> The fact that women are now encouraged to devalue caring work has exacerbated a widespread societal crisis in caring that has deep political roots. . . . If women abandon caring for competition, rather than working to encourage all of us to share in the real work of the human community, then who will care? What kind of liberation have we purchased? (Gordon 1991: 14–15)

Her main thesis is not that women are mainly homemakers and should avoid the public arena, but that women should organize to change the public arena and should transform the 'rat race'. Unfortunately, many North American women who were committed to changing society in the USA in the 1970s had entered administrative or management jobs by the 1990s and were eager for success within mainstream organizations. They were therefore less vocal in their criticisms of the organizations in which they worked. Gordon refers to the way the magazine *Ms* altered its position to account for these changes:

> *Ms* and other feminist journals carried numerous articles about feminism and power, and consciousness groups grappled with these issues in weekly sessions around the country. Many tried to distinguish between power, celebrity and self-aggrandisement and assert a definition of power as empowerment. But, as the seventies moved into the eighties, the consciousness-raising groups . . . were disbanding – in part because women's struggles in the marketplace were so time consuming this kind of transformative politics was relegated to the margins. (Gordon 1991: 20)

In the UK women's struggles or campaigning also reflect this same conundrum and the same social pressures which pulled women both in the direction of conformity in order to gain status and credibility and towards arguing for social change. Socialist and radical feminists in the European countries remain profoundly ambiguous about the notion of 'equality' and have always been sceptical about being 'equal to or like men'. In Britain by the 1980s Equality Feminism had been born and nurtured by the press and by those who wanted an individualistic form of feminism which would utilize women's skills at work. However, the systems and working practices remained intact.

Most feminists believe there to be profound differences between men's and women's experience. The argument for them was concerned with whether these difference were genetic or to do with socialization (Segal 1990). However, those that were involved in campaigning for charters and legislative change sought to persuade the establishment that women required these changes, precisely because they were a special group in need. Again, women found that while decision-makers could accept some working women as a special group in need of welfare, they were unable to accept that women could have their own political and legal rights. The 'establishment' was more attracted by the idea that gender did not result in differences than the fact that it did. Many women in Britain who were active in women's groups and campaigns in the 1970s later became public sector managers (Segal 1990) and many of these women experienced the same conflict as the American woman below:

> She found that her ideals of caring and empowerment were scorned as counterproductive in the business world. The same kind of pressures operated in medicine. . . . Someone would ask, 'who can do a lumbar puncture?' A lot of guys would raise their hands, including those who couldn't to the procedure. I could never do that, I thought it dishonest. Yet, they didn't see this as dishonesty; men saw it as a mark of self-confidence. When I admitted I couldn't do it, it was seen as not aggressive enough. After a while I realised that the problem wasn't that I couldn't act like this but that I didn't want to. (Gordon 1991: 73)

Women joining corporate USA quickly learnt that men are uncomfortable with femaleness. It is hardly surprising that in order to survive or be understood American feminists made appeal to similarities with both individual men and male cultures. American society is still driven by socially determined individual achievement. The government's role is only concerned with the protection of the individual and some think it has no role in providing for the community or the common good. Given that this continues to be the case, in the late 1980s there followed a crisis in the community of social caring work generally. Women were competing at work and because so few concessions were made to their other responsibilities little time was created for non-family commitments or even family commitments (Gordon 1991). There followed a reactionary swing and a call for women to return to the home as nurturers. This wave of reaction arose from feminists who were tired of constraining themselves in an alien world and from those (men in the main) who wanted social problems to be solved, yet again, by women.

Reasserting difference

Carol Gilligan (1982) led the way for women to reclaim their actual experience. She described women's lives as paths of caring and nurturance and argued that women and men distinguish themselves by their gender identities. Although not all women conform to female gender stereotypes, most do feel strongly about their communities and social responsibilities; they prefer connectedness to disconnectness. On the other hand western (white) men tend to identify with and prefer distance, abstraction and separation from others. Many feel underconfident about making moral judgements, preferring general rules to guide them:

> My research suggests that males and females may speak different languages that they assume are the same, using similar words to encode disparate experiences of self and social relationships.
>
> Because these languages share an overlapping moral vocabulary, they contain a propensity for systematic mistranslation, creating misunderstandings which impede communication and limit the potential for co-operation and care in relationships. At the same time, however, these languages articulate with one another in critical ways. Just as the language of responsibilities provides a war-like imaging of relationships to replace a hierarchical ordering that dissolves with the coming of equality, so the language of rights underlines the importance of including in the network of care not only the other but also the self . . . In the different voice of work lies the truth of an ethic of care, the tie between relationship and responsibility, and the origins of aggression in the failure of corrections. (Gilligan 1982: 173)

Yet in the USA Judy Rosener (1990) was as controversial in her announcements to managers that women had a different management style from men. This was controversial not because men and women doubted it, most in fact believed it to be true, but because those who were fighting for a change in the status quo saw such statements as dangerous within the North American context. Gender difference remain controversial, particularly in the USA. Bacchi (1990) pointed out there is a difference between the arguments about gender similarities and differences which are culturally determined and statements defining male and females characteristics: 'Instead of creating "lesser" and "greater" feminism, we ought to increase our sensitivity to the way in which feminist arguments reflect and are constrained by particular political, economic and social circumstances' (Bacchi 1990: 91)

The debate about 'difference' and 'similarity' is again perpetuated in the thinking of those interested in theoretical accounts of gender and management and by women aware of gender relations in their own thinking. The problem is that the use of 'different' qualities appears to justify the status quo. If 'good' managers appear very masculine, not to appear as masculine is easily associated with being a poor manager. This crude assumption is apparently one of the main reasons why there are so few women in senior positions in management in almost all countries. As Chodorow (1978) and Gilligan (1982) point out, gender differences are usually illustrated by polar opposites such as male equals autonomous, formal, decisive and assertive, whereas female equals attachment, informal, attentive and diffuse.

The stark polarization between men and women and their differences has obscured the profound differences between women. bell hooks (1987), a black woman writer, asks which men do women want to be equal to? There is a generalized tendency to think that those who are oppressive will be themselves less oppressive and that the oppressed victim has a form of moral superiority, which certainly has been exploited by some feminists. This is not necessarily the case. Such an assumption led to the idea that the Jews were incapable of dehumanizing their Arab neighbours, which has been proved false. A feminist psychoanalyst, Jessica Benjamin, suggests that in fact the opposite is often true because the oppressed 'remain in love with the ideal of power that has been denied them' and thus replicate the behaviour of their oppressors. A similar explanation is used for child abuse, which is often said to be repeated by victims on their own children. Communities do have very difference gender cultures, but the concept has not yet caught on in the press which prefers to continue the battle of the sexes as if they were at war. In fact the conflicts are as much over values and ways of behaving in the public arena as they are exclusively to do with men and women. The dominant gender culture influences the values attached to social relationships and care, as well the actual personal relationships between men and women.

Narratives which undermine social 'values' and care

To understand how the tension between responsibilities and right sustains the dialectic of human development is to see the integrity of two disparate modes of experience that are in the end connected. While an ethic of justice proceeds from the premise of equality – that everyone should be treated the same – an ethic of care rests on the premise of non-violence – that no one should be hurt. . . . This dialogue between fairness and care not only provides a better understanding of relations between the sexes but also gives rise to a more comprehensive portrayal of adult work and family relationships. (Gilligan 1982: 174)

By the 1990s active socialist feminists in the USA suggested that the women's movement had failed because it undervalued women's domestic and caring work; it had contributed to the undermining of women, especially poor women, and American society's appreciation of basic human values: 'Our inability to liberate women's traditional work from patriarchy's firm ideological grasp, we tried to liberate ourselves from its occupational constraints, has resulted in a profound division within feminism and among women' (Gordon 1991: 131).

Gordon thought that equality policies and programmes which encouraged women to become like men would result in losing sight of their more traditional links with social and community values. In doing so, she states, many women managers are now behaving little differently from their male colleagues. She suggests that this is not women's liberation, but a loss of social values and social caring. In her view women have enslaved themselves to work because equal opportunity feminists have equated it with liberation while labelling caring and domestic tasks as the work of slaves and victims of patriarchy: 'This has resulted in a profound division between women – and our progress is now charted by the distance we have travelled away from care giving work – and towards male activities and preoccupations' (Gordon 1991: 131).

The fact that women have rejected their social values and 'caring' roles is to their own detriment as well as society's. Social workers and teachers are in short supply in the USA because they are undervalued and paid poor wages. The lack of social concern for children, the old and the poor has led many feminists to reconsider their opinions, tactics and political positions. The hallmark of the American male professional was his rejection of caring values and his individualism. The work environment generated by such men presented obstacles to those men and women who desired social change and wanted to revalue care:

> The resistance comes not only from the market economy that is hostile and indifferent to care, but from some female caregivers themselves who have been so influenced by our emphasis on the bottom line, power and independence, that they have come to identify with the aggressor and try to elevate their status by denigrating care. (Gordon 1991: 157)

Gordon links the failure of women to assert their values with the American and British obsession with regulation and restriction as against quality services. The narrow economic criteria dominating both social services and the business world have led to further reduction in time for community caring. The social services are driven by market economics, and practitioners are forced to make judgements on economic and efficiency grounds. Consequently, caring and quality fall further down the list of priorities unless practitioners are especially aware of being led away from their social commitments.

In many ways this is an American phenomenon and the American context is even more extreme that it is in Britain. In the UK this trend can be observed among managers who do not appear to have the same social value framework and can be ruthless in their pursuit of efficiency drives. Equality Feminism is not far removed from this attitude, although the climate is changing and there is more interest in the sociale economie than there was during the 1980s. New Feminism is born out of the attempts of working professional women to remodel feminism under a glossy cover where women are presented as wanting to be both determining and feminine; it is interested in the image of women rather than their realities and appears as a reaction against the old feminism. This is misleading as the same social realities still exist and patriarchal relations have not disappeared. The media tendency is to endorse a form of Equality Feminism and to adulate career women as role models. This perspective has recently been repackaged in New Feminism and the press is now obsessed with high-flying, rich and powerful women. These executives are applauded while those in middle management, struggling on the front line or at home with the contradictions between social values and efficiency are left feeling undervalued and ignored. The complexities of women's lives, thinking and political strategies are apparently of little interest to popular journalists who continue to seek out isolated and extreme examples of successful women or women victims.

Women and feminists have rebelled against the media's versions of Equality Feminism and are angered by the notion that superwoman is a feminist icon. Socialist feminists have always been dismissive of glossy pictures of successful women and forms of Equity Feminism which only promote individual achievement. Such women have been subjected to years of press criticism and continue to be labelled 'worthy', 'humourless', out of date or puritanical. Earlier feminists did of course shun the trappings of glamour because to have adopted them in Britain would have undermined their case against the promotion of women as 'sex objects'. A similar reaction can be seen among Muslim women. Although women feel freer to express themselves by what they wear in the 1990s, the reason for the blue/black suit remains; they still feel obliged to desexualize themselves in public and at work.

Some feminists may had a strong puritan streak, mirroring other social movements. Women's politics is after all rooted in Labour politics, but the puritan streak is also a response to the fluffiness of the 1950s. The New Feminism presents the liberated women as sexy and high flying, which in France would be laughable. British culture has a problem with sexuality generally. This is not the fault of feminists, but it is the world in which British feminists live. The New Feminism attempts to present a friendly face which is not surprising. Younger women have grown up in a more egalitarian world and do not expect to be discriminated against. They expect to have what they want and many do not encounter resistance until they have children or move out of the London experience.

The problem with New Feminism is that it does not address what is to be done if the philosophy does not work. Equality Feminism, like New

Public Management, is hype, a dream and a mission statement. It provides little guidance on how to achieve New or Old Feminism or how to overcome the ambiguous nature of gender roles and male preferences that continue to exist. Mothers, unless very well paid, are automatically excluded from the success picture. They have no choice but to challenge the status quo because it does not work for them. Equally, those who disagree with the colonizing frameworks and are rebels, mavericks or whistle-blowers are equally vulnerable. New Feminism does not provide an analysis or agenda for those who want to challenge the current thinking in management, negotiate new deals, forge new boundaries or change the furniture at the workplace because such behaviour would be confrontational and likely to cause conflict. If anything the working environment of the late 1990s is more not less ruthless and anyone who does not conform to managerial thinking or work long hours is extremely vulnerable.

New Feminism is really about definition, not about change, and as such is accepting of the very cultures and social dimensions which continue to oppress men and women, especially women within the public sphere of politics and business. It is in effect a merger of personal therapy and the postmodern desire to redefine the disagreeable out of existence. It is a redefinition of what to call feminism rather than a new trend and its mission statement promotes the personal philosophy of feel equal and confident and you will be successful.

Confirming or negating social realities

Gender studies research usually communicates one of two messages: it can describe a prevailing reality or convey possibility and change; or, in the case of more postmodernist writing, one floating perspective divorced from power relations and social context. However, one of the attractions to postmodernist thinking was that overdetermining models of gender relations trap women in negative versions of themselves and their capabilities. For instance, many female students are demoralized by accounts of how equal opportunities policies have failed and consequently become pessimistic about feminism. On the other hand, idealistic assertions about women's potential can misrepresent the power of traditional culture and women's own collusion or acquiescence in traditional gender roles and relationships. Rigid theoretical positions on gender relations frequently have a negative effect on women themselves. Parkin (1994) reports that her students are less interested in equal opportunities because so many older feminist lecturers have told them that the last twenty years of equal opportunities have brought no positive results. Similarly, some labour market feminists write that women's position is getting worse; women managers are in collusion with the bosses and any attempt to engage with restructuring is counter-productive. This is damaging to women's confidence in effecting change if it is not set in a perspective that acknowledges possibilities. Equal opportunities policies may not have changed the overall gender culture within management, but they have provided a framework on which to hang strategies for more profound change and given women a confidence in the workplace. Suffice to say that theoretical positions and philosophical accounts are far more powerful in everyday life than is acknowledged and many of those involved in academic work should be aware of this and more responsible in their attempts to account for reality. If the possibilities for social change are not incorporated into research and evaluation, they stifle possibilities and misrepresent the more challenging activities of those engaging with social change.

Postmodernism has tended to be associated with radical thought, with marginal people and states of flux rather than established traditions. Rejecting social analysis and generalizations it focuses on intellectual narrative and personal experience. While postmodernism is a peculiar brand of British and North American disease it is none the less significant. The most depressing feature of postmodernism is that it reinforces alienation rather than attempting to construct social realities and change. Within an authoritarian culture this approach is highly prescriptive and critics are attacked for being 'modern' or of not accepting diversities, etc. It is a deeply reactionary approach which attempts to delude those with difficult realities into thinking that they can work their way out of the quagmire, but stops short of supporting activities which would help them to move forward. This approach treats thinking as if it were the process of change itself; as if individuals can think their way through problems as a substitute for social activity – a form of mind over matter.

Pessimism also penetrated the Left and feminism. Even those who would previously have campaigned have become tired and despondent. Both the Marxist left and forms of Radical Feminism leave a negative legacy in terms of their overdetermining analyses. Although their perspectives do not deny the need for struggle, the overwhelming message is that workers and women are victims who need support. They are rarely presented as capable of personal creativity and innovation because the weight of tradition and power is against them.

Many postmodernist views of gender relations reinforce the notion of the isolated woman as victim operating in a sea of male culture, powerless, passive and inert (Barrett 1991). Its analysis of men's and women's relationships often amounts to the reinforcement of embedded gender stereotypes. The postmodernist deconstruction of relationships often leads to a denial of women's own experience as a generalizable phenomenon (Moore 1994). In the Kantian tradition, the denial of social realities and the reduction of analysis to the literary, separated individual experience from its base in social realities affecting agency and social change. Barbara Epstein (1996) argues that postmodernism on gender has been destructive to the women's movement, encouraging rarefied feminist theory in place of real activity and empirical evidence:

Intellectual discourse has come to be governed by shifting fashions. Work is judged more by its level of sophistication than by the contribution it might make towards social change. . . . This sub-culture that emphasises the charisma of individual performance but does not place much value on ability to make sense of reality. . . . Though difference is endlessly celebrated in feminist/radical post-structuralism circles, there are strong pressures toward intellectual conformity. (Epstein 1996: 86)

The deconstructionist approach is useful as a consciousness-raising exercise, but it is too focused on the assumed symbolic nature of roles and structures and is unable to unpack the complexities of social processes or to assist those interested in their capacity to change the status quo. This is unfortunate since many followers of postmodernist thinking claim that such (individual) deconstruction does assist change:

By the late sixties, theory was taking precedence over reality. . . . What is striking about the present discussion is that this time the separation of theory for experience for which radical feminists once criticised the left is now taking place within feminism itself, and that this polarisation has become even more extreme: feminist (theorists) are trying to develop a theory which explicitly renounces experience as its base. (Epstein 1996: 97)

The apparent obsession with obliterating the social dimensions gives rise to a form of reactionary interpretation from theorists who consider themselves radical. Critics of postmodernist feminism observe that deconstruction at best can demonstrate oppression and raise consciousness about oppression (Nicholson 1992). It is not capable of generating alternatives, which are necessary if social transformation is to occur. The feminism of the 1970s was in essence a postmodern movement, but as soon as the theoretical feminists became removed from the everyday realities of women's struggle, the battle for social changes become hampered not just by patriarchal traditions but also by a theory which was individualist and pessimistic in its messages to women. This not to deny the variety of gender narratives and their significance, but if these are dislocated from real social conditions and influences they merely become a collection of stories, not a philosophy for social change which can unite and provide a basis for more collective actions: 'Material Existence and the social organisation of people in grassroots struggle are remote from the high status production of "theory". You don't get anywhere these days unless you have a text; or a discourse and the more incomprehensible the better' (Rowbotham 1990: 39).

The phenomenological roots of postmodernism and of individual voluntarism appear to be its strength precisely because they understand change to come from individual determinism, not through collective struggle and consensus. Many postmodern perspectives are subjective or personal, almost akin to the approach a trainer may use in a workshop in order to encourage individuals rather than to analyse: the trainer may say 'think change' to facilitate learning. There is an 'as if' or illusory quality which appears to satisfy a desire in those frustrated by overwhelming social and political realities. There is an argument in training and therapy that mind over matter can lead to greater confidence and therefore to personal change. However, the suggestion cannot be made that social realities will disappear merely because of either individual or collective thoughts.

The postmodern tendency is to reinforce the idea that today's reality can be sealed from yesterday and tomorrow and abandons historical analysis and social reference points. This is not real liberation from the shackles of work, oppressive relationships and debt which continue to exist in reality no matter what narrative is at play. The hostility to women does not disappear because you wish it to, although to ignore it may provide some solace. The idealized version of realities does not remove the real constraints presented not just by a lack of money or housing but also by social relationships and personal histories. To understand oppression may be a liberation, but usually to ignore its reality is nothing more than a retreat into nostalgia. The current obsession with dismantling structures is a readjustment too far and only makes sense if done in the pursuit of new relationships and possibilities, not as mere armchair dreaming. The loss of confidence in the 'social' and the 'others' has become a retreat into abstraction and analysis which has the destructive consequence that individuals experience realities as separate and different; they feel not confirmed but isolated.

Individualistic mindsets hinder emergent relationships between those separated by professional establishments, working practices and contracting. The drive for understanding individual difference rather than making sense of connections and barriers to new relationships removes the individual from envisaging alternative social realities. Without vision people are passive observers in their own lives. The dominant and rather individualist narratives emanating from managerialism and equalities at work are powerful obstacles to those seeking to transform organizations. The tendency to declare class and gender to be redundant concepts only adds to the delusion. They do matter, if not in theory then in practice, and they certainly affect relationships and the possibility of changing them. Social realities cannot be bypassed or ignored; neither can the fact that everyone makes value judgements about events and other people. To assume gender–class power relations are now egalitarian is dreaming. Because the balance of power between some men and women has changed does not indicate that inequalities have been irradicated. There are also huge national, ethnic and cultural variations. Women as a group continue to be poorer throughout the world, in spite of the fact that a few women have become richer and better qualified. The attitude that there are possibilities for all and that everyone has potential is the basis of therapy, assertiveness training and other management techniques and for any individual's own philosophy and hope. But this is very different from assuming that all have the same opportunities and potential, they do not. Traditional and unequal relationships persist between the classes, between black and white, between men and women.

The strength of the Women's Liberation Movement lay in their confidence in the possibility of change and in their ability collectively to change social definitions and social realities. The movement produced a crop of experienced activists who moved into public administration in the late 1970s. Many then became involved in equality issues at work and equal opportunities policies. The more radical women's liberation movement demands were squeezed into equal opportunities and affirmative action programmes, reducing feminists' arguments to those of work, pay and status. They distorted socialist feminism in Britain and radical feminism in the USA. Fortunately, the younger women of the 1990s are more outspoken, confident and determined. By comparison the young men appear confused, underachieving and underconfident. There is a plethora of articles on the plight of men: men as fathers, as divorcees and as unemployed workers. Women's determination to seek more egalitarian relationships at home has left the men who are unwilling to change feeling vulnerable. But while men may feel vulnerable and undermined, women continue to live in a world defined by patriarchal relationships and male institutions.

It would be a positive move to shift the discussion from one of gender differences to one which revolves around gender cultures which affect boys as much as girls. There are clearly huge gender differences between men and women, and between women, but so long as the debate continues to focus on who is to blame, rather than on how to achieve a balance in gendered relationships which is concerned not only about work but also social life and values in the public world then change will not take place. The current popular gender analysis merely feeds press sales and the battle of the sexes. Men are more powerful than women, but they are also oppressed by gendered thinking and gender cultures, which many women also collude with. Young men are depressed, stressed and anxious, not because of women or because they are unemployed, but because their role models encourage them to traditional definitions of manhood and masculinity. It has been suggested that managing masculinity at work is just as much of a problem for male managers as it is for the women working with them. However, although this may be true in some cases, there are few men campaigning against this oppression. Unfortunately, most men do not appear to be conscious of how far masculinity is in fact an issue for them, whereas women are extremely aware of gender dynamics and the need to manage their gender image. There is a need to break out of the straitjacket of rigid convention and social determination, but new practices will only develop through changes in social and ideological realities. Deconstruction will assist the process, but it is not social transformation. Transformation can only come from a shift in power relationships between men and women, but gender narratives dominate and dictate this struggle.

Barbara Epstein (1996) has demonstrated how reactionary feminist theory becomes when it is detached from its roots in the women's movement and relocated in postmodernist thought. Postmodernism follows in the romantic tradition where dreaming replaces reality. New Feminism is part of this tradition where the desire for change is thought to be enough. But changing definitions and narratives is highly significant in that radical and change agents have to define their emergent relationships based on their values; they have to articulate their strategies if only to undermine the boring perpetuation of 'same' and 'difference' arguments.

The discourse of gender struggles is also integrally linked to that of managerialism. Both inhibit social transformation and negatively stereotype change agents and radicals for questioning the status quo in public and managerial life, especially the role of women as innovative change agents. In the following chapters the interviews with women managers demonstrate how women's thinking and popular narratives influence their judgements and responses to them as challenging women struggling to transform management within local government in Britain in the 1980s.

7   British public sector reforms

If Enhoven were correct about *Homo Economicus*, excellent specialist and famous teams in the NHS would not exist . . . presumably, the same arguments applies to tenured professors like Enhoven as well. If they teach well, they simply get more students and have more papers to grade . . . indeed, excellent professors like excellent doctors or nurses are swamped with work. According to the doctrine of *Homo Economicus*, they must be neurotic or irrational. By the same logic, introducing competition into healthcare forces providers and managers to accentuate economic self-interest and starves the other 'irrational' spiritual or emotional motives. The culture of commercialism makes 'dedication' seem quaint, even foolish. There is a good deal of denial about this obvious effect. (Donald Light 1995: 152)

In Britain the Conservative government introduced privatization and the internal market in order to reduce public services spending, dismantle the large bureaucracies and disempower the trade unions and professional associations. By the mid-1980s the market model and managerialism had come to be accepted thinking within Europe, as well as in the USA, South Asia and Australasia, as the correct framework on which to hang the parameters of public sector investment, accounting mechanisms and performance management criteria. State regulation and planning were rejected for the market model, at the expense of public services and social infrastructures. The blurring of the edges between private and public sectors was very much the introduction of private sector thinking into the public sector. Although all organizations have undergone dramatic change and internal restructuring, the 1980s market ideology dented the public sector ethos by undermining social values within a profit or finance corporate framework. There was, however, a growing awareness of the need for greater corporate accountability within the private sector if trade was be socially responsible as well as wealth generating. By the 1990s multinationals were proclaiming their concern for the environment and for local communities. Although few believed their propaganda and corporate ethics and the British public remain sceptical about corporate hype. However, there is a growing awareness that private trade and business has wider responsibilities than those to shareholders. There is a new awareness and a recognition of the independent sector of not-for-profit organizations or non-government organizations (NGOs).

While the pressure to liberalize and reform the public sector continues in European countries following the lead from Britain and New Zealand, there was a growing rejection of the market model in the UK which was demonstrated by a change of government in 1997. Public interest grew about the state of public and community services as it became clearer how far the 'market model' had resulted in increased poverty and social exclusion and how short-term financial interests had undermined social relationships and alienated deprived communities.

The consequences of public sector restructuring or structural adjustment programmes are to be seen globally, particularly in the south but also in northern cities in the USA and the UK. Social exclusion became more obvious as the gap between rich and poor increased exponentially during the 1980s. By the late 1990s even the World Bank had acknowledged that national governments could not deliver adequate social infrastructures: 'The crude neo-classical model is enormously elegant but totally unrealistic' (Lunt et al. 1996: 374).

However, the fact that many political economists doubted the sanity of the free market model appears to have carried little weight during the 1980s. Those who chose to prioritize social values over financial interests were seen by policymakers as the dinosaurs, worthies, or at worst socialists. Unfortunately, those who argued for free 'quality services' were viewed as old fashioned or ill informed. In spite of the narrow economistic trend among policymakers, the people of Britain remained attached to the welfare state, and especially to the NHS which provided a common service and focal point for the nation.

The British welfare state which grew up in the 1940s may have been bureaucratic and paternalistic but it did deliver basic, free services and consequently had a levelling psychological effect across the class divide. Although only a few middle-class professional mothers needed child benefit, it united mothers from very different backgrounds. This is not to say that people were content with the bureaucratic practices and red tape of public administration, but they were glad of the security that the welfare state provided and could not envisage any other way to organize services on a national scale. The post-1945 public administrations are beautiful examples of classical bureaucracies and these rigid command–control organizations were regarded as the most efficient and rational way of ensuring standards and probity.

A major criticism of the public administrations in most countries was that huge hierarchical organizations encouraged 'buck passing' and created cultures of inertia where staff rarely came into contact with the consequences of their work. Civil servants and administrators tended to close their eyes to the impact of red tape and kept the systems ticking, reacting badly to any change or deviation from normal procedures. Civil servants and officials justified their cold detachment from users as 'professionalism'. In Britain they are trained to adhere, to be partial, to avoid any show of feeling or political affiliation. In fact the so-called professional psychological detachment conveniently mirrored the characteristics of middle-class men and their attitudes to the largely working-class recipients of mainstream services. The British class divide generated the psychology of welfare as much as the bureaucratic nature of public administration systems. The legacy of paternalism can still be felt in some communities where people remain grateful and uncomplaining about poor standards and the aloofness of staff.

By the 1970s the New Right theorists and the left-wing community activists had begun to recognize that public administrations were far from efficient and that those working within large bureaucracies and corporations were institutionalized and cut off from customers and clients. In the UK media jokes abounded about lazy workmen who drank tea all day, about arrogant officials or rude carers. The national press reported daily how public officials had it far too easy and were protected by trade unions disinterested in service quality. The problem was said to be twofold: public services were costly; and they were unresponsive in a changing world. For while the state machinery was capable of delivering basic services, it failed to be responsive enough to any type of demands from users, new or otherwise. The effect of centralist planning on localities and of red tape procedures on staff acted as a brake on those more innovative employees. The work culture itself had a disabling effect on staff, particularly on women. The rule-bound culture and its authoritarian relationships within the administrations, reinforced as much by class-bound societies as by structures and procedures, resulted in officials or civil servants abusing their power. This was as true in Britain as it was in other countries where civil servants and local bureaucrats tended to:

- patronize clients and tenants and act as dictators;
- follow rules irrespective of appropriateness;
- blame those who were innovative;
- excite department rivalry.

Both the Libertarian Left and the New Right are critical of the authoritarian nature of public administration systems and wanted to dismantle the bureaucratic structures and cultures, but in completely different ways. The New Right perceived the cause of public sector inefficiency to be due to socialist planning traditions, in spite of the fact that many large private sector organizations were just as cumbersome and there was no proof that the health service and local government were grossly inefficient when compared to large private companies. The New Right saw the solution to 'welfarism' in a change of ownership; public administrations were to be privatized. A confusion was created between the effects of the culture of bureaucratic administrations and the welfare policy itself. The policy and how services are organized and delivered remains confused and undifferentiated.

Dunleavy (1995) has studied British administrations as an outsider and believes that they were insensitive to both users and the wider community.

This tendency persists, even after restructurings, and managers and policy-makers continue to be:

- led by those preoccupied with rapid policymaking;
- reinforced by an adversarial political system;
- socialized in an overconfident, removed and expert elite;
- controlled through a highly centralized state;
- lax when checking the implementation of policies.

Transforming the British public sector was constrained by a number of other factors, notably a British class culture where the weaker user and staff voice were ignored. There exists a rigid divide between doers and policymakers (thinkers). There resulted a lack of foresight about policy impact and the processes of change. Unfortunately the thinker–doer distinction is strong in Britain and reflected in the different mindsets of politicians and managers.

While both the Right and the Libertarian Left were critical of the bureaucratic nature of public administrations, their solutions to the problem were very different. The Libertarian Left wanted to develop local democracy and involve local people in the planning and organization of local facilities and services. This distinguished them from the more traditional Marxist Left, which continued to believe in centralized state planning, rational by design and authoritarian in delivery, as well as from the New Right. Both communist and socialist groups tended to ignore the necessity of involving people and were more concerned with political ideology than with individual human experience and quality of life arguments, which were viewed as liberal concerns by the Marxist Left. The Libertarian Left was small and often denigrated by traditional Marxist groups as being either individualistic or anarchist.

Libertarians rejected the legacy of Russian Communism, state planning and overregulation, which they believed ignored the reality of individuals and the complexity of power relations. Women in the various social movements frequently observed that when individuals and human concerns were ignored and bypassed in the name of political utopias then decisions became less humane and sometimes ruthless. They also noted that if a person avoided contact with realities it was possible to confuse ways and means with political ends, resulting in a lack of judgement. Within authoritarian regimes and contexts people can sometimes appear as 'cogs in the machine'. Their subdued reactions enable others to bypass and ignore their interests and not to differentiate between the state's interest and the complex needs of local people. A similar if less frightening situation operates in administrations where planners and politicians avoid the social realities and experiences of local people.

However, in the 1970s the political perspective of the Libertarian Left was dominant in the Women's Movement, the Peace Movement and later in the Green Movement. All promoted the idea that the political process was as significant as political theories generated in previous eras. Those who were politicized and active in the community were never confident that local democracy would result from the plans and thinking of a small elite group. Local activists focused on building relationships in campaigns and projects as well as on 'ends' and were suspicious of idealized theoretical models which never tallied with social realities. Community activists learnt that participation and process were as important as theories in social change, especially in the development of democratic relationships. While they also had dreams, these were tempered by reality. Community activists who struggled over planning proposals, housing standards and community facilities were met with hostility from local politicians who appeared to want to ignore the impact of authoritarian management and were less than open to the idea that internal democracy and local democracy were connected. Local politicians were not interested in service management, which was the concern of managers, although there was some recognition that centralized services were inaccessible and that there needed to be local offices and information points.

A radical period in the 1970s led some cities to attempt to transform local government. Local groups and organizations demanded that politicians and officers should become more open about local planning, but they rarely overcame the entrenchment of government structures and had to fight to be heard even in their own local service plans and consultations. In response to local activism some authorities did embark on a decentralization of services as one way of taking officials closer to the people. However, even where there was agreement that services should be decentralized, politicians and managers were reluctant to relinquish their powers and control over staff by dismantling centralized management structures. They remained hostile to local activists and very uncertain about how to respond to services users and community groups. Those active in the social movements rather than the adherents of political creeds or cults tend to be more critical of neatly packed theories and have fewer illusions about people, irrespective of their race, gender or class, in the knowledge that good and bad exists in all communities, however victimized.

Many women activists became aware of the need to involve people in change and to relate to their thinking and values as well as to their material needs. They wanted to reorganize and democratize public administrations and make them more open to local communities. They sought to develop a third or alternative way for local communities to relate to government and organized local forums, groups and projects. Unfortunately, there are poor records of this activist history since most activists are practical people who are more concerned with change rather than with documentation. However, the significance of community activity was understood by the New Right. Although they never acknowledged it, they realized the potential within voluntary and community organizations as substitutes for state service providers, not as a powerful vehicle for local democracy or their ability to socialize public sector management.

The New Right in the USA advanced the idea that social infrastructure would only develop if the state was dismantled. Only then would people be motivated to provide for themselves and their communities. Those of the New Right in Britain persuaded the public that the welfare state had created a dependency culture which reinforced bureaucratic rather than community interests. It was not difficult for the Right to attack public administrations. They could tap a rich vein of public irritation. The public were sympathetic to any political party which acknowledged their dissatisfaction with 'rigid services' and 'rude officials' and they voted in the Conservatives in 1979 on an anti-union and privatization platform. The New Right argued that the introduction of a market within the public sector would remove bureaucratic practices and that central management and financial control would generate more efficient public services for less cost. The Conservative central government felt confident and secure enough in the 1980s to privatize the utilities and to introduce contracting and market testing within local and central government and the National Health Service through:

- denationalization through the sale of public assets;
- deregulation and the introduction of competition;
- contracting out of service to private companies.

Underpinning these moves was the desire to reduce or control spending in the public sector. Central government became more prescriptive about how monies were to be spent within local government, setting levels and caps for expenditure. Hennessey (1996) argued that a colonization of minds took place within policymaking and the civil service within Britain during the 1980s. The language of trade and financial transaction invaded all relationships, not just those of financial transactions but also those of personal and social relationships. Financial value became the anchor of judgement and financial gain was supposed to be only incentive for individuals and agencies. The effect of this was further to undervalue longer term social relationships within economic relationships. This emphasis did not necessarily demonstrate a real shift in political allegiance, but a lemming-like tendency to conform to the language of trade; the market had colonized public thinking and private lives. Suddenly being realistic meant being businesslike, no matter what your job. The public were hostile to this change and women in particular fought against such conceptualizations at work and in conversations. The pill was to be softened by the language of 'quality and choice' and the New Right asserted that deregulation and privatization were beneficial to society:

- a reduction in the Public Sector Borrowing Requirement;
- provide greater choice for individuals as consumers;
- open up the trading markets;
- stimulate better services through competition.

Some would say that international financial conditions forced such moves on national administrations and that politicians were less free in their decision-making than they liked to proclaim to their electorates. There continues to be an international trend, largely driven by the international financial markets, that government should press for market mechanisms and financially driven managerialism within public administrations (Le Grand and Bartlett 1993). Britain under the New Right was more open to these pressures than other governments in European countries.

New public management

National government's answer to controlling expenditure was to dismantle the large public administrations, resulting in arm's-length companies, quangos or trusts which would deliver services. These agencies or service providers were directed by central government targets and financial controls and management mechanisms. Integral to the public sector reforms were tight managerial control and a move away from local political accountability. There was an emphasis on improving performance outputs and reducing costs and away from planning and managing the labour force. The central management mechanisms became known as New Public Management or managerialism, which publicly emphasised service choice and quality but was driven by a desire to cut costs. There was a shift away from the needs and securities of the workforce. The focus was to be on the service user; the public sector workforce was to become the servant of the state.

The New Right justified public sector restructuring and health reforms on the grounds that these would bring a businesslike approach to public management and would therefore improve service 'quality' and 'choice'. The argument was that public sector directors should become like private sector executives, able to make strategic decisions, control costs and in theory develop quality services. Various utilities were privatized in order to improve efficiency and raise capital. Services managers were expected to move from projected budgets to cash flows and trading accounts and the performance of staff, managers and operations was to be measured. The way in which managerialism was introduced and interpreted in Britain resembled a form of white-collar Taylorism.

Throughout the 1980s British politicians and public sector executives discovered business management thinking and the texts of American management gurus became bestsellers. The total quality creed, as expressed by *In Search of Excellence* (Peters and Waterman 1982), was adopted by public sector managers as a bible about how they were to behave in future. Managers were encouraged to focus on:

- a drive towards action rather than inertia;
- a customer focus and customer closeness;

- a focus on what the organization is best at: 'stick to the knitting';
- be value driven;
- creating loose structures and innovative staff;
- reducing layers of decision-making.

By the 1990s the Peters and Waterman cult of 'excellence' had been replaced by the more directive thinking of Osborne and Gaebler (1992), who believed that government administrators should be entrepreneurial, 'mission not rule driven' and service activities should be contracted to private decentralized agencies. For Osborne and Gaebler (1992) government was to be impact driven and performance measurement was to be based on 'outputs' and targets, whereas previous public administration measures had been on workforce numbers and existing activities. They suggested that local government should break from the staged incentive schemes associated with personnel career management and that individuals and tasks should be monitored.

The government shifted power from the local politicians to central government and appointed executive managers. Generalist managers were empowered to override local politicians and to work to central government targets. The number of local government elected committees in Britain was reduced and the process of readjusting the balance between local politician and managers began; the streamlining of public sector departments has been almost universal. Within the health service senior managers were seduced by the promise of more control over staff and service organization. A new agenda for managers emerged. Public sector managers who had previously worked alongside professional practitioners after the reforms became generalist managers with much more power over staff. They were given the power to hire and fire, change contracts, introduce short-term contracts, flatten career structures and grading systems. They also changed promotion criteria, flattened management structures and introduced new performance criteria for agencies and individuals, which were frequently based on accounting criteria in order to assess performance outputs more easily:

> However, it was only in the 1980s that Conservative governments made a concerted effort to promote new management practices throughout the public sector. As most readers will know, this was associated with the introduction of tight fiscal controls in local and central government, general management in the NHS and the widespread use of performance indicators. A key aim of these reforms was to ensure that public sector services were 'managed' in the interests of 'efficiency' and 'bureaucratic' structure of the public sector and, in some cases, actually reinforced it. (Kirkpatrick and Martinez Lucio 1995: 2)

By the mid-1990s many public sector managers and professionals had had to become more critical of generalist management and the never-ending road to efficiency and 'excellence'. Exposure to business thinking and the benefit of hindsight drew their attention to the fact that guru-speak and management theory painted rosy pictures of ideal practices, but did not provide realistic guides on how to manage change or how to manage resistant people. Management fads did not measure up to difficult staff or difficult realities. None of the various management techniques told managers how to achieve excellence or how to motivate demoralized staff who were resistant and antagonistic to restructuring. As the levels of staff dissatisfaction grew, managers began to recognize that service improvements and increased output were dependent on staff commitment and motivation. Public sector managers realized that the constant flux of entrepreneurial activity was hardly a way to run complex public sector organizations which were different from retail and other private companies. They became more suspicious of general management training and began to communicate more with the practitioners. Public sector organizations are subject to changing political forces and executives are rarely totally free to determine their 'business agendas' as those in private sector corporations; nor do they have the luxury of being able to choose their 'customers'. Public sector bodies have many stakeholders and serve multiple clients (stakeholders), including the electorate, direct users or consumers, policy makers, politicians and purchasers, as well as their own management boards.

Tensions over objectives

Public sector organizations require a new type of manager who can make sense of business costs but is also committed to the particular service and can prioritize service quality within a business framework. The change process is also complex and there are continuing tensions between managing the 'as is' realities alongside 'future visions'. Managers are currently receiving very contradictory messages. They are told to provide quality services but also to control them within budget, within set protocols and national targets. This was seen as an impossible task by managers, many of whom chose to retire. Others who were serious about service development began to challenge performance management criteria and started to involve practitioners in output measures. Conflicts throughout the public sector services generally, but more particularly within education, local government and health, concerned who set performance measures and standards – the government and the managers or practitioners and the community? The financial underpinning of most performance management fuelled the tensions between managers and other staff. Public sector staff and professionals were suspicious of the government's motives for the constant restructuring and management changes. The introduction of the internal market and the purchaser–provider split separated staff in many services who needed to communicate with each other. The practitioners or specialists felt out of control, removed from strategy and undermined by the peer review of performance management. The purchasers were dissatisfied because the felt cut off from the frontline service and therefore from interaction with the services users, which undermined their capacity to relate strategy to reality. Professionals and staff had major doubts about public sector reforms, which they suspected were introduced not to improve quality but to cut costs, reduce staffing numbers and to undermine the autonomy of the professional groups, whether social workers, doctors, teachers or nurses. The suspicion was that the public services were being slowly undermined by ideology, not a lack of funds. In the 1980s the ruthlessness of restructuring and the rigidity of management systems offended those who wanted to introduce a greater flexibility into management practices in order to develop public services: in the practice of public management the 1980s and 1990s have become the age of the financial manager. 'Accounting, budgeting and auditing dominated the discourse about the delivery of public sector services and changed the language and rules of resource allocation in areas as diverse as education, health and policing both in the UK and overseas' (Gray and Jenkins 1995: 88).

The contracting environment was one of endless overdetailed specifications, protocols and measures for fixating behaviour within well-known boundaries. The accounting systems demanded breakdowns of budgets and the notion of decentralized locality units dovetailed nicely with this thinking. Many departments began to cost each other for no other reason than it has become accepted practice. The pricing of public services was meaningless because the estimated costs often had no bearing on the real costs of staff and overheads which were impossible to untangle. But the effect of internal trading did have an effect on staff and their attitudes to change and risk; it increased competition between departments rather than forged relationships. Those who made mistakes were blamed and attacked more frequently as people's jobs became vulnerable and contract stability was undermined. A culture where a fear of transgressing the rules becomes a blame culture is unhealthy for staff, managers and users. Margaret Wheatley (1992) reports that the current emphasis on quantification, categorization and definition in order to fulfil and monitor contract is as controlling as were bureaucratic practices, and is not a good way of encouraging new practices, collaboration and partnership.

Both 'the market' and 'bureaucracy' appear to work against the type of collaborative relationships required by future public services. There continues to exist a deep chasm between policy objectives and those of managerialism. This has resulted in a mismatch between management systems and the willingness and capacity of staff to collaborate and therefore to deliver integrated care. There are difficulties of developing management systems that meet the conflicting demands of cost and national standards while also being capable of responding to local demand. The present approach to UK public sector management is too managerial and driven by a systems mentality which encourages forms of reductionist thinking.

Health service reforms in the UK

There have been enormous changes in health and social services in Britain since the late 1970s. The Griffiths Report (1983) concluded that 'planning' and consensus management had failed in the health service and a more devolved authoritarian style was required by all health agencies. There was a lack of leadership and direction in the NHS and the Report recommended the creation of general manager posts in all hospitals to counter the influence of the medical profession. The following reforms were introduced:

- the purchaser–provider split;
- general practitioners would become fundholders and therefore purchasers of acute service as well as provides of primary care;
- provider trusts would be independent with governing boards.

General managers became chief officers accountable to the Department of Health and their own trust boards. The health trusts were in effect quangos and were introduced in 'waves' in the early 1990s. The providers of healthcare within the National Health Service were split into three groups: general practitioners (GPs) and primary care centres, acute hospital trusts and community healthcare trusts. The health authorities (HAs) and family health service practitioners associations (FHSPAs) became the purchasing or strategic bodies which took over the role of the former planning authorities; later these were merged. The GPs were given the dual role of providing primary care and purchasing secondary or acute hospital care. The motivation behind this move was to shift power from the acute medical sector to the primary and community healthcare sector. Within localities where politicians and health managers were antagonistic to contracting and the internal market they resisted setting up trusts until the third and fourth waves in the mid-1990s. Health professions and the public noticed that often health boards were chaired by local businessman who were 'friends' of the New Right and members of the Conservative Party; non-executive posts were in effect political appointments (NHS 5/E/60 1996).

The heavy control and financial restrictions were accompanied by the softer side of 'quality initiatives' where the patient was the focus. The Patient's Charter was introduced in 1990 and monitored health providers on key activity levels set by central government such as waiting times, standards and improved staff–patient relationships. Central government sent NHS trusts and purchasing authorities weekly directives on financial and performance targets and policy recommendations as working guidelines. The contracting environment made it extremely hard for managers to focus on health or quality targets and, while many of the government policy documents on service development and community care were endorsed by professional staff, they feared that policy changes were in reality an opening for the next stage of cuts rather than service development. The problem for public sector managers remains one of how to function effectively and initiate service development within finite and contracting resources. A business approach was difficult when costing was equated with cuts and the problem for managers was that staff feared any 'costing' of services and doubted that even good initiatives would be adequately financed.

However, by the late 1980s in Britain most health professionals no longer resisted change itself and became more actively involved in attempting to adopt measures and contracting to meet service and user needs. Smaller trusts came under pressure from regional executives and the health authorities to merge with other trusts in their localities. This pressure created its own tensions, especially insecurity and job loss, and occupied much of senior managers' time, resulting in further agency competition rather than partnership. The emphasis on hospital mergers undermined professional relationships. A survey of chief officers revealed that they thought mergers were actually unlikely to release huge amounts of cash, but would create a further lowering of morale and take up inordinate amounts of senior people's time (*HSJ* 18 September 1997). The community trusts were more likely to suffer most from these mergers, irrespective of good service or collaborative staff relationships, but unfortunately the rationalization of services and reconfiguration had its own appeal, even when it released little finance.

In spite of these difficulties, output in terms of consultant episodes and operations increased and clinical performance increased dramatically. Those clinical directorates that exceeded the contract quotas were put in the ridiculous situation of overshooting their contracts and not being paid or of clinicians not working. Chief executives were faced with the difficult dilemma of either dismissal for overspending on elective work or cutting the number of patients to match the quota stated in their contract. If they did the latter then they were likely to fail to meet the government's targets for service improvements and also 'fall foul' of the public and press for not. Managed care refers in effect to the co-ordination of operations in order to deliver integrated care and appears to work well in easily defined ailments and procedures in the acute sector and much less well in the community of priority care sectors where systems are less important than relationships (*HSJ* December 1997). Integrated care services are dependent not just on synchronized systems but also on the capacity of agencies to agree strategies and on collaborative relationships between practitioners, managers and staff. Without more open management practices sensitivity to users and carers is unlikely to emerge.

Purchasing

In the early 1990s public bodies were encouraged to distinguish between the purchasing and needs assessment side of their responsibilities and the service providers. Service provision could then be provided by local state, private agencies or independent not-for-profit agencies. In health agencies purchasers and providers were distinct whereas those in local government varied according to local enthusiasm for the system, for instance some New Right authorities in London became strategic bodies with little inhouse service provision, while others merely divided into purchaser/provider staff in name only. Dominant players within health authorities tended to communicate more with the acute hospital sector and with hospital consultants. Although commissioning varied from city to city, and region to region, the acute sector and the medical model continued to dominate commissioning and healthcare models, reinforced by the fact that performance indicators in hospitals were more easily reduced to visits, operations and consultant contacts. Those in social service departments were divided into assessors and providers and often based in different locations removed from each other. They realized that they needed to communicate regularly and that a total split between function made this more difficult. Purchasers became adrift from local need and from the realities of service provision. By 1993 NHS purchasers began to recognize that they had to encourage, support and develop providers and secure long-term relationships within provider agencies. In many smaller towns health purchasers had no choice other than to buy healthcare from the one and only hospital in the town. The purchasing authorities realized that they had to work more in partnership with providers in developing planned services and that they also had to halt competition between provider hospitals and create consortia and partnership bodies. This was not a real market, neither could it be; trading transactions are purely financial and do not reflect social care values or complexities. Purchasers were given the different task of assessing good and bad providers and many discovered that it was better to commission services from the providers they knew, rather than from new and untested private agencies. By the mid-1990s pure forms of the purchaser/provider split were recognized as ineffective and the concept of purchasing was softened and the terminology changed, purchasing became commissioning. The public would never have accepted clinical treatment being provided by the private sector and the introduction of private services was on the fringes of healthcare, it was the direct support services such as in catering and cleaning which were put out to tender.

Chief executives shifted their thinking and began to look for other mechanisms apart from contracting out which would of itself generate service improvements. The Audit Commission (1994) made similar observations that 'horse-trading' between private healthcare agencies had undermined both the quality and development of services (Poxton 1995). Health commissioning began to concern service configuration, risk management, strategic directions and developing partnerships. However, the development of more mature forms of purchasing was slow and patchy. In many cities provider units had to negotiate with several purchasing authorities (in

London a great many), which was time consuming, costly and pulled the organizations in different directions. The staff in health authorities were split between those who tended to be more developmental in their approach and those who were influenced by the 'medical' model of care. Provider agencies worked more constructively with their health authorities where senior teams were united and had a clear position (Maddock and Morgan 1998). Where the commissioning authorities were overbearing, the relationship between purchaser and provider was fractious. Commissioning skills did evolve in the 1990s, although most reluctantly among the general practitioners. This was hardly surprising given that general practitioners were isolated, overworked and not at all enthusiastic about business administration.

The Audit Commission announced (1996) that fundholding had not resulted in better primary health services largely because of the lack of motivation and enthusiasm of general practitioners. The future direction of health commissioning will be placed in the hands of general practitioners and community nurses who will hold the total healthcare budgets for each primary care group instead of the health authorities.

It is likely that the transition to primary care groups (PCGs) will be bumpy, given the poor morale among primary care doctors who in Britain remain independent contractors and not on the NHS payroll. Enthusiasm for local commissioning groups varies enormously around the country and it is uncertain at the time of writing how this will develop. Although doctors and nurses are to play a joint role in deciding local health priorities, it is difficult to see how the nurses will be anything other than handmaidens to the doctors given the traditional imbalance of power relations between doctors and nurses.

The shift of focus to community services

The community care reforms (1990) were based on the belief that dependent people should be supported in their own homes rather than institutions. They were widely supported and viewed as good in principle but difficult to implement, especially if no additional funding was made available. The reforms were intended to give people a greater say over their care, where it was provided and by whom. They also endorsed a primary care-led health service and required practitioners to work collaboratively in order to deliver integrated care. The Community Care Act (1990) had the following key objectives:

- delivering community domiciliary services;
- support for carers;
- assessment and care management systems;

- performance management;
- value for money;
- stimulation of independent providers.

Since the Community Care Act (1990), many other reports and government papers (NHS White Paper 1997) call for partnership and there is a growing recognition among policymakers and practitioners that integrated services depend on the collaboration between agencies and professionals (Wistow et al. 1992). However, the problem is that managers remain uncertain about how to develop collaborative relationships, neither do they appear to be particularly good at partnership themselves.

The health debate in the UK tends to be rather simplistic and focused on medical operations, hospital facilities and finances. The policy shift from acute healthcare to community and primary care was a brave attempt to move the power from the hospitals to the primary and community services. Unfortunately it was slow to materialize due to inadequate funding and a lack of support from hospital consultants who remained sceptical about the capacity and capability of their GP colleagues and their lack of knowledge about the work of therapists and community nurses. Professional barriers are difficult to shift when the press and the public think of hospital as the providers of healthcare and tend to be less aware of other services. The medical model in health distorts resource allocation and is extremely difficult to change as a mindset. The public equates healthcare with medical intervention and hospital closures excite much opposition in the community. Those who argue for hospital closure in order to move public money from the acute to the primary care sector have not convinced the public, the press or politicians that such a shift in funding is justified. Few primary care services are adequate or visible to the public. This fuels suspicion that a local closure is nothing but an expenditure cut.

The health reforms did stimulate at interest in the quality of care. More recently a need for evidence on good and bad services has given rise to what has come to be called evidence-based medicine (EBM). The questions of who makes the decision and what constitutes evidence of 'good' and 'bad' practice remain underdeveloped and dislocated from the processes of care. Much of the policy rhetoric focuses on 'patient choice' and 'service quality', but too often quality is determined by central formulae which undermine the ability of staff to respond flexibly. Performance indicators have been fought over hard and doctors appear to have won the argument for clinical rather than management measures in health.

There is less discussion about how management measures and practices work for or against caring relationships. The tightening of systems may have resulted in greater productivity with fewer qualified staff in both the community and on the wards, but it has also eroded the quality of care and the time for caring patient relationships. This lack of sensitive performance measurement continues to be a problem. Final consultant episodes are a nonsense, even in the acute hospital setting, but are completely meaningless within the context of social cases and therapies in the community where quality services are dependent on the processes of care not episodic contact with consultants. The measurement of activities such as contact times, waiting lists and final episodes obscure the value of those services in the community which are more difficult to quantify. Because the impact of community and primary care services is difficult to quantify, investment lags behind need. These concerns are voiced in a recent government White Paper:

> In paving the way for the new NHS the government is committed to building on what has worked, but discarding what has failed. There will be no return to the old centralised command and control system of the 1970s. That approach stifled innovation and put the needs of institutions ahead of the needs of patients. But nor will there be a continuation of the divisive internal market of the 1990s. That approach which was intended to make the NHS more efficient ended up fragmenting decision making and distorting incentives to such an extent that unfairness and bureaucracy became its defining feature. Instead there will be a third way of running the NHS; a system based on partnerships and driven by performance. (NHSE White Paper 1997: 10)

The question remains how are managers to generate a synergy of interests between staff, patients and service configuration. The systems approach to healthcare management developed in the USA may be focused on integrated care, managed care and evidence-based procedures, but it ignores the voice of users and their need for caring relationships as well as efficient and safe procedures. These depend on time and staff motivation.

Besieged local government

Within the UK context local government and the National Health Service are completely different in their cultures and working environments. The separation between them has been exaggerated since the public sector reforms. Local politicians view health managers and NHS board executives as unaccountable, while health managers see local government managers as lacking authority and unable to act, trapped within old bureaucratic procedures (Holden 1997). Local government remains rooted in local needs and retains its local accountability but is still a highly bureaucratic management culture. Managers in local government are experienced in transactional and mechanical management and are excellent at report writing and procedures. Unfortunately, they are also underconfident about managing change and stepping beyond and outside the traditional boundaries of their departments and individual responsibilities. The culture is still fearful, especially within social service departments which interface with health.

Even after numerous restructurings many of the metropolitan authorities tend to remain highly bureaucratic and driven by top-down restructuring. Officers in these administrations spend inordinate amounts of time on policy debate and very little on practical implementation. The divide between politicians and managers and 'decision-makers' and 'officers' continues to dominate the way in which change is approached and the way user and public consultations are conducted. There is often a lack of trust between politicians and managers and vice versa. Although local politicians may be extremely sensitive to local voices, they continue to be hesitant and confused by their inability to change management practices. This lack of comprehension by both managers and politicians about the extent of the impact of the system's approach and the reverberations of the blame culture is due to their being unaware of the problem – each is chopped in two. What politicians do not know about the blame culture they do not ask about or discuss.

The New Right sought not to improve effectiveness but to undermine local government through various legislative and financial controls in the 1980s and 1990s. The effect of many years' attack from central government led to a deeply entrenched position in the large metropolitan authorities. The growth of market testing, the contracting out of local services and increased managerialism all contributed to a 'siege mentality', low morale and high levels of stress among politicians and staff. The result of the internal market ideology and competitive contracting was the development of arm's-length agencies, the purchaser–provider split within some services, devolved management of schools and colleges and a corporate approach within senior management. Previously service directors had control of their own departments, but by 1990 chief executives had become much more powerful and service heads were corporate deputies playing to a corporate management tune:

> The preparation and adoption of a corporate strategy is regarded by district auditors and consultants as the *sine qua non* of serious management. Whilst old-style corporate plans have a long history, current thinking favours a less mechanistic approach. Strategy is now seen as more a matter of flexible adaptation to changing realities. (Young 1996: 358)

In some authorities a new corporate layer was developed, working over directors the corporate team decided on strategy and departmental integration. However, in the 1990s few northern authorities were enthusiastic about radical change or managed to flatten their management structures. Kirklees did develop a corporate team who attempted to discuss a separation of powers between managers and politicians and involved backbench members (Boviard and Hughes 1995). Despite a few examples of authorities where managing was discussed by members, most local authorities remained highly bureaucratic with authoritarian cultures.

Impact of public administration reforms

The introduction of centrally controlled performance management and tighter funding mechanisms dramatically influenced public sector morale and confidence in their ability to change. Commentators began to ask whether attempts at restructuring had:

- Resulted in a user/customer focus?
- Brought client and manager closer together?
- Facilitated inter-agency working and partnership, given that the level of collaboration between agencies remained poor?

As the internal market took root in most public sector agencies it became clear that the answer to many of these questions was negative. The impact of the internal market on staff has been disastrous. The internal market and contracting out have had a dramatic effect on those labour controlled local authorities which the government sought to undermine. The institutions in the larger authorities are also unwieldy and slow to change. Some of the county councils adopted managerial techniques sooner than the northern metropolitan authorities and the London boroughs, because the local politicians were less 'hands-on'. There are also northern metropolitan authorities and the London boroughs. There are also significant regional variations; southern cities and counties differ from those in the north and Scottish and Irish executive bodies still retain distinctive regional cultural preferences.

On reflection, many of the supposed benefits of contracting and purchasing proved to be illusory. With hindsight, commentators observe that Thatcher did not reduce the Public Sector Borrowing Requirement (PSBR) in Britain. Few health or local authorities managed to purchase a wider range of services at a reasonable price in areas where people needed them. Areas of deprivation found that they did not have money for comprehensive and free social care for the elderly, schools and health. Whether the contracting culture within public services has delivered greater choice depends on who you are, where you live and how much you earn. There was a general recognition that those living in rural areas lost services and their choice of schools, hospitals and transport was reduced, not increased.

There was also a growing concern that the public bodies and many of the new quangos delivering public services were not politically accountable but controlled through central government performance targets and budgetary controls. The social infrastructure continued to deteriorate and the physical infrastructure of rail and road has yet to improve. It would appear that to cut government spending further is an unsound economic strategy resulting in poorer services and facilities. In addition, the notion that competition improves performance in the service sector is highly debatable. Competitive relationships in health and social care have been shown to result in less partnership and collaborative practice, a prerequisite for flatter organizations delivering integrated care. Whether this divide between internal purchasers and providers has reduced the dependency culture is debatable: 'The irony is that in its eagerness to get away from the nanny state, the government has encouraged privatisation, and a contract culture in which many providers' and carers' business depends on dependency. Social workers are no longer problem solvers but shoppers' (*Community Care* 1996).

The fact that contracting involved additional costs was ignored by the government. The competition between smaller contractors that was visible in the late 1980s collapsed in the early 1990s when larger firms took over smaller agencies and began to compete for work around the country. By the mid-1990s there were only four or five major catering companies competing for contracts in the NHS and universities. The most notable change in services is that there is in fact more paperwork, generated by contracting, market testing and constant evaluation. This is certainly the case within the police force, social services, education and local government. A form of generic management started to develop whereby managers attempted to standardize assessment, management and care. Junior staff were exposed to increased workloads, protocols and work sheets. Public sector management had changed beyond measure in Britain between the early 1980s and 1990s. The large public administrations dependent on command-type management structures and centralized planning mechanisms were exposed to market testing and quality initiatives. They devolved into smaller entrepreneurial departments if the work was not commissioned from new private or independent agencies. Direct service departments bid for their contracts and the language of public sector management changed dramatically from that of planning and need to purchasing, consumers and choice.

It would appear that the internal market resulted in far too much administration and was just as rule bound, again reinforcing closed thinking and the blame culture. In spite of restructuring, the legacy of bureaucratic cultures and traditions remains and the blame culture within public offices has not disappeared, resulting in a siege mentality which has had a dreadful effect on many local government officers' confidence and their ability to be strategic. The restructuring has demanded that officers do become more strategic, especially those in senior or executive positions. But in many ways the local government context has been reactive where politicians and managers have been forced into the internal market and contracting. Consequently they have been less inclined to dismantle management structures and the cultures have remained largely intact. This has made it difficult for those wanting to transform rather than restructure, but the value base, public ethic or ethos also remains. The debates around democracy, user consultation and service quality are well developed within local government, but the management machinery is still highly structured and traps managers rather than enabling them to enable change.

Facilitating change and the learning environment

The contracting environment led chief officers to accept the view that local authorities should become enablers rather than providers (Clarke and Stewart 1988). A Local Government Management board survey (1993) demonstrated that chief officers had moved in the direction of believing local government should have professional managers developing core services and strategies, and need not be the sole public sector provider in the city (see Table 7.1).

The Audit Commission which monitors health and local government for central government has become much more proactive since the early 1990s and encourages this enabling role. The Commission began to adopt a dual approach to auditing of facilitation and 'watchdog' in the mid-1990s. This approach was not compatible with the 'annual' contracting process for it required confident relationships and a 'people approach' to change. The introduction of an organizational approach to audit was a major shift and very different from the watchdog approach adopted by other national public sector monitoring bodies. There is a growing body of literature on how contracting has resulted in individualist and competitive relationships rather than collaborative cultures within the public sector, especially in health and social care (Le Grand and Bartlett 1993; Walsh 1995). The processes of contracting have in fact undermined staff morale and created a climate of mistrust. The desire for efficiency savings have forced practitioners into mechanical relationships with clients and alienated relationships between colleagues, which for many are even more frustrating than the inertia of the bureaucratic departments. Charlesworth, Clarke and Cochrane (1996) demonstrated that The Community Care Act (1990) has dramatically affected the relationships between agencies, between local authorities and the voluntary sector, between health and social services, and between managers and professionals. Where the contracting system operates as a purely economic market system it measures only output or task efficiency rather than service outcome, impact and quality.

> Because the analyses of far have been directed primarily to discovering the logic of such markets the prevailing form of competition, contracting regulation and organisational strategies), they have tended to reduce the complexities of relationships and social processes involved in mixed economies to their specific economic dimensions. (Charlesworth, Clarke and Cochrane 1996: 77)

Since the 1980s the internal market and competitive contracting have resulted in 'marketised forms of relationships' (Wistow 1995), which encourage competitive and combative forms of behaviour and prioritize immediate measurable results rather than process and development. The assumption was that the 'provider agencies' should be 'entrepreneurial' in their approach to clients and contractors. What emerged within the mixed economies of care were various types of entrepreneurial organizations

TABLE 7.1 *The changing role of the LEA 1988–94*

	Strongly agree		
	1988 %	1992 %	1994 %
As traditional provider	76	20	31
As strategic manager	80	88	77
As partner	54	95	82
As enabler	46	93	72
As adviser	76	95	80

Source: Young, 1996: 354

within the private sector and entrepreneurial behaviour within the larger authorities which remained bureaucratic. Both worked against inter-professional relationships and sustaining work cultures.

Joint planning across agencies was never a success in Britain and government departments are the worst offenders for blocking emergent practice. Each government department or ministry has its own vertical funding streams and is extremely insular and competitive with other departments. A recent report (Glendinning et al. 1997) records that the barriers to collaboration in primary care between local government and general practitioners are due to:

- a lack of agreed or shared values;
- a lack of professional understanding and contact;
- a lack of inter-agency co-operation.

Even those desirous of inter-agency collaboration tend to reinforce management mechanisms which work against joint work and partnership. Similarly those committed to community-based partnerships and partnership generally focus on new service configurations but forget to address the huge cultural geographical differences in Britain and the obstacles likely to be encountered by those actually implementing new service arrangements. Putting social objectives centre stage within contracting requires a change in national budget allocation and policy objectives, but it also requires active work by politicians as well as staff, professionals and managers. Probity and accountability are real concerns and public administrators have to ensure standards, but these are more likely to improve when there is local sensitivity and a confidence in staff at all levels. Local decision-making and sustainability cannot be achieved within the command and control administrations.

Socially inclusive management

Clearly, complex services have to be organized but the question is how management techniques can be utilized and adapted within a social value framework for the public sector. The current challenge is how to transform management systems in such a manner that they are driven by locality needs and staff involvement. While task focused management-by-objectives may have been a good starting point, it is merely an empty system that needs grounding in the particular needs of service users within local service contexts.

The new government in the UK has not changed the legislation which exempts white-collar officers from compulsory competitive tendering of their services, although the language has been softened and the internal market is being replaced by assessment of service provision on the basis of 'best value' for the community or consumer from any provider. Local authorities have put forward services which they consider demonstrate best value for assessment and to indicate how other authorities can move towards better partnerships with users and agencies. The indicators of best value have yet to be determined, but should involve a combination of national indicators and local measures gathered from audit and impact studies. How best value is to be achieved within a context of demoralized public sector staff is yet to be revealed, for the motivation and energy is still low, although a change of government has lifted spirits and the willingness to engage with new initiatives.

Public sector management could be harnessed to social objectives but policy-makers lurch between handing power to managers or to one group of professionals (doctors). Managerial techniques are a contested area, precisely when seen to be driven by financial agendas not quality services. The various stakeholders have different criteria for success and in their definitions of positive outcomes. Performance measurement is also a contested area for the public and for staff. There has to be a balance between standards and flexibility, between protocol and judgements, and between staff and users. This means that executives and politicians have to listen to staff values and thinking if public sector employees are to positively engage with major changes. As many in the health sector have discovered, corporate change programmes fail if they alienate staff. Alienated and overworked staff cannot, and will not, work collaboratively if they themselves are not valued.

There is a need for social inclusiveness inside of organizations as well as in the community. For a recognition that employee–manager partnerships are perhaps more important than inter-agency working. Without a readjustment in thinking about staff relationships and a revaluing of public sector staff many of the government's agendas in health and local government are likely to fail. Responsive services are dependent on responsive staff. Managers and staff need to reach agreement over change processes as well as service objectives, if internal democracy is to be achieved. The change process and its guiding framework is as much a policy matter as are service priorities. Both managerial and bureaucratic cultures have failed public sector agendas and need to move onto a more inclusive form of management as outlined in Table 7.2.

The problem within public administrations and in other organizations is how to encourage a shift in thinking towards a perspective which acknowledges the role of all stakeholders in change, including those who are mistrustful after bearing the brunt of redundancies during periods of restructuring. Both the market and bureaucracy have been shown to work against the type of collaborative relationships required by future public services and New Public Management (NPM) has had a negative effect on staff relationships (Coote and Hunter 1996). Staff morale in the public sector is very low and stress levels are high. A 'systems' approach dominates management thinking about how to change realities. There is a tendency to deny cultural barriers until they are strangling the observer and to think in terms of structural or economic levers and that personal change and new relationships will follow from these. A recent UK government White Paper (1997) *The National Health Service: A Service with Ambitions* called for a 'high quality integrated health service which is organised around health needs of individual patients rather than the convenience of the systems of institutions'.

Making it happen

Too little time is spent on thinking about joint work and making it happen. Although there is a growing interest in new service configurations and organizational forms which support inter-agency and inter-professional relationships, policy-makers give little time and energy to thinking about implementation. It is not just a question of rearranging the furniture but of making the furniture fit and the way in which the workers manage the move. One local configuration of services may be appropriate in one region but totally unsuitable in another where the power nexus of relationships is very different. While there remains a powerful opposition to contracting out core and strategic services in local government, the realignment of service purchase and provision is far from complete, clear or defined. The process continues and has become more sophisticated. Each authority and location has developed its own network of agencies and key figures, which vary enormously in favour, especially in the north and south of the country and between country and metropolitan cities.

Future public service organizations depend on the creation of a strategic management framework which enshrines an approach to change and does not endorse economic and management mechanisms which conflict with a learning ethos. This necessarily results in a shift from the need to control to a desire to teach, train and support decision-making and learning within the agreed value and objective framework. A shift from a systems to a people approach is desperately needed in all public sector services, but most specifically managers need to have more confidence in staff than in systems. In many instances this would involve a reversal of power relationships and a reinforcement of challengers:

TABLE 7.2 *Towards a social inclusive management*

Bureaucracy	Managerialism	Characteristics of Obstacles to	Inclusive management
Approach to employees Rigid roles Need for control	Individuals competitive Competition	Fear, anxiety	Processual approach to learning Sharing
Managed by Supervision Set procedures	Task and targets within financial limits	Internal cultures Professional mindsets	Shared objectives Multi-professional teams
Performance measurement Line management and national standards	Central government performance measures	Dependence on accounting systems	To be re-negotiated, process measures Local-determined indicators which value social relationships
Communication with public Lack of user focus connection	Policy of user focus but in reality systems disregard community	Professional mindsets	User/community involvement
Policy set by Local elected members Politicians Ignored management	Managerialist control Lack of accountability Lack of interest in systems impact	Local politics Hostile parties	Partnerships through learning Renegotiation between hostile parties
Service development By planners	Purchasing Care management for those most at risk	Low morale No contact No time	On-going quality feedback Audit and communication systems with inclusive locality groups

From	*To*
Rigid/standard	Diverse/responsive
Central control	Bottom-up processes
Plan/models	Learning processes
Regulation monitoring	Individual judgements

Such a shift in emphasis cannot be agreed in principle but has to be worked at – the behaviour of managers has to change. Modern managers need to develop an ability to negotiate and discuss effectiveness with the public, with users and with staff, not just policymakers and powerful professionals such as doctors. This process also needs reinforcing and acknowledging as valid within performance measurement, appraisal and audit.

Partnership and Berlin Walls

Social transformation has proved no more fruitful under market conditions and appears to be dependent on employees and managers renegotiating their working lives on the basis of new social and sustaining conditions which facilitate learning and change rather than inertia and competition. The barriers between agencies and practitioners need to be acknowledged and addressed if partnerships are to survive. Moving beyond the market requires an approach which will overcome the years of hostility between agencies and the professions. The interface between agencies, staff and professionals needs managing and new partnerships will ultimately be dependent on organizations becoming more permeable or osmotic to stakeholder views and local knowledge. If managers remain detached from service and user need they will remain unaware of the impact of both services and management systems on users and staff. Shared learning is desirable, not just as an end point but as a learning process; shared experience is invaluable in reaching more balanced judgements. Unfortunately, too many senior managers are detached from the impact of their own systems although some do have a limited understanding of the services them manage. The conditions for partnership need to involve an ability to move beyond the professional, cultural, managerial box – cross-cultural exchange is critical to shared learning and new practices.

The philosophy underpinning much of the thinking in public administrations is towards closed systems. Restructuring through changes either in contracting or the management furniture is assumed to drag people into motivation. This could not be further from reality; demoralized staff are rarely responsive in their relationships. From this one can only conclude that internal democracy is critical to the development of locally responsive services. The challenge is to develop strategic frameworks which listen to users and utilize the potential of public sector staff; a social framework which assists transformation and staff participation. Otherwise, joint initiatives will reflect either the dominant accounting interest or the dominant professional body. The conundrum of finance, care and priorities is not solved by the introduction of new systems but through facilitating processes based on the participation of staff, many of whom are already working towards a renegotiation of roles and responsibilities. Partnership is not achieved merely through new models or structural change but through shifts in thinking and the relationships between a number of groups:

- the public and the policymakers;
- policymakers and managers;
- managers and staff;
- practitioners and managers;
- men and women.

The problem of what is beginning to be called 'interface management' involves not just a willingness to communicate but also a realignment of power relationships between groups and whole regions. The cultural attachment to the group or professional necessitates not only a structural change from command to a market economy, or a shift to some new idealized system such as a network form, but also a shift from a systems perspective to one focused on developing people and their relationships, regardless which stakeholder group they belong to. A shift from systems to a people approach is desperately required, but more especially managers need to have more confidence in people and reflect on how to socialize or humanize the systems in place.

A people and process approach is required which recognizes the need for an acknowledged 'social settlement' (Mackintosh 1997) between structure, value and agency. The network form of agency is particularly suitable for future public sector organizations (Alexander 1991), but the question remains of how to develop stable relationships in a changing world and, more specifically, how to match system to processes: inside organizations in management practices as well as outside organizations through changes in contracting, organizational form and service configuration.

Social democrats endorsed a change in approach but appear to continue to believe in market economics and to rely on top-down change, central targets and a blind faith in current interpretations of managerialism. The contracting environment has been extensively criticized as a framework within Britain, but its management mechanisms have colonized political cultures and managerialism. The extent of this colonization has been observed even when cost cutting has not been a priority. The following chapters suggest that many women managers working with health and local government are well aware of the connections between learning and effectiveness, between employee relationships and quality services, and of the need for managerial techniques to be rooted in local detail. Unfortunately, many social and management innovations are not acknowledged because they are led by women. These women managers experience extreme frustration when attempting to transform management practices in health and local government due to dominant male work cultures.

8   Innovative women are challenging women

The challenge can be expressed as the paragon of the new professional. She is committed to the poor and weak, and to enabling them to gain more of what they need and want. She is democratic and participatory in management style; is a good listener, embraces error and believes in falling forward; finds pleasure in enabling other to take initiatives; monitors and controls only to a core minimum of standards and activities; is not threatened by the unforeseeable; does not demand targets for disbursements and achievements; adjures punitive management; devolves authority expecting her staff to use their own best judgements at all times; give priority to the front-line; and rewards honesty for her, watchwords are truth, trust and diversity. And thought this paragraph she can also be a he. (Robert Chambers 1995: 32–3)

Orlando Figes on his commentary on the Russian revolutions (Figes 1996) observed that radical women sought social change through development rather than through violent struggle whereas young men spurned and rejected learning for the romantic ideals of more violent revolution.

The recurring observation that women and men organize differently is evident throughout the world and appears in general to transcend class and ethnic origin. Of course, the notion that political processes are as significant to revolutions as political ends was the basis of the women's movement. Yet the fact that many of the visions or ideas of women about management correspond closely to contemporary thinking appears to go unrecorded, although noticed by management gurus and some executives. Tiefenbrun (1993) observed the impact of women's involvement in communication and decision-making processes within his own company:

The serial approach to doing one thing at a time in a defined sequence is not untypical of male behaviour . . . the female approach is the complete opposite. This is one reason why the future manufacturing methods should be more female than male. My company has long since abandoned the linear approach. Our methods and structures are tree-like and involved gathering processes as opposed to serial processes. Our objective is to use every individual at the highest possible level. (Tiefenbrun 1993: 5)

Unfortunately there is little research on how women manage women's organizations, but one of the few studies revealed that they develop consensus frameworks and prefer to operate in teams (Iannello 1992). Another analysis in Britain by Jo Freeman (1978) showed that women have a tendency to dismantle formal structures, but they also sometimes collapse into what she termed the 'tyranny of structurelessness'. It is probably worth noting that she was writing in the early 1970s when breaking down barriers and challenging authoritarian structures was still more pertinent than developing existing structures. Perhaps it still is. In situations that require new practice and negotiation, those who encourage resistance to the 'other' generate stalemate, dispute and drama. The postmodern world is diverse and varied in its cultural nuances, especially with reference to gendered habits and attitudes to difficult interpersonal relationships. What can appear as momentous major change in gender roles in capital cities is hardly visible within more traditional communities in the same country. The phenomenon of the 'new man' is hard to find even within urban communities. Women in Britain may go out to work but they continue to do the lion's share of housework and caring.

Social change and transformation are dependent not only on new narratives and dreams but on willing parties working towards shared objectives. One party in negotiation is not negotiation; women may seek egalitarian relationships with men when the men do not understand that this is being required of them. Consequently they remain resistant. Similarly, employers may require employees to work collaboratively, but the process of negotiation is easier to describe than achieve because it demands shared values, trust, egalitarianism and a rebalancing of real power relationships. This requires a confidence in being able to jump from behind the Berlin Wall, overcome defensive behaviour loops and risk criticism. Marriage may involve a complex relationship, but at least it usually only involves two people. Initiating change in organizations requires the active engagement of motivated employees, who may be hostile one to another and are trapped by traditional cultures and rigid management structures. New relationships require learning and the conditions for learning – no matter how energetic and innovative, individuals need allies and a support context.

The learning organization sought by sensible employers is an idea or a virtual form. Existing work cultures more commonly reinforce defensiveness and suspicion among staff. Transcending suspicion requires confidence, risk and challenge from managers. Senge (1990) describes this as having entered the fifth discipline of learning. The real distinction between traditional approaches to change and social transformation concerns the change process itself and the energy of those who are willing, active and capable of removing the barriers to more open relationships and partnerships. The transformation process requires innovative people who can motivate others to work beyond their own grade, profession and status. Innovation in management is not just about the dismantling of old structures, but also about building new relationships, and requires hard work and perseverance.

While the learning models are well developed, the experiences of those who struggle against resistance within the context of institutions are either individualized or packaged as a group and their reflexive agency less visible. Conceptual models are often based on snapshots of reality and relationships at one particular time. Consequently they infer that the move from closed to open is a passive shift of behaviour or one which originates from the passive osmosis of learning and/or 'knowledge transfer'. In reality, such shifts are the result of active struggle by challenging individuals whose experience is often ignored, especially when they have no status or are marginal.

The personal and learning framework are useful tools for individual action but they avoid the realities of power struggles and the general nature of resistance to radical (women) precisely because they are radical. Too often the models of learning and change do not account for the reflexive nature of agency within organizations or how those who attempt to initiate partnership and egalitarian relationships are represented or misrepresented within the context of shifting power reductions. For instance, there is a great deal of talk about the notion of feminizing management, but there is less about how this is achieved or how those who attempt actively to transform practice meet huge resistance. The resistance to women affects the direction of transformation itself and draws attention to individual battles between men and women and away from that transformation. Social change is not a passive activity but is one in which challenging individuals are actively involved. The social transformation of agencies is dependent on the active relationships of those struggling with the barriers put in their way by politicians, structures, operations and cultures. Often the process of social innovation remains hidden until is uncovered, especially if common narratives or conceptualizations only refer to 'input and outputs' and avoid the process of moving from one step to another. Feminizing management has come to mean a change in style of interaction from 'closed' to 'open' approaches, but social transformation is much more than a change of style. It involves a reversal of values and structures and an ideology which is rooted in social capital and human values – it is a process, not an event.

This chapter gives voice to public sector women managers in the UK who were not only seeking a change in management style (in fact many did not find the 'feminine' style in management very useful), but also wanted to transform public sector organization through open relationships with service users, internal democracy and an injection of social values into public sector practice.

Those actively seeking transformation were not necessarily in senior management and were often invisible within the hierarchical status organizations. Women innovators were frequently bypassed precisely because they were challenging women, pressing for radical change in management style, practices and measures.

During the early 1980s in Britain thousands of women entered local government as managers, specialists, advisers and community workers because they endorsed radical municipalism and the community politics of the 1970s. Some of the larger metropolitan authorities introduced women's units, strategic policy units and decentralization programmes. Many of the managers had experience in the women's movement, local campaigning and managing innovative community projects and organizations. Aged between 24 and 45, 80% of middle managers had children while only 50% of senior managers had children. The women worked for Labour-controlled local authorities in the North of England and were typical of managers in local government in the 1980s. They were chosen for interview on the basis of their commitment to public sector management and interest in improving practices long before the reforms and managerialism had hit Britain.

The women selected were committed to public service values and their local communities, representing a new breed in public administration. They had a vision, although they did not necessarily demonstrate a feminized style of management, and were driven by a desire to see social values incorporated into management thinking which they thought was integral to developing democracy, inside and outside of the organization. Central to their thinking and actions was a desire for a change in cultures and structures as well as in inter-personnel behaviours. They not only challenged the male mode of interaction but also the institutional frameworks and value systems. They wanted to forge new practices and break down barriers between departments. They questioned traditional management structures and were committed to ethical business and open forms of management. They wanted to transform management in such a way that managers were confident enough to listen to clients and in turn be listened to themselves:

> I copied men's ways of working, I didn't know another way, but I couldn't express women's voice in this way. I am convinced that women do have a different way of working. We pay attention to detail, can be firm but also tender. Women put things together. Men don't do this, they don't pay attention to detail, they are trained to look away from the world.

Social transformation for these managers was not merely a question of a feminized style but amounted to a synergy between praxis and policy, finance and social objectives, and forms of organizing which were rooted in social need and service detail. Women managers found themselves constantly arguing with their colleagues about the need for more discussion and debate within their authorities over management practices. Their desire for discussion was not due to underconfidence but because they knew that they had to talk in order to open up thinking and persuade their colleagues of their case for change. The perception by male colleagues that brainstorming was time wasting merely confirmed women managers in their conviction that male cultural definitions of manager role and behaviours were rooted in avoidance tactics and a desire for inertia and continuation of the status quo. Discussion was not an objective in itself but was seen as essential if the services were to become more reflexive in response to the changing needs of the community. Women wanted local government managers to treat their tenants and clients with greater respect. Many managers were dismissive of users and without an improvement in communication between officers and users public service delivery mechanisms would remain rigid and closed. They were pushing for similar social change in management and reported in summary that in their experience women managers did have a different management style or focus from their male colleagues:

Female focus	*Male focus*
Facilitate/encourage	Categorization
Recognize process	Outputs
Discuss	Snap decision-making
Collaborate	Traditional roles with colleagues
Seek information	Given information
Find allies	Impression and status
Question and ask	Assume and direct
Be understood	Colleagues and next job
Pursue social objectives	Detachment/professional role

These particular women managers were adamant that public services should be locally appropriate and equitably distributed. They agreed that the way in which services were managed and organized most influenced service quality. A coherent picture emerged from these women as a group, rather than as individuals, which suggested that they had a vision for service development and an idealized version of open management. However, the majority recognized that few women managers found it possible to practise what they preached. What was significant about these women managers working in northern local authorities was that those in middle management wanted social change more than career advancement, irrespective of status and grade. This commitment to change provided the backcloth to their own personal gender strategies at work and fanned their prejudices about men:

> Men find it hard to change, whereas women want to develop. It's harder for men. Women are open to both sides, I think, and know staff work best if you support them. Organizing at a local level one cannot help but observe the fact that most women, irrespective of feminist of not, attempt to develop more democratic ways of working and organizing.

The finding that men and women would prefer to work in different ways is hardly a revelation, but what was significant about these managers was that they were struggling to change management structures and practices, often at their own expense in terms of career prospects, in order to make management more sensitive to community need. These radical women were challenging and seeking not just a change in management style but a total paradigm shift in thinking about public service management. Their thinking and strategies have since been reinforced by much of the 1980s and 1990s management thinking, emanating from work around learning, total quality management, organizational development and open systems:

> The real problem was that in many authorities the formal procedures and patterns of work were based on unchanging conditions and no longer match a changing environment. Unfortunately, those attempting to break down formalities and integrate services are often in the community working on the margins of the authority, this causes them to be vulnerable as officers, and their projects vulnerable to closure.
>
> In further education there is no area committee, no representative, no structures at all for discussing the work or the service. They presume the councillors can do that – they never seek real in-depth information. There is no connection between policy maker and provider. I either conform or am warned. This is not trade union business so the unions are not interested. It's a mess and, because they will not listen, the service will die and the people round here will lose all their community education provision. Yes, it's connected to gender. All the further education outreach workers, lecturers and co-ordinators are women. Some of the managers are women.

The fact that these women have been little acknowledged is largely because they tend not to write in academic journals; they work within their own organisations and localities and lack senior status. In other words they are not visible within the general narrative and the mainstream. In the 1980s they also avoided promotion. Many middle managers were highly critical of quality work and equality policies which merely promoted women per se. They wanted social transformation for everyone which would free men and women from oppressive gender roles and rigid work boundaries.

This is not to say that all women managers are radical, or that every woman manager in the study was channelling her energy in the same way, but the group did characterize a particular type of innovative and challenging woman who entered local government management in the 1980s. They were employed as managers at a time when it was difficult for women to be intellectual leaders and visionaries. The senior women interviewed were less radical. Many had adopted a quiet role when in middle management. Most became more aware of male gender cultures and associated restrictive practices where they experienced hostility to themselves personally once in senior positions and exposed to crude battles between directors in board meetings.

Pressing for a paradigm shift

The majority of women were insistent that collaborative ways of working were essential to service quality, but only those more challenging women were prepared to argue for changes in management structures, reward systems and performance measures. Many suffered and were punished for their efforts and attempts at social transformation. The difference between these women and others was that they were confident enough to argue for such a shift in practice. The recognize that a paradigm shift in thinking and experience is required if they are going to persuade others to change their practices and relationships at work. This could be summarized as a paradigm shift moving from:

Formal	to	Organic
Detached	to	Connected
Objective	to	Social value base
Event led	to	Process awareness

What was striking about the accounts from women managers working in very different organizations was their agreement that management was dominated by male cultures which inhibited social change and collaborative relationships.

These women managers wanted time to focus on the implementation of policy and how 'to make things work'. They knew that this involved active participation of staff in change processes. They were not antagonistic to assessment and performance management, but they were extremely hostile to irrelevant measures, central control and forms of management which demoralized staff and reinforced the blame culture. Women were extremely critical of the cultures within the larger authorities, which they said influenced managerial practices, and they welcomed the arrival of the contracting culture. They claimed that command–control management in the public administrations had resulted in inertia, impression and crisis management and a disrespect for service users and all forms of partnership. Management by objectives and greater transparency were therefore positive changes.

Women managers attempted to introduce their personal values into their work judgements. They wanted to be 'fair to be effective' and were attentive to the appropriateness of the criteria they used when appraising need, people or projects. They wanted their work relationships to be 'professional' but human and to continue to be connected with local needs. They were aware that there was a need to rebalance systems with real information, local detail and the experience of staff:

> My aim is to break down the secret codes that operate, which men know how to operate and women do not. When I came here no one read the minutes. Now I circulate them to all staff. This helps them do their jobs because they have a better understanding of the basis of their work. I would never have persuaded other officers to do this – I had to do it myself.

From policy to process

These women managers were not seeking a total feminization. They were aware of their capacity to be zealous in the search for 'justice and value';

what they wanted was a rebalancing of gender interests and a total change in the approach to managing people. They already had a wealth of experience in developing organizations and were strategic in their thinking and clearly connected to their local communities. They held strong social values.

The biggest frustration for the middle managers was that they recognized that a real shift in thinking was required, from the command control model to a perspective which recognized human processes of change. But if the bureaucratic management structures and line management systems did not change, then communication between officers and service users was also unlikely to improve and change would be impossible. There was agreement that line management and hierarchical structures trapped employees in boxed ranks and focused their minds inwards instead of outwards. Women reported that only when managers were interested in what was happening in the community would they be sensitive to what users and the public were saying. A lack of interest in 'process' and how to overcome common bureaucratic red tape was frequently mentioned as a frustration. Women managers focused on how to manage, how to bring the detail and the general policy picture closer together. They demanded cross-departmental work and taking policies forward, as opposed to operating existing systems which would have required less discussion and planning.

Unfortunately those women concerned with process were seen as practical and useful, but their thinking was not valued in an intellectual sense. Male colleagues justified their fear of process and practical implementation by snubbing women's efforts and being derisory about their holistic thinking:

Men don't have any reason to change – they find it hard to change – I'm generalizing, some men aren't like that, but most men say that they'll do something different and then go back to the old way. Women open up and look at problems differently.

Women were frustrated by existing structures and procedures because these were used to avoid difficulties rather than to advance solutions. These women managers recognized that the public administrations had grown into prisons for staff and they wanted radical changes:

- flatter management structures;
- less rigid job specifications and more flexible roles;
- a focus on task not status;
- collaboration and informal and human communication between staff;
- an emphasis on clients, users and the community.

Women managers wanted a workplace environment where working relationships were less formal and trusting enough for staff to discuss implementation problems as well as policy objectives. They agreed that conflict at work often resulted from men and women adopting different approaches to managing staff and their departments. Their experience was that women focused on the relational aspects of 'how to do things' while men tend to think 'what to do'. Challenging women are the persistent managers who press for practices which reflect relationships, social objectives and demand social change within management:

> When I arrived there was a crisis in confidence in the LEA, especially with the head-teachers – that's when I noticed that some of my best managers were women. This was a general realization and I also have some good men but the crisis brought women out into the open and made their skills more visible. I've always believed in encouragement rather than dictate and this was the only way to work with head-teachers in a contracting environment. In the old days we would have instructed, especially in education departments which are renowned for their traditional and autocratic practices. The difference was that in the past my style had been one of personal preference, LMS made it a necessity. I realized when we have an overspend of £4 million and a crisis of confidence in the schools that I had to lead and not just set an example. I asked three senior managers to take early retirement and set up a new management group, bringing women tier officers. I had a big meeting of all the officers and head-teachers, some were threatened but in general constant communication of facts works.

Women wanted to get things done and to solve problems, not avoid them. They saw their male colleagues as sidestepping and avoiding difficulties until a crisis occurred, leaving aside anything that was not within their job specification, being slippery about the impact of their actions or more importantly their inertia and lack of initiative:

> I think what women share is a deep rooted desire to solve problems, and they want to get on with the job. Male managers are more interested in crisis management than services.

Without exception middle managers saw men and women's actual management style as very different. Women managers tend to 'sex stereotype' their male colleagues, because they felt the sex stereotypes of female (person oriented) and male (systems oriented) matched the reality they experienced. Interviewees felt this difference in style and strategies tended to vary according to political sympathies. This thinking makes them potential leaders, change agents and innovators in the public sector:

> I like working in a team and with women. Women learn from training, they want training, men don't. This is true in the voluntary sector as well as here, they still bang their fists on the table and shout.

Women were bemused, surprised and confused by colleagues (usually male) who did not even reflect on 'how' they were going to put a new policy into practice or more commonly how to improve unwieldy procedures which users had complained about. Local government managers had a tendency to proclaim policy, objectives and events but did not bother to think how to achieve them:

> There is the difficulty of persuading other managers to work together to develop foresight and planning. There's no understanding of process – in local government the political agenda dictates that everything had to be done yesterday.

Women new to local administration were shocked by this attitude and lack of interest in service delivery. They mostly put it down to a lack of awareness of 'process', which was a general male characteristic, reinforced by the rigid role bound culture of public administrations. In the 1980s local government managers were poor at planning and did tend to ignore service users of patronize tenants:

> We never discuss how the next piece of government legislation will affect us. Instead we let it hit us in the face, and then we end up having to do more firefighting again – (crisis management) and so it continues.

Women fought against the bureaucratic formalities and found it hard to adhere to what they saw as an unnatural and irresponsible obedience to rules and roles. By contrast their male colleagues viewed their detached objectivity and acceptance of procedures as integral to professionalism, again reinforcing the Bass and Avolio (1993) view of the male preference for transaction and the more female focus on transformation. This is hardly surprising as women are often disadvantaged and disconnected from the professional world and consequently seek social change and transformation. Complacency among male colleagues was another often mentioned grievance of this manager group:

> They do not see the point of analysing, dissecting operations. As far as they're concerned we just carry on as normal – it's dinosaur mentality – calling a meeting means dragging them into the world of planning and taking them away from firefighting which they seem to thrive on.

The 'process' approach was difficult to make visible when male colleagues either feigned or proclaimed a total lack of understanding of what their female colleagues were telling them, preferring instead 'firefighting' and crisis management. In the 1980s women middle managers reported that many of their female bosses had acquired the same disingenuous lack of interest in the realities of conflict and process dynamics within their departments and among colleagues. They preferred to imitate the male model and become the 'queen bee' figure rather than challenge the status quo with management. Women in middle management complained of:

- crisis management and a lack of planning;
- a disregard for detail;
- no awareness at all of process;
- other managers having a lack of personal responsibility;
- a 'culture of blame' and scapegoating.

Senior women officers were more concerned about inefficiency, the culture of blame and the resistance to change than they were about personal style and individual differences. They were more frustrated by traditional management structures than by personal slights or forms of discrimination. They could see how the organization was operating overall and how service delivery appeared to be dependent on changing management practice and service operations.

Those managers who were serious about services were forced to be more astute about the barriers to change; the relationships involved in change; the need to agree policy and to audit change strategies. Moving forward or gaining credibility in management involved analysing barriers, finding allies and new relationships. Systems were required which would reinforce positive processes and record minute changes over a period of time. There were huge differences between the women and the departments they worked in. Those who felt free to do their work reported feeling less stressed and frustrated. Those who worked in education departments experienced a less aggressive but more patronizing culture which was formal and polite, somewhat gentlemanly but very restrictive:

> It's a very old fashioned environment of paper pushing and formality. You cannot get anything done by talking to people. It has to be minuted and passed around – being direct, I think, is sometimes seen as offensive by the older male officers, they don't expect to get much done and don't want to be shown up.

Some felt overwhelmed by the pressure to avoid reality and hide behind old practices. A recently appointed woman felt that she had lost confidence in the process and in herself:

> When I was interviewed for the job, they laid great emphasis on my not having enough management skills, but what they meant was that I was not dictatorial enough and too participatory. I soon realized I had slipped back into a deferring role to two men in the team, one younger with confidence and the other very experienced. It was only when these two men left that I realized I had to fight back to gain a more key role in the organization.

The senior women in this study who had the energy to pursue strategies at work for management change had no children. Other directors were prepared to wait and accepted slow progress for their management of change programmes:

I cannot presume to tell my managers how to manage – they are independent professional people. They do get rather bored by my talking to them about management. They are changing; they do not see discussion as soft now. Sometimes it is rather like a boys' club but it is much more encouraging for women than my last authority.

Ignoring women's innovation

There was little disagreement between women concerning the inadequacies of local government management. All mentioned the following problems:

- organizational cult;
- centralization;
- departmentalization;
- rigid and closed hierarchical procedures;
- a blame culture.

But it was women in middle management who were stressed, trapped and reported being ignored, patronized, undervalued and misunderstood as managers with ideas and desirous of change. They were frustrated in their efforts to effect change and the majority reported being actively blocked, undervalued and labelled as troublemakers. They complained of lack of interest in discussion and collaboration and too little planning within their departments. They also reported a complete lack of appreciation of processes on the part of many of their male colleagues who appeared more skilled at impression and crisis management. Their problem was less how to be heard and more how to be understood. They needed allies if they were to persuade officers and members to be more aware of the significance of organizational cultures. Each authority had its own local version of management cultures, but the same frustrations were reiterated by almost every women middle manager interviewed.

Unheard and ignored

The most quoted complaint was that in meetings women managers were bypassed or just ignored. The overwhelming majority of middle managers complained that their managers did not listen to their comments about their work. The impact of such daily negative and denying reactions left them feeling undermined, marginalized and underconfident. The consensus was that this occurred because men thought that women had little to say or wondered what on earth they were talking about. Women's comments on organization and management in the early 1990s were innovative. They involved a confidence in process and change which their colleagues did not share and did not believe in. Their male colleagues just did not understand what was being suggested, or when they did could not believe that such changes would work. One woman chief officer summed up the catch 22 problem for women in middle grade posts:

> There are two reasons why women go unheard: they are women and not men, no one really understands what women are saying – they hear the words but have no understanding of what is meant by them, so they ignore them. This does not necessarily mean they have no respect for the woman, just that they don't want to make fools of themselves by asking what on earth are you talking about. Men don't in my experience, like uncertainty, and don't ask other men when they don't understand either. It helps the man to think, 'Ah it's a woman – that explains it – it must be rubbish – ignore it.'

The male manager's sense of 'being right' seems to stem not from his credibility as a manager but from being a 'man' in a male world. Such male confidence would soon run out on the shop floor among women workers. Within traditional male cultures, the majority of men do not open their ears to women, except where who has an added social status which forces them to do so. Although the experienced women managers recognized that much behaviour was merely deferential to those with formal and informal status, they knew that women were doubly disadvantaged by its dynamic. An experienced officer who had worked for local authorities in equal opportunities since the 1970s said that even though she was well aware of authoritarian tendencies among officers, she was still amazed at how many chief officers (in spite of the fact that they had managed major change and been exposed to all the new management thinking) continued to refuse to listen to women managers and found listening to anyone extremely difficult:

> Then I realized that they didn't listen to what anyone had to say – it's not just gender it's an institution, of not listening, of saying your piece, and then sitting back with arms folded waiting for the time when you can make your next intervention. They are hostile to everyone, very judgemental, we never have any sort of discussion when they're there – its completely different for everyone when they are away.

The authoritarian response is to belittle those with assumed 'inferior' status (female) or to make statements or pronouncements to colleagues. This dismissive attitude is most acute in authoritarian hierarchical departments where managers tend to categorize women as having less competence without even seeing them. Female staff, including managers, were generally held in low esteem until they proved otherwise:

> They assumed because I was a woman I couldn't handle figures, even though I'd told them, I had taught maths. Basically he listens to male colleagues.

Women know this and compensate by gaining more and more qualifications – women middle managers accumulate postgraduate degrees. It was also common for male managers at all levels to misjudge or underestimate senior women's capabilities. This was less common in departments where there had always been women managers:

> I've found that unless I really push the women at interview, other male colleagues have a tendency to assume she lacks of experience, toughness, and ability – even when she is bristling with qualifications.

The majority of senior women recognized that women in junior and middle management needed support and encouragement and allowed direct access to themselves:

> I observe how people treat women managers. For instance, I have a woman who is very good, but her line manager gives her no reinforcement at all. She is clear about her targets but needs a more open management style to make them work, and wider evaluation criteria. I discussed with her the process and agreed her programmes, I knew she'd been blocked by her own manager.

Some women who were not used to such sexist stereotyping were surprised at how far male colleagues continued to doubt women's capabilities:

> I think we stereotype men and women too much, but the problem is many women have changed and so many men haven't.

Those women who had worked for some time with male colleagues with whom they got on well were shocked when later they discovered that when interviewing other women managers they had expressed the same prejudices and doubts about employing more women: 'We've already got three women in this department.' Yet, when such negative stereotyping was commented on, women middle managers were accused of 'moaning' even when they referred to how a project had not worked or they sought advice. Women complained that when a woman made a criticism it was 'moaning', but when men challenged schemes they tend to be seen as 'fair comment'. Although men were often difficult, their behaviour was not characterized as representing all 'male' behaviour but a particular man who happened to be a nuisance. By contrast, women's actions were not judged on their individual merits but as the expected behaviour of all 'women'. Each woman carried the responsibility for all women. This dynamic had the effect of distancing those who wanted a quiet life from radical women who undermined that possibility. A woman manager who voiced a view was characterized as either 'difficult', a nuisance, or plain 'silly'.

> They think we are whinging women. Most managers absorb problems. A group of women managers went to the director with the same complaint of too little communication, too little feedback, not enough discussion, and we were treated like silly women. It's not that some of the men don't want to say the same things,

but they know they'll be abused so they don't bother – they leave it to us to complain and be belittled. If you try and pose a question they see it as a sign of weakness, of not knowing, when of course you are trying to consider alternatives to a problem.

It is within this gender context that women managers who are committed to social change and public sector transformation have devised tactics and strategies in how to handle the gendered environment in order to be effective and to remain sane.

Resistance to innovation

Innovative women managers were trying to develop new ways of working within a very bureaucratic and autocratic environment. They were often ridiculed by colleagues who said they were 'far too busy to engage in time-wasting activities such as discussions, training courses or strategy development', there was 'far too much work to do'. Women managers' vision and knowledge of service detail were often the basis of rejection at interview. This was because the ideal version of a manager (much reinforced by the idea that any executive could be introduced into the public sector, no matter whether they had experience) continued to stress a form of detachment which underrated those with specialist knowledge or who were interested in operational or service details. The thoroughness of many women and their interest in the detail of service operations consequently counted against them:

> I was interviewed only because a candidate dropped out and I was on the reserve list. The first evening at dinner was the worst, I don't think I said more than two words. Then the next day we had a lot of psychometric tests, on the following day we did practical. We had to draft a letter to a blind secretary about a problem in the Asian community – I didn't finish mine because I wrote something long about single sex education. The other male candidates came to find me and said no chief officer would waste their time on such detail. I thought they were probably right but I got the job.

Women met with huge resistance both to their suggestions in middle management and their actions in senior management. Those women directors who were responsible for major restructuring programmes frequently met with personal hostility and political resistance from politicians and managers, especially when they tried to incorporate more open management and democratic practices into this process:

> The corporate team made such a fuss about my structuring proposals, but I had a sense I had to stick to it. I disbanded the grade of deputy and brought in third-tier people, many of them women, and created a management team of nine

people. They said this was too big and kept throwing it out – but my department were with me because I had involved them and the unions from the beginning. In the end I won because I agreed to seven with two secondees. The most frustrating thing was that the corporate team never got around to talking about management principles. They hated it because it came from me, they would have disliked it though whoever stood up to them in this way. They tried to say things like 'your team is too big', and I would say 'why'? and they'd say 'well, it just won't work'. Then they said the trade unions would eat me, but they didn't. What I was most shocked by was that they had told me they were interested in flatter more open structures, delegating responsibility and valuing staff, but when it came to it – they didn't.

This particular director, although she found work with her own corporate team difficult, grasped the problems of the closed hierarchy in education and attempted to bring her staff together to improve communications. She became a director in 1992 and was sacked in 1993.

A college principle talked a lot about developing education relationships with schools and head teachers, but many of her efforts were blocked by accountants who thought that the information she was relaying to other agencies and parents was confidential and belonged to the authority. After introduction of the internal market the issue of confidentiality became more controversial, particularly when local government had to work with new partners who wanted to know what costs were involved. Treasurers continued to hide financial information from outsiders and were reluctant to release any information. Trust in new partnerships were impossible when each party did not know what amounts were being spent on what. In the early 1990s many schools wanted financial information which was withheld from them by secretive local authorities. Politicians and bureaucrats continued to think that divulging financial information was contravening some basic trade secret. This was an instinctive response, not a rational or financial one, when in fact a shared knowledge of costs and overall budgets was much more likely to demonstrate integrity and goodwill in new relationships:

The treasurer did not want to release information to the heads – because psychologically it made him realise that they were in effect now our managers whereas in the past the education department had acted as their bosses – this movement of power was expressed in terms of who had the most information about money. In the end the chair and chief officer backed me and the information was released.

Political relationships

Many radical women were convinced that their colleagues were institutionalized pawns working within a system who could not square local democracy with internal democracy. Women found that while local accountability was frequently discussed, internal democracy was always avoided. It was the politicians who were the least able to comprehend the practical difficulties of delivering services through a highly controlled and inflexible bureaucracy. Too often they saw their role as problem solvers and tended to avoid thinking about management:

> It was the elected members who were the biggest problem. They were less aware of the importance of style and culture and that values have to be translated into policies and action. Politicians tend not to understand processes, they understand structures and still think that they can dictate direct from on high.

Local politicians often appeared to have a disregard for management and service organization. They rarely attended to how services were managed, which is surprising given that their local surgeries were probably full of people expressing dissatisfaction about a lack of response to their complaints about schools or housing repairs. Labour leaders and senior managers often lacked experience or contact with any community or local projects and consequently had no confidence in alternative forms of organization and ridiculed co-operatives as 'silly'. Their lack of support for innovative women managers' plans usually indicated that they did not understand them. They heard the words but did not have the experience to make sense of what they meant. Management was viewed by councillors as a world of predictable routines controlled from the centre. They believed their role as councillors to be to find out what people wanted and to decide policies. Management would then put their wishes into operation. Women managers could not persuade local politicians of the significance of management organization to service development. They reflected that this political lack of interest in 'management' was probably far more of an obstacle to social change than the resistance they encountered as women.

Such at attitude lay beneath many locally elected councillors' thinking in the 1970s and 1980s. Politicians were concerned with winning political arguments and getting their policies adopted, not with how to implement policies. Women managers reported that local politicians appeared to think that the 'inside of organizations' was nothing to do with them, as if management was politically 'neutral' and not connected to policy.

Although civil servants in Britain are not supposed to communicate directly with politicians, some women managers became so despondent that they sought political clarification and contacted politicians directly:

> I'm so fed up about the way the service is going I wrote to the chair of the committee. I got a phone call from my boss, who said I was supposed to be an officer seven days a week and not allowed to communicate with politicians directly. But who am I supposed to talk to? There is no structure for discussion, no forum. We have no academic board, nor any representative and the trade unions are not negotiation bodies for services.

This woman was reprimanded by her senior manager for writing to a politician. Other women became so disillusioned that they decided to go part-time and spend more time with their families:

> After a while you get disillusioned. I've been working on decentralization for four years – and still believe in it – but they won't recognize that it won't work without a change in management practice and culture. I spend more time with my children now and work part-time because I've sort of given up. I did *not* become part-time because I have children – in fact my children give me more confidence than do my work colleagues.

Radical policies such as those of decentralizing services were bound to fail if command-type, hierarchical management structures remained in place. The frustration of a great many women was that any discussion about the relationship between internal management practices and service delivery was impossible, especially with local politicians. Those who attempted to explain the connections were reprimanded for even trying:

> We would attempt to bring up our concerns with team leaders and the senior team at every meeting but we knew they were not going to restructure beyond opening local offices. The closed culture made everyone suspicious and the training was all about where the offices would be placed and line management, not about training, sharing and learning new ways to work with users. In the end we gave up and Sally had another baby, you can't spend you whole life explaining new ways of working to those who do not want to hear.

One councillor was outraged when it was suggested in 1989 that a development model could be adopted on the estates in Yorkshire to set up new businesses. He replied: 'That's for underdeveloped countries, not *my* city.' This tendency among local politicians to ignore the need for development and the impact of management practices on services was harder to overcome in local authorities which were more authoritarian. The traditions of social planning and the 'command economy' were difficult to shift, especially in northern cities where the women managers worked. Further entrenchment set in during the 1980s when central government restricted local government finance. Many northern Labour authorities entered a period of siege mentality and became more intransigent, rather than less so. By contrast, in other less politicized country authorities senior officers were allowed to take the initiative and introduce radical management restructuring and various forms of new managerialism. Those who did this in the metropolitan authorities without significant political backing were liable to attack from elected members and ridicule from their colleagues, as many women directors found to their cost.

Opportunities after the reforms?

One of the reasons why female managers were more likely to embrace new public sector management was that it looked as if it would undermine the male traditional establishment and closed management practices. Many women saw the advent of managerialism as a liberation from male bureaucracy and the professional establishment. At first they perceived public sector restructuring to be to women managers' advantage – because they assumed that restructuring was driven by their own social commitments and values. After witnessing the market-driven, top-down changes instigated by the New Right, they became doubtful and feared that the public sector social infrastructure would collapse. Those in more senior positions could see that there were opportunities here because they could undermine the hated red tape and bureaucracy. Other women were more hesitant, agreeing with the management philosophy of individual growth and development but worried by the market framework, the way managerialism was hyped up and, more importantly, the cutting of public sector resources.

> The trouble is we're taking management thinking from the American private sector without thinking about how it relates to public sector values in the UK – but in discussion about the relationship between management and service outcomes this has to be a good thing.

There was a real tension between those interested in 'quality initiatives' and service users and those focused on financial control and dominating restructuring. The interest in 'output' and later 'outcomes' focused managers' minds on achievements and performance. They could identify those who were blocking and resistant to change. This focus on outputs and later outcomes made senior managers more aware of the impact of organizational culture on staff motivation and the potential of those managers who could galvanize staff relationships with users. Management by objectives did result in a greater transparency of work methods and performance criteria. For some it also resulted in a greater awareness of how traditional practices and gendered behaviour trapped competent women.

The introduction of business thinking into the local government and the health services was in itself 'innovation' even though driven more by cost cutting than any interest in the community and public service effectiveness. Attitudes were changing:

> Service agreements have sharpened people's minds and TQM has become of interest and they want staff ownership of the strategic plan, which, of course, is impossible without a more open form of management. The one thing I still haven't tackled is that one colleague winks at me whenever I enter the room.

There were waves of internal restructuring and managerial practices which were initially welcomed by women in local government. In general new public management thinking was viewed as a positive step for both services and women wanting to democratize management. A union officer pointed out that competitive tendering in the Northern Ireland NHS provided an opportunity for women to assert the value of their work in local union negotiations. She recounted how they put together an inhouse tender for the cleaning contract and succeeded in retaining the contract despite demonstrating a need for higher costings. Experienced women did not undervalue their work, nor did they 'cut everything back to the bone' in their bids for contracts, although many others did:

> Because women relate to people differently from men, branches run by women tend to be organized differently. The Northern Ireland women favoured informality, mixing sociability with business. They ran meetings of different types: coffee mornings, meetings with speakers, small groups. A male trade union official described the new atmosphere: when women have control of the branch the whole system just falls away and there is much more openness about trying to take the union to the people, and to take on board issues which historically have not been mainstream of the union, but may be the mainstream of what the women membership want to take on board.

Many local authorities employed large company consultants to devise better operations and management systems, initially on the basis of total quality management (TQM). Unfortunately, the deferential British culture determined how TQM and continuous improvement programmes were implemented, most often not through dialogue but diktat. Changes tended to conform to what managers already believed they needed, rather than involve a radical change in approach from 'systems' and 'people' focus. Those consultancy companies which recommended organizational change and a people approach were paid for their reports but not their practice. This interpretation of TQM resulted in a very narrow focus on specification systems which increase the control over frontline staff and undermined staff involvement. Overspecification, detailed work sheets and rigid evaluation reduced the time for personal interaction at work and lowered staff morale. It was no coincidence that the majority of managers interpreted total quality to mean an increased control rather than a tool for improving motivation and morale. Women managers agreed with the total quality agenda but not with how it was interpreted and implemented within British public sector organizations.

Many of the directors interviewed had been involved in restructuring programmes and quality improvement initiatives. Some were trying to introduce new more open management practices while also reducing staff levels and meeting new service demands. The changing context and the demands of local management of schools led many directors and chief officers to look for managers who could transcend boundaries and work on conflictual situations in a responsive and responsible manner. Senior women were looking for people and opportunities to undermine the blame culture and for those who would develop practices which would shift staff and managers out of their traditional patterns of work. Initially the trade unions were perceived as a threat to these endeavours. The power of local trade unions depended very much on the way that change was advanced, how it was communicated and the general morale within, say, housing or social services. Senior women found it easier to convince their managers and other colleagues of the validity of new management practices:

> It is clear that men in executive positions are also irritated by bureaucracy and they see new management techniques as a way of breaking down red tape. This is usually to enable the individual manager to be free to be creative, but, as a perspective, it is only marginally closer to women's demands for collaboration and planning. In fact, in some managers' thinking it justifies less planning and negotiation; it is the 'go ahead and prove yourself' approach, or the policy written 'on the back of the envelope' syndrome. This is not just restricting for women but for all managers, and whether the services will benefit is another question.

There was still powerful resistance to change which they attributed to the persistent male gender cultures:

> I've been very reinforced by reading about TQM but no one has ever attributed the changes to me or other women who led them. The issue when you work in a male-dominated culture is to persuade people you can do the job in your own way. I think the macho way is a facade anyway. The seeming refusal of many managers in the period 1989 to 1992 to face up to reality and address problems has left local government in an even more vulnerable state. I think, we all want a better deal for the kids and the service. We want to be close to the school. I feel absolutely with Labour in fighting opt-out, etc., so they can't see me as the political enemy, although I know some do. The trouble is the men are still playing a totally different game here. Either you join in and play their silly game or you get attacked. (Director, suspended June 1993)

But by the 1990s women managers were disgruntled by a lack of concern for their values and the social traditions of the public service within the performance and contracting management systems. The contracting environment resulted in a more macho culture, which again mirrored the values of the male establishment bodies. Women working in health and local government grew tired of the rhetoric of the New Public Management philosophy, which promoted autonomy, devolved power and employee responsibility when the reality was of increased central control, increased workloads and more responsibility, not power. They welcomed the fact that NPM brought a greater transparency of practices and criteria, but disagreed with those used in performance assessment of users and agencies staff.

The women who could see the opportunities of a reappraisal of management objectives had the problem of persuading more sceptical staff who perceived the reforms to be based purely on the desire to make financial cuts and undermine existing working conditions. Low morale resulted which made team working and collaborative practices difficult. Thousands of frontline staff and middle managers lost their jobs and everyone's workload increased. The tension grew between those wanting to make the service change in the interests of local people and those attempting to meet government financial performance measures. A stressed community organiser reported:

> The workload is terrible and getting worse, but it has made an enormous difference having a woman director, she listens and tries to improve things. I know not all men would support us in this way, but she does, because she seems to believe in open management. Women's commitment to 'open' management is one which involves team work and devolving responsibility in order that employees have a sense of 'ownership'.

As the public sector reforms progressed, many of the women who had welcomed new public management with open arms grew more and more sceptical about whether their own politicians and managers cared about service development or service quality. They were all extremely antagonistic to the Conservative government which they viewed as lacking social values. Managerialism, which appeared as a liberation from red tape and bureaucracy in the 1980s, has in fact generated performance management systems which rewards cheap activities, fast results, macho and individualist behaviour and evaluation systems which justified the contracting process and standard dimensions.

Leadership roles

Leadership skills become critical during times of change and much more significant within public administrations. The chief executive's style and approach to staff has become critical to successful organizational change management. Those women working in transactional cultures have had to hide their transforming skills no matter how senior. The climate and culture of senior management make a huge difference to a woman's confidence in career prospects and in her work.

The senior women interviewed between 1991 and 1992 were older than their middle manager colleagues and had learnt to function in the command/control male cultures. They were more able to cope with mechanical attitudes to change and more likely to be experienced in manipulating the system. However, they were less experienced in dealing with radical change and motivating staff. Those women who had experience in the social movements or non-government organizations were more confident of strategy and more adept at managing the transformation processes.

The problem was that innovative women were not in leadership positions. They were also threatening to other managers and met with hostility when they attempted to bypass convention and suggested radical change. Women executives were well aware that had they been more challenging when in middle management they would never have been promoted. Many had more mainstream careers and were unaware of discrimination because they had not previously represented a threat:

> I don't think I was aware of gender until I came here. Before I worked with other women in a local team – now I am surrounded by men who are unused to women managers, who doubt whether we/I can manage any size of budget.

Directors had only become more aware of gender as they entered the boardroom. Other older women managers had learnt to adapt and respond to the traditional and hierarchical administration traditions, often at their own expense, and they found it hard to readapt to changing expectations. Senior women recognized that the appropriate responses in middle management were totally inappropriate in senior leadership positions. Those challenging middle managers who questioned and queried practices were change champions, but they met antagonism rather than praise for their leadership qualities. Within traditional public administrations middle managers are not expected to make decisions. Middle managers have to persuade their senior management team of the logic and justice of their arguments. This is extremely difficult when the senior manager is personally threatened by innovation, unwilling to listen and doubtful that alternatives to the bureaucratic practices are feasible. This response left many women frustrated, angry and likely to explode out of exasperation, further undermining their own case:

> When you start you think it's a question of politics, then you think: I'll fight a few targeted battles – then you just get angry with the senselessness of so much bumph and meetings and totally lose your grip. It may make you feel good sounding off, so you do it to cheer yourself up and get a sense of self-respect again.

These innovative middle managers were in a 'catch 22' situation. Senior women could see that this was a waste of potential and demoralizing for creative women with leadership qualities but they often did not recognize the extent or depth of the dynamic. This lack of power resulted in middle managers pressing for corrections in definitions and reporting, which others thought a complete waste of time because they did not understand the significance of recording new activities. Significant activities are often left from minutes because they had never been recorded previously. Within transactional management the formalities and records enter traditional practice and omit emergent relationships. Those who seek change have to be insistent, and women who are insistent are a nuisance.

This creates yet another conundrum for women: do they seek more authority in order to push through changes or battle away in middle management? Often the transition from the middle to senior ranks is difficult, especially for those remaining with the same authority. Many women in the late 1980s were doubtful that they would have more power or more authority within the authorities where they lived. Some were lucky and were 'headhunted' by executives who wanted radical and challenging women directors. These executives admired their tenacity and aggressive customer focus, but were unprepared for the hostility to appointments from more misogynist managers. There was a tendency to see women as the new dynamic but ruthless force, able to take on all resistance and willing to cope with whatever was thrown at them:

> The chief executive has had several meetings with all staff and he has tried to explain how he wants the authority to be run. It's good for people to see and hear him – and I think he is committed to a form of less oppressive management. But he still thinks that to succeed you must be macho and tough. What he wants to get rid of is all the government restrictions so macho officers can do their own thing, unhindered by accountability or discussion.

Unfortunately, supportive executives did not necessarily understood that strong leadership was not the only requirement for change and that there was also a need for sustaining environments. Those women most satisfied were working with senior managers (men and women) who had experience of managing change and understood the possibilities of more democratic management:

> The chief executive comes from local government, but it's an advantage that he has also worked outside. He backs us with his leadership and is totally committed to management by competence, not by club or clique. Too, but they are tied – the corporate team dictate and we bow to their power.

However, many of the radical women remained doubtful about entering senior management in the early 1990s and as a group they were more united in their desire for real change in how services were organized and to have their work valued by managers. Many saw a career in senior management as amounting to a collusion with political policies and management practices with which they disagreed: 'I know many women here still think that being a senior manager is colluding with a system they dislike.'

Women managers appeared to be more at ease with new forms of leadership which were visionary but not autocratic and the competitive climate made it difficult for them to envisage how they could function effectively within the contracting environment without being compromised. Many felt trapped in the never-ending contradiction between status and what they saw as their lives, authenticity and integrity. Was it worth the 'pain', 'slog' and discomfort in the male world of senior management and if they reached a status post would they be free to be themselves and innovate in the way they wanted? Within the northern authorities suspicion about senior management persists, and if anything has increased during the course of privatization and public sector reforms. In 1989 many middle managers were reluctant to seek promotion. This was especially evident in the more authoritarian authorities where a punitive blame culture endured and there were few women managers at any level. In some authorities the isolated women already in post were often hostile to female applicants, but by the late 1980s this was changing and most senior women in local government were encouraging women applicants. Networking had begun to galvanize women managers and there was a growing awareness that only when a critical mass of more radical women was evident would the male and authoritarian cultures begin to change.

Valuing work not promotion

In the 1980s women suspected that they would never be accepted in corporate culture. Others did not want to move to cities and many were reluctant to enter corporate teams which they knew were responsible for cuts and redundancies. Those women committed to social change but not careerists often accepted senior positions without the pay; this was called 'acting-up'. Acting-up involved accepting the senior responsibility without having either permanent status or increased pay. It is unclear whether any men accepted such positions and where an exciting opportunity was presented to a woman she often accepted it irrespective of pay or promotion. A number of women working in local government strategic units in the late 1980s were 'acting-up' and were in strategic posts which had not been advertised, but were endorsed or initiated by energetic politicians. It was not uncommon in local authorities for chief executives to 'fast track' capable women into senior responsibilities without actually promoting them. Senior managers singled out able or competent staff to carry out strategic work or to lead difficult change programmes without going through formal interview procedures. Women directors tended to promote women, not ask them to accept responsibility without the protection of formal status, and few men were offered 'acting-up' positions:

> I know that a man probably would not have accepted this job, but it needed doing and I know that if someone else had done it a lot of the issues to do with democracy would have been lost. The problem is that it will not show up on my CV as a senior post. I don't have a problem with senior men, they're rather respectful towards me, but other women in middle management think I'm being fast-tracked and rather resent it, or else think I'm a fool for doing it.

None of the women interviewed wanted status for its own sake and so if the opportunity arose for more interesting work they accepted it; they valued social relationships and stuck to their jobs because of the satisfaction service development gave them. Although they did not desire rapid promotion or huge salaries they were hungry for reinforcement, for some appreciation of their worth. On the whole these women were not working to career plans or being tactical about the next stage up the promotion ladder; they were interested in the quality of their work and their lives, not personal status:

> I was asked the other day what were my career plans. I've never had a plan, I've had a series of odd jobs. I first worked when my children were one and three in Birmingham which I thought of as a bit of a lark, this is what I call my first proper job.

> It is not just the male culture which put many women off seeking promotion, many entered the public service sector in order to work with people and improve service quality, although in managerial roles some were not attracted to senior management because it would remove them from direct contact with service users. This is especially true of women doctors.

Some reluctance was of course due to a realistic appraisal of life with young children:

> I don't want any more responsibility. I've got enough already managing seven people. I am looking for a job with less responsibility so I can take it easy for a while. I think women worry more about getting things right and worry more when they're managers. If they have domestic burdens as well they (we) can become very stressed.

However, while women were willing to adjust and balance their lives with other commitments they did want to be valued.

Many women in middle management felt angered by the fact that they only had credibility at work if they were career minded and sought senior management. They felt that the obsession with senior management and high-flying women undermined the worth of other women and other employees, which was also to the detriment of the service. Their frustration stemmed from the fact that their managers did not appreciate their work and their commitment and they were angered by the attitude that anyone not in senior management by the age of 40 was dismissed as irrelevant. They felt that they were made to feel failures because they remained as middle managers by choice, not just for family reasons but because they wanted balance in their lives and felt they could not accept many of the senior management functions:

I'm ready for less responsibility rather than more. It's a question of what you feel ambitious for, life or work. I like seeing my children, but I also want to see my friends.

In general women wanted recognition and respect for the work that they did at the time and did not want to be constantly pressurised to become the 'boss'. They were certain that given the right circumstances many of them would gladly accept formal power later on in their careers, but in the meantime they did not want to be pressurized into feeling 'failures' for being middle managers and fodder for equality targets. They believed that good managers should value staff at all levels.

The pressure on these women to achieve was great. Women in senior positions wanted them to swell the numbers of women in senior management because they could see what potential many of them had as change agents. Senior women reported that it was a pity that so many women in middle management did not realize how many of the frustrations of middle management evaporated when once in a senior position:

> Although the organization remains bureaucratic and patriarchal, senior woman do have the power to initiate change. The culture has not changed that much in the north of the country.
>
> I think the reluctance of women, particularly feminists, to enter management is greater here than in London. I have felt very isolated since I came here. In London in the 1980s there were secretaries moving up the ladder to become officers. Here everyone is too impressed by status. It's lessening in some places in the north, but not in others.

Competent women acting as leaders in middle management can be seen as very threatening and a huge problem for middle managers was that they were acting like senior managers by adopting the roles of strategist and change agent without the status to reinforce them in those roles:

> I accepted the role of leading the local restructuring of schools because I thought it was crucial both to the survival of the education service and to schools, but it does rather irritate me that no one has suggested upgrading me, and if I left I would still be on a senior grade and so would never get an equivalent post.

What was clear was that many creative change agents are thwarted in middle management. The emphasis on 'superwoman', women 'high flyers' and senior women bosses in the 1980s irritated many women in Britain and the interest in top charismatic women continues. This beam on the exceptional woman does not convey the differences between women and the complexities of most women's lives within a male world. Where men and women were unused to women in decision-making posts, those newly appointed to senior positions were given a hard time and found it harder to make the shift in role to senior managers:

I'm interested in what women have to offer organizations and it's sad that so many women still put themselves down, even when they're working harder than everyone else. Some women have got this view that managers are people who oppress you and we could never be one. I know one woman who became a junior manager and made herself sick with worry about how she was treating staff. She was in fact very good; she left after six months.

In spite of women's general mistrust of senior managers, others in middle management recognized that status would give them not just power but also the opportunity to develop such a change at a critical time in local government:

The carrot got brighter as I worked up the ladder. Once you are in a more senior position you can see the service overall and that's exciting. You feel you can do something. I began to realize that if I had more power all this would not have to happen to me. I could do something.

Those middle managers who argued for strategic and practices change in order to improve service quality were within traditional manager roles but behaving more as senior managers. This could and did antagonize their colleagues who perceived them as 'upstarts'. One woman now an assistant principal said: 'I hated being in middle management because people like me are such a "challenge" – I can understand why the manager wanted me out. I threatened him and questioned all this actions.'

Those in middle and junior management positions are expected to conform as an official not be innovative. This role conflict was most acute for those women who had previously had a leadership role in independent organizations where 'initiative' had been an essential skill. They were more aware of the contradictions between administration and transforming management. More positively by the 1990s some women reported that their innovative work and critical stance had actually assisted their promotion. Two women interviewed had rapidly risen within the Greater London Council and gained confidence in the political environment, where discussion and debate were more valued than they had been in the northern authorities where they had previously worked:

I was always bringing up issues, which are taken for granted in London but are still challenging in the North. In the end I had to leave. I was fortunate and worked for the Association for Local Authorities as a policy adviser, where I was valued. Here I wasn't seen as threatening or mad. It was an exciting time for me. I know it gave me the confidence to look for a chief officer's post.

As management changed and tasks and objectives became focused, the potential of women in middle management became more visible at least to executives (except in the very traditional authorities) and middle managers were supported by senior manager mentors and became much freer to innovate and direct change programmes:

> When I first came to the Town Hall the chief officer was very arrogant and blamed everyone except himself for bad services. When he left the new CE came in with a very different style. He changed the atmosphere so much everyone became more open, more motivated and more confident. He treats us like individuals and we appreciate it.

Senior women began to 'mentor' younger women and pulled out those able women to middle management:

> I think women are good at taking projects and running with them. They often have to do this because they cannot get backing from their bosses – flattened and more open management will be good for women; if it happens I'm always drawn to looking at the staff and seeing what effect changes have on people, even if I was the treasurer I'd still want to see how money affected people. I think this is a very female point of view but one which all executives are now having to adopt.

By the 1990s many women were beginning to feel as if a door had opened and that competent women were valued. However, they were still not seen as capable of innovation or leadership. Many chose to work in strategic policy and decentralization units in order to be instrumental in change at a local and policy level. They were surprised to find that many of their colleagues were not so motivated. They did not have their experience, were institutionalized, had moved through the organization and remained in the same pool. Few of them were confident enough to challenge tradition or motivated to do so, with the consequence that inter-departmental competition persisted.

Challenging and innovative managers

These women were challenging organizational frameworks and management practices. They supported other radical women and equality programmes which were linked to service improvements and the community. Women may share the common experiences of juggling domestic life and work, but they are far from being a homogeneous group and not all are innovative. The women interviewed were innovative in the sense that they were not merely reporting frustrations but also recounting their strategies and practices to change social realities. A challenging manager was one who spoke her mind in meetings, asked questions and spent time and energy on improving practices. Transforming practices usually involved removing structural barriers, addressing culture blocks and improving communication systems, especially between frontline staff and managers. At first challenging managers had been circumspect and waited for the appropriate moment to intervene, but when this moment never came they reached a point when they could not do their work without clarification and began to ask questions, criticize and be tactical in their behaviour:

> I started off being non-questioning and friendly but in the end I couldn't do my job properly without further clarification, I had to ask questions and in effect challenge his judgement.

Most had learnt over time when to question and when to keep quiet. When their work demanded clarification, new protocols and a change in practice most said that they really had no choice but to adopt a critical stance in relation to management practices; not to have done so would have left them demoralized, untrue to themselves. Those who remained silent felt 'low' and observed how those men who attempted to humanize management practices were often subjected to the same belittling hostilities:

> Dave, a good manager, was asked to leave his post and moved to another area. He did attempt to have a more open style of management and after some months people had some confidence in it and it was working. But we needed him to protect the rest of the department and our new boss is the opposite. He doesn't confide in us and has no interest in education at all (he came from training). We are all jaundiced and fed up and threatened.

Those men who openly defended women colleagues and their more open practices were often also labelled 'oddballs'. Although the women were aware of the link between management and gender, most remained silent and did not make public statements about gender relations or the way that gender cultures affected management practices. Their commitment was to public service development, and if they felt that drawing attention to gender inequality was going to affect their credibility as managers, they tended to remain silent about the personal slights and gendered behaviour, although most could see the implications of this tacit collusion:

> I know that in a way I have been colluding with the system by allowing much to pass by – and sometimes I feel bad about this but you cannot keep your credibility if all the time you are shouting about women. We have all learnt to be strategic. But we are also our own worst enemies – because the culture has remained male in spite of massive change. And the consequence is that women end up being more antagonistic to each other – this is such huge agreement about what we want – but so little discussion about how differently we act – some of it is personalities some of it politics – in the end you end up working with those most committed to the service and its relevance to the local community.

These women were pragmatic, practical and highly strategic in the interests of public sector transformation but they were well aware of how their own gender management strategies influenced the direction of change and of the complexities of juggling their role as managers and their long-term vision. Innovative women are not necessarily women 'at the top'. Many of the most challenging women worked as middle managers and were bypassed for promotion precisely because of their challenging attitude to management. In the 1980s the women in middle management were most aware of the need for change and were the most challenging, but they lacked support. The women who were promoted were often more likely to be those who were known to endorse more traditional practices. This caused resentment and hostility to women directors among women middle managers in the 1980s in the more traditional authorities.

Commitment to service user

Women directors frequently mentioned that although they were not idealistic about all women managers they did believe that women are more likely to be closer to the users of services and therefore have an instinct for 'quality' and the connection between staff morale and service outcomes. Women directors in local government were clear that there is a very strong link between quality services and open, participatory management styles; they could cite examples from their own service departments of why and how this was the case. The women did not suppose that their male colleagues lacked commitment to public services, but many of their male colleagues appeared to be unaware of how traditional practices affected effective service delivery:

> We're trying to open up communication with schools but I've had to fight to get the finance department to even let head-teachers see the budgets. How can they make financial decisions if they haven't seen the figures? I've always been in favour of competitive tendering for efficiency. We should know what things cost. When I came here I didn't believe how inefficient things were – we have to be more confident and open the books, otherwise we'll never deliver better services – they will get worse. It's so obvious.

Senior managers quickly came to the conclusion that social change was dependent on a quality working environment for staff as well as an openness to users and customers, although some senior women were loath to make such a direct correlation between male gender culture and service delivery and male and female management styles. But when pressed further on who they had designated to lead major management of change programmes, it transpired that they had allocated women from third-tier positions:

> It is interesting, though, when I think about it, the two officers who are most comfortable with quality issues and are running with them are women. I think on reflection, that a lot of women identify more with users and believe in the problems they encounter when faced with us (the local authority). Of course there is a tendency for the old guard, managers and politicians not to value this but to think of these women managers in the same way as they think of the public, as a nuisance.

Some women felt very strongly that they were best suited to direct service work and wanted to remain working at grassroots level, with people. They feared that if they became managers they would lose this contact:

> I like grassroots work. I get a lot of satisfaction from knowing people and seeing them change and develop. You never get that in administration. All we want is respect. Just because you work in the community doesn't mean you're dim. I've probably got more qualifications than all of my team leaders – this is a problem. They don't value the service enough.

Qualities and experience

Women working in local government exhibited precisely those qualities that management gurus extolled: social commitment, self-motivation, autonomy, openness to change and desire to be a change agent. The women who were most confident of social change were experienced in negotiating and flexible management and had some confidence in alternative practice. In addition they were connected to a social value base. The difference between them and others was that they were searching for not just efficiency but a form of social management where business methods were used to meet social objectives. They were willing to engage with business methods, but wanted the finances to be controlled in order to meet social objectives. They sought a synergy between systems and outcomes – and for outcomes to be based on what the users or customers in the community deemed priorities. These women had a clear attachment to public service and were intent upon developing forms of public administration in a manner which was flexible and open to new demands. They realized that this was not possible by traditional bureaucratic command and control systems or change programmes directed from the top down. Those most innovative in their attempt to build partnership and internal democracy were motivated by similar goals and, in particular, a process perspective and a confidence in people relationships. They tended to share the following attributes:

- a social commitment based on social values;
- experience of alternative organizations;
- a confidence in social change;
- a process perspective on social and managerial change;
- a local connectedness with the community in which they worked;
- a sense of vision and strategy;
- learnt from experience and independent from other people's definitions;
- confident in alternatives;
- defined themselves as rebels, radical and challenging;

- awareness of user's interests;
- awareness of gender and the power of gender cultures.

Confidence in social alternatives

A significant number of the managers had previous experience of working in community organizations and local non-government organizations (NGOs) or various other sociale economie agencies where they had learnt to work collaboratively. Many of those entering public administration in the 1990s had been involved in social movements and had experience in negotiating within a work or industrial framework. In effect these women from the social movements and the community sector took a strategic look at their work and their lives and demonstrated a transference of learning or knowledge. Many had been instigators of social projects and new innovative organizations and networks. Those with experience of alternative working practices and managing conflict were more confident in their vision for public sector reorganization based on social value and objectives. This may have been gained in local organizing around housing, planning or childcare schemes within voluntary organizations or in developing countries. Many of those most confident of achieving joint practice, team working and complex negotiation had experience in the not-for-profit independent sector, for example:

- overseas development projects;
- local community organizations such as housing, law or advice centres;
- rape crisis or women's refuges;
- community transport and planning projects;
- play schemes or crèches;
- local retail and environmental co-ops;
- credit unions and community enterprises/co-operatives;
- trade union resource centres;
- campaigns and advocacy work;
- community education or as community development worker.

These women community workers reported that without some appreciation of development and process their work would have been impossible. They had a clear idea of how people could work together and the problems encountered when attempting to work collectively; for example, one woman who had worked in an non-government organization in Bradford said:

> I worked in a collective for some years and, although it was hard and we had terrible arguments, it taught me how to negotiate, how to campaign and how to plan for work. I'm sure most managers in local government have not had enough

experience of working outside of an institution to realize that it is possible to be more informal and open and yet effective.

This view was reinforced by many other women who had community development experience in not-for-profit organizations, including juggling social and financial responsibilities and grappling with future visions to translate them into the 'here and now'. Those managers were the least oppressed by male gender cultures and tended to be clearer about their roles, responding less personally to slights from other people. Although only a few had well-formulated management, all had a clear vision for change.

> I don't think all women have an alternative vision of organization – but what is certain is that women all in my experience do express frustration with the way things are done and want change in current practices. They are frustrated by lack of communication, which is crucial if we are to meet changing needs and work in a complex environment.

The women more comfortable with the systems approach tended to be those who had worked in heavily regimented professional organizations. By contrast those women experienced in the interface of management and negotiation between local people and central offices found the formalities of administrations cumbersome. They were aware that the complexities of people's lives never matched the national standards and fixed criteria often set by national bodies.

Building relationships

Those who had learnt through experience of projects knew that often the end results would be at variance with what was originally anticipated and recognized that the process was important rather than the outcome. They suspected that the majority of their male colleagues had not had such experience, resulting in their having less confidence in alternative ways of working. The emerging models in NGOs may have been fraught with conflict but they represent an attempt to democratize organizations in a manner which was both efficient and fair to staff.

Those who had worked for years in large bureaucratic administrations found it more difficult to imagine where the breaking down of role-bound management structures would lead and were more hesitant and less confident of change. Those with experience in small independent organizations had learnt how to juggle priorities, change tactics and develop strategies within a group with other people. They could handle conflict, ambiguity and change and tended to be more able to sustain their spirit and sense of purpose in spite of such blocking people and cultures. Those active within trade unions or political parties tended to have developed more formal skills for managing procedures and rules, reinforced by historical concepts of 'insiders' and 'outsiders'. The trade union and Labour movements tend to be dismissive about community organizations and continue to believe that public bodies must be controlling of staff and centralized. Although many may think this is a legacy from a previous era, those working in local authorities and the Civil Service report that these attitudes persist, mostly because the distinction between line management and co-operation is so stark with little experience of the middle ground of negotiation, balancing of priorities and controlled discussion. By contrast, those working in community organizations inevitably have more experience of people relationships which results in a developmental rather than confrontational approach to people and change. Community workers tend to develop skills in negotiation, outreach work and education within networks where organizational boundaries are osmotic. Unfortunately, the radical sociale economie or community sector remains marginalized within academic writing since few academics are acquainted with domestic community-based organizations.

9   Barriers to transformation

The crisis mind can offer no solutions. . . . The metaphors and concepts of minds deprived of the feminine principle have been based on seeing nature and women as worthless and passive, and finally as dispensable. These ethnocentric categorisations have been universalised, and with their universalisation has been associated the destruction of nature and the subjugation of women. But, this dominant mode of organising the world is today being challenged by the very voices it had silenced. These voices, muted through subjugation are now quietly but firmly suggesting that the western male has produced only one culture, and that there are other ways of structuring the world. Women's struggles for survival through the protection of nature are redefining the meaning of basic categories. They are challenging the central belief of the dominant world-view that nature and women are worthless and waste, that they are obstacles to progress and must be sacrificed. . . . And while Third World women have privileged access to survival expertise, their knowledge is inclusive not exclusive. The ecological categories with which they think and act can become the categories of liberation for all. (Shiva 1989: 223)

New partnerships are dependent on learning, social interaction and a confidence in the future. However, establishing a collaborative culture which supports emergent relationships is more difficult than it appears. Those struggling to develop innovative practices meet with resistance and a lack of understanding about development processes. Real partnership is not about 'hype' and declaration, but involves those who were previously hostile to one another actively collaborating on an equal basis, listening to each other's experiences and valuing the contributions of those who have been marginalized, sometimes for centuries. Women were advocates for ethical trading long before American gurus such as Fukuyama (1995) started talking about social capital and its significance within the world economy. Similarly, radical women were struggling to democratize management practices long before the public sector reforms. Women managers in the UK found public sector management frustrating and struggled to be heard within formal administrations. Consequently, they were enthusiastic about 'management by objectives' and to some extent the internal market. Much of women managers' thinking on management was not new, but what was significant was their approach to change and their commitment to injecting 'value' management criteria and practices. Many women soon became disillusioned with the New Public Management (NPM) and managerialism which focused more on efficiency. When they attempted to transform management structures they met powerful resistance which appeared to be rooted in:

- powerful gendered cultures which permeated the professions, management and politics;
- a legacy in public administrations of bureaucratic practices such as blame culture;
- forms of New Public Management or managerialism which worked against not with the grain of improved staff or user relationships;
- the persistent tensions visible in public sector organizations before and after reorganization including impression management or hype, role identity confusions, more responsibility but less power for managers and forms of reductionist and generic thinking, all of which undermined staff confidence in themselves and emergent relationships.

Women managers reported a deep-seated male culture at all levels within local government and in the health services. Not only is the glass ceiling still firmly in place in Britain, but so too are powerful gendered cultures which underpin organizations and approaches to change and management. Male cultures vary from organization to organization, but there are common themes, one of which is that men may value individual women as friends but continue to underrate and undervalue them in general. Women have to seek out new posts in order to gain promotion and credibility. When they are promoted it was often on the basis of peculiar local power struggles. An education director described how she had applied for many posts because she needed to leave an authority where her boss had made her life a misery:

> I applied for principal officer jobs but didn't get anywhere they all went to men. In the end I got my present post as director because the leader and chief were in dispute and one appointed me to spite the other. Most women in local government if they are considering more senior posts are unlikely to find directorships in their own authority, moving is usually a must. Women continue to believe that by proving their qualifications and competence that this will get them the job. The move to performance management systems does make this more likely, but a woman can collect qualifications and still not get the post.

Alison Halford (1993) recounted a similar story. Her appointment to a senior management post in the Merseyside police was due to the chief officer wanting to outdo his equivalent in Manchester; she was a token woman. Although opportunities did present themselves to women in the 1980s, most continued to encounter many obstacles when they sought promotion. They had to be persistent in their efforts if they wanted to secure a director post:

> When I was interviewed great emphasis was placed on my lack of management skills – but I soon realized that what this actually meant was that they disagreed with my management style: they thought I was too participatory and not dictatorial enough. I never didn't connect to my gender, but I was made to feel

uncomfortable and marginal. I had already left one city because I knew I would never get promotion there, I had been too challenging – and the system was corrupt, the interviews were rigged and they didn't operate proper procedures.

By the 1980s the number of women in management made discrimination less overt. However, women had to seek out allies and supportive environments if they were to be able to be innovative. Although formal status provided senior women with some added authority, this was offset by the informal gender cultures which worked against their credibility. Local government reorganization did provide women managers with opportunities, but once in senior posts they found themselves subject to levels of hostility which most had not previously experienced:

> The college was the worst place for women ever, it was snobby and snotty. It was a tin-pot regime and run by a priest with no idea how to manage and another manager who locked himself in his office all day.

The women who were more forceful in their desire for change and passionate about local government were the most threatening to their colleagues. Passion is challenging in any local government officer, but in women it is particularly threatening. Innovative women can easily be demonized as strange creatures in administration where passion is an alien concept. In Britain, being outspoken is challenging in itself and government officials are expected to conform. Not only were outspoken women demonized, but also those radicals from ethnic or working-class backgrounds. This was especially true in the Civil Service and local education departments where politeness and humility are valued above creativity. Managers noticed that those politicians and officers who were sensitive about their class origins tended to compensate for their own sense of insecurity by talking-up their work and national connections and sometimes bullying junior staff. Such officials were often more antagonistic to women managers and especially to those who questioned the very practices they were endeavouring to emulate. Within British institutions, class identity continues to influence personal interactions and relationships, but this is rarely discussed as a management issue:

> I don't think women suffer more from oppression than other groups, we have to find and build alliances. Too many assumptions are made about class. White middle-class women often assume male managers must also be middle class, when actually they are working-class men trapped in working-class identities.

Women from working-class communities recognized that local government was dominated by masculine management practices, but observed that men's and women's work relationships were rather less 'sexist' than those with neighbours or former managers from the private sector:

It's my husband and his friends who tried to stop we working – in the place I worked before all the managers assumed that women worked for 'pin money' and patronized us a lot, that is a lot less here.

Those who worked in private companies tended to be more tolerant of macho behaviour generally, saying that they had encountered much more extreme versions of sexism in their previous posts. One director thought that her experience in an accountancy firm had given her a better platform from which to judge local government management:

Of course, we still have to push for women's rights and support each other, but at least in local government we have the starting point of equal opportunities policies. In the private sector there are few equality policies and you have to be 'liked' to get on. If you antagonize a boss, you've had it – at least you have recourse to policy here.

Women valued equal opportunity policies, not because they were effective in changing cultures but because they legitimized a woman's right to be a manager and endorsed women's right to work. Within private sector firms women did not speak out because they knew that their rights were not enshrined in basic policy. Equality policies provide an anchor from which women can demand change. Where such policies were less acceptable, women felt less comfortable about making demands and were more likely to adapt themselves to the company culture and imitate male management models, not wanting to be different and therefore less likely to be promoted:

Although I was promoted, if you are not liked in the private sector you have no chance, even if you're good. You depend on largesse, therefore women conform and adapt more.

A manager's ability to develop practices was directly related to the type of management culture with which she has to deal and her authority within it. Male cultures which are physical make it even more difficult for a woman to be heard because she may be intimidated by displays of male strength. For instance, it was not unusual for male colleagues to use body language to dominate meetings: they might sit away from the table, splay their arms and legs, talk loudly or interrupt a lot. Even in local government management, which is not a very macho environment, it is common for male colleagues to trivialize women's work, to make jokes as a way of avoiding serious interaction and to direct discussions towards either greater or lesser formality:

Whenever I go and see him, he is always over informal, jokey and never stays on the subject for long; I'm sure he's not like this with other men, or perhaps they all joke and never talk shop. I think not, it's a way of keeping us outside decision-making. I think men are still deeply connected to simulated warfare –

when you try and pose a question they shoot – it's not that they mean much by this, it's just the way they behave – it's a habit that's not very constructive.

The lack of debate on gender relations has a negative impact on women, making it difficult to comment on management practices or internal relationships, or to refer to intimidating behaviour. In the 1980s women lacked the language and the confidence to articulate what they felt about gendered dynamics and about the way the male cultures oppressed them. Many departments developed confrontational and arguing cultures which did not intimidate women but made it impossible for them to be heard:

Basically it's an arguing culture – I used to have a boss who every week would argue and banter with me – in the end I decided to put a stop to these sessions because they were exhausting. Then he said how much he missed our meetings, he enjoyed them. They all behave like this, it's sort of gladiatorial. The difficulty women had when criticizing this approach to work was that male managers were 'good at it', there was not time to discuss anything and the basis for promotion was the ability to either be good at decisive crisis management or at least appear to be good at it.

The culture set the scene and context for all discussion and oppressed as many men as it did women:

It's not that individual men are so bad, they just conform to a culture they feel comfortable in. There is so much bravado and 'bullshitting'. In a punitive and paternalistic environment few people had the confidence to work in a different way from their colleagues, this affected a great many women's lives in the 1980s and continues to do.

Although management development was beginning to address flexible work practices, the need for training and crèches, these tended to be used by more junior staff; women managers felt obliged to prove that they could work full time. They were afraid that if they sought special treatment their work would suffer. All women had to struggle within the long hours culture, in addition to the tacit assumptions about them as women. They rarely raised the issue of gender or mentioned their own feelings in this context, which would only have further undermined them and their projects. The anger, stress and tension that this caused was mentioned by almost every women interviewed; to add insult to injury, when women's ideas were effective they were claimed by senior managers:

I've been very reinforced by management thinking and have set up quality initiatives which have been praised at quite senior levels but no one has ever attributed the changes to me or other women involved in them. Women still don't count as innovators at work; we are the servicers, the doers – we don't think or initiate, we serve and usually cope and make do.

Senior men tended to have wives who serviced them, did the shopping, cooking and child care. They were able to work the long hours which reinforced the 'long hours culture'. This culture of 'work, work, work' was said to be gender neutral when in fact it was gender insensitive. No exceptions were made for other commitments and managers could be expected to work from 7 am to 7 pm with those who rebelled being made to feel vulnerable.

Warring women

In spite of the long hours culture and the pressures on women, some were less critical of their male colleagues. Those with the most negative views on men tended to be the worst offenders:

> First you have to remember that men are like dogs, they fight in packs and the mere presence of a woman calms them down – trade union officials nor executives feel obliged to prove themselves to a woman.

Women dismissive of men doubted that gender relations would ever change. They had low expectations of men and put up with their ways. The believed that if anyone was going to make a difference it would be a woman, yet they criticized women for inertia or naivety. It was not the feminists who were hostile and dismissive of men but conservative women, because they had less confidence in social change and were therefore more frustrated and angry. Frequently this anger appeared to be directed at women rather than men. They felt that work negotiations were less complicated with men who saw events and relationships in stark and uncomplicated terms, compared to women who discussed difficulties and their own gender management strategies.

> Men make the decisions in pubs and bars and if you can't be bothered with all that you have to win by force of argument, by your personality. I've always worked with men, in fact I find it easier than working with many women. I'm not interested in all this weeping and gnashing of teeth. But I am interested in achievement. The one job I did not get was when I was interviewed by a woman.

If changing the playing field or the overall framework is impossible, then the only alternative is to respond with pragmatic solutions which involve much less thought and certainly less confrontation. Almost all women resent having constantly to appraise their gendered relationships, but most are forced into tactics and strategies in order to cope and survive in male environments.

Senior women were repeatedly criticized by women middle managers who had unrealistic expectations of them as managers. They wanted their female bosses to be both successful and powerful and also sympathetic.

They wanted women directors to be caring managers, in spite of the fact that the male culture made it impossible for them to be both effective and pleasantly laid-back at the same time; this was a schizophrenic role.

> I met a woman at a party and she started to harangue me about something. I just wanted a rest. I'm not friendly any more because it's not friendship they want, it's my patronage. It's very unequal sometimes they're wrong.

Middle managers were critical of their female bosses for not being 'soft and caring', for being weak and not confronting managers who opposed or criticized them. They did not want weak role models, they wanted a socialist Margaret Thatcher. Sometimes senior women found that they had run out of energy, were overwhelmed and intimidated by colleagues and oppressed by female staff:

> My boss is a very able woman, but she gets in a state, which makes her look incompetent. The men notice this at once. She then gets very confrontational and sets up unachievable objectives which she can't meet, so she gets aggressive and feels a failure. It's sort of self-defeating and rather depressing.

Women were clearly more upset by conflicts with each other than with men, which often involved support or administration staff and not colleagues. Secretaries can either be extremely loyal or hateful to women managers; they are rarely impartial. Isolated women in management frequently have to battle to get adequate support from those who automatically continue to service male colleagues. Doctors experienced this most acutely – unpopular female doctors are not helped by nursing staff.

In the 1980s few women adopted a feminized management style; none, however, doubted that women in general did want to democratize management practices. Women managers talked about a female distinctive approach, but many rarely felt it was appropriate to use it; in fact most did not find it easy to develop their own style, to be more open or more democratic. They had to win arguments in order to finance their projects and felt that being open about tactics was totally counterproductive in a male world.

This suggests that there is no such thing as a female management trait, but only different learnt responses and gender management strategies. Changing roles involves changing strategies and tactics, which is difficult. Many women had moved cities in order to be accepted, promoted or to make the transition from coping middle manager to strategic director. Those who had been activists and had then become senior managers in the same authority found the transition from one role to the other especially difficult when they continued to work with female friends. Renegotiating relationships with peers was stressful. Often senior women felt that their junior female managers had no idea of the constraints they were under:

> I promoted one woman who I know would make an excellent manager, she was experienced and sensitive, the problem was she knew all her colleagues and her prejudices about managers – after six months she resigned.

Women had a number of choices, some believed that the only way to real change was through ruthless, centralized direction, but this did not mean withholding information and being devious. Others thought that stealth was better than transparent targets. They had to choose appropriate tactics and strategies. At the tactical level clear differences arise between women, and this is especially the case with those in middle and senior management positions. Women managers learn to respond in accordance with the dominant management culture. A woman's political thinking does not necessarily determine her tactics. An analysis of manager qualities which is out of context can be misleading. Individual managers adopt many of the very practices they criticize precisely because they feel unable to challenge them. Successful women can be obsesses with work, zealous in their search for objectives and passionate about change; they can appear as driven:

> You can understand why men get so fed up with women constantly telling them to make improvements – I think we (women) should relax more. Women have to be careful, they present problems in a too diffuse and confused fashion, trying to encompass a perspective rather than be specific about something that needs tackling. While these women were scornful of some women's tactics and behaviour in general the women interviewed were extremely sympathetic and understanding of other women even when they disagreed with their own proposals. In the past women have appeared to be more critical of other women than were their male colleagues.

The tactics women use vary enormously and this causes deep divisions between them. Women managers tend to respect those who are astute, with naive women being held in disdain. There was a lack of sympathy among managers for the political woman because they often appeared naive, in spite of the fact that naivety was probably an asset during times of transformation. Those not held back by personal fears and motivated by a passionate desire for social change are often very effective at putting their views on the agenda. Although politicized themselves and concerned about value, most of the women managers were concerned with implementing change and persuading others of its necessity, not campaigning. Social change is driven by passion and commitment is all the more needed within static cultures. Politics and change are not rational activities.

Conflicts between women colleagues tended to revolve around whether they were people oriented or managerially driven (Franzway et al. 1989). Australian feminists documented the movement of activist women into administrative jobs within the state sector in the early 1980s and a similar shift occurred in Britain. They invented the term of 'femocrat' to describe those women administrators who became more concerned with efficiency than with social change. As many had been community activists during the 1970s they were seen by some to be turncoats. The women interviewed were less 'democrats' than politicized managers, but they did learn how to manipulate the management systems in order to achieve change. Femocrats could be said to be careerists by radical women while those who were more concerned with efficiency were often irritated by the innovators' insistence on social change:

> Some women do fit into the 'efficiency' and male environment better than others. Those women who relate to work in an individualist way and do not bring with them a commitment to a social values set and different way of working are not barred from promotion. In education women have been promoted for many years as administrators – but it does tend to be those women who are most concerned with preserving the status quo – and even they just miss the most prestigious posts. (Leeds manager)

There was a criticism of those who did not talk to women outside their grade or profession and could not empathize with the diverse gender management tactics of female colleagues. A general lack of openness about gender management strategies reinforced unnecessary hostilities. Within a hostile environment each woman has to assess how far she can push through changes and what she can expect as support. Those who have struggled up through an organization are often suspicious of women who are outsiders, or intellectuals or just appear too radical. This is especially true of those who have grown used to the dominant male cultures and do not necessarily want change. It should not be assumed that because gender cultures are biased against women, they do not get satisfaction from manipulating within traditional closed professions:

> There is a mythic, composite, able-bodied, middle-class, white male resister to change who are believed . . . to be ranged against all female, black and disabled people. In feminist literature women shine with all the virtues – as oppressed, as wronged, as victims. (Parkin 1992: 6)

Dowling (1982) called the dynamic generated when women collude with their own subordination the 'Cinderella complex'. This results in many women being more critical of challenging women than are men. Younger women who expect support from older women are surprised when they are shunned and find it difficult to comprehend this dynamic.

The caring conundrum

The conundrum for women is how to be credible in a male world; when to be credible they need to be accepted, they need to conform and to be effective they need to be challenging and imaginative. Management is a complex environment especially for women, who face the choice of 'making the system' work or challenging the framework and being marginalized.

Unfortunately the gendered pressures on women result in those who are most challenging appearing to be the least 'caring'. Current images of feminists portray them as the wreckers of marriages and homes. It is interesting how the popular view of women has shifted from their being a conservative force holding men back from strikes for the sake of children to the contemporary view that women are responsible for a lack of care, divorce rates and social instability. At various times in history women have had to struggle with their social realities in variety of ways. Women have to make difficult choices: to be married or single; to be childless or to have children in order to be successful within the public realm. A complex dynamic has grown up between those willing to prioritize ambition and success at the expense of social relationships and those who would call themselves socially committed.

Some can find the macho culture exhilarating and being highly efficient very rewarding. The pressures to work hard are irrelevant while great satisfaction is gained from making difficult systems work well. Those women who witnessed the shift in public administrations from red tape to a task-focused efficiency could see how tempting it was to become a workaholic for people with no dependants or social life. The go for it culture was grasped by many women because it provided real opportunities. However, there was a price for excelling at 'making do' and coping with all the contradictions new public management brought with it. Women saw many of their colleagues made redundant and others leave stressed or for early retirement. Some began to yearn for the former, less frantic, culture which was less efficient and in which male managers were not macho, just paternalist.

The contradictions presented by the managerial culture are not dissimilar from those in the professions. The 'care and cope' response is common in female professions while those in male professions are encouraged to question, decide and think:

> It is of course the traditional woman's role to service and care, and the job I have as a committee secretary is by its nature servicing, the whole of the Civil Service is servicing. We are all servicing politicians, it is a feminized profession. Of course, I feel by being so unthreatening in the way I do the job I am in effect colluding with both traditional gender relations and the 'system'. The more efficient I am, the better the system works. Women are trapped in perfecting systems at work which are oppressing them as officers and as women. (Davies 1995)

The reality of women's lives pushes them towards social relationships, not abstraction, and their lack of power towards conciliation rather than conflict. Many women do have a deep sense of right and wrong and are irritated and confused by those with less certainty and conviction. Often women managers were confused by their colleagues' lack of interest in the services and their arrogance towards the public and were irritated when they had to explain what appeared obvious to them. Some reflected that their own clarity and passion about public services had led them totally to misunderstand the traditional role of public officials. As many became more experienced they realized that what they had assumed to be valued skills and qualities of being committed, qualified and competent were in fact threatening; they expected to be capable, caring and conforming, not well-qualified strategic thinkers. Many women also wanted others to adopt female roles at work since radical women often pay for dissent by being rejected by other women. Those who were more successful at avoiding judgement in the past were in the main upper-class women who were never expected to have a domestic role and were therefore already closer to a male world. Patricia Hollis (1997) reveals the extent of the 'blue stocking' tradition in England in her biography of Jenny Lee, which demonstrates the trait of detachment from other women and from domesticity. The conclusion to be drawn from this is that the divide between women is still largely influenced by class, education and opportunity.

Caring can be a bad tactic

Traditionally women who sought public status had to shed their female role and associated conciliatory behaviour. By doing so they could lose the warmth of other women's support, which was the price they had to pay. These dynamics are subdued but they are not dead. Managers were quick to spot that those who exhibited 'attentive' behaviour in the boardroom may be liked but they were not effective. The banging and shouting boardroom tactics persist because even those who would like to challenge them do not. Women had to choose their tactics and strategies carefully; caring too much has been used to justify not promoting them.

Coping can also be equivalent to adapting to authoritarian cultures and behaviours. Those struggling in middle management or in female professions such as nursing may be 'caring' of clients or patients, but they can also be bullying when managing staff. The matron who was deferential to doctors was trained in a military style of management and was known as the dragon. Although harsh, this caricature demonstrates the contradictions faced by women at the top of traditional professions and organizations. Nurses may be caring but they are also deferential and underconfident and it is this inability to be free of the authoritarian culture which results in their finding ambiguous situations difficult to handle. Many are fearful of change and lack confidence in the future (Williams, Robins and Sibbald 1997). The present uncertainty within nursing in the UK is due to a confusion over roles and the justified fear that public sector changes will undermine the nurse's caring function. The lack of nurse status in service reconfigurations undermines the very working relationships desired by policymakers.

Doctors are trained to be leaders, not participants, which presents a problem to those wanting to develop emergent relationships based on consideration and care. Doctors rarely have an egalitarian approach to relationships. This is unfortunate. Although nurses may endorse the need for professional partnerships they do not want them to be at their expense, or to the detriment of caring relationships. Community nurses have been battling for integrated care for many years, but they do not want one-sided partnerships where they remain handmaidens to doctors or to have become managers which will remove them from direct contact with services users.

However, there is another perspective on these responses: although coping can indicate powerlessness, it is at least an active response and could be described as conciliatory or negotiatory. By contrast, the more male responses to powerlessness are to refuse to negotiate, to remain detached and disengaged. Disengagement is counterproductive to learning and a detachment from the needs of others does little to overcome difficulties, to generate discussion or to find new ways of working. Only in macho cultures are women exploited for their willingness to respond and 'make do'.

The problem with the coping response is however that it narrows the women's vision and results in their being too deferential and accommodating, it is not transforming but reactive behaviour, it lacks strategic direction.

A more strategic response was demonstrated by the local government managers who risked 'act-up' without pay increases in order to develop new initiatives and projects. They were strategic in their thinking and able to handle conflict and make the necessary personal adjustments in order to be involved in emergent practices. Most are not. The future of partnerships depends on management recognition of those who are already struggling for egalitarian practices. The gendered nature of public debate and of organizations marginalizes much of the collaborative work in community and pilot projects. The innovative practice of bringing together the professions often takes place on the margins of mainstream organizational life. Yet this is where women in particular are bringing about cultural transformations. As long as emergent activities remain unrecorded, innovators will continue to be oppressed by authoritarian professions, organizations and cultures.

Professional power relationships are less pronounced within local government, but the experience of changing roles and the caring conundrum is just as relevant. Local government managers are also reluctant to give up the security of preset agendas and the safety that time-honoured practices provides (Macalpine and Marsh 1996). Management is still divided between those who are seen as 'soft' or 'hard' – although in many organizations this is changing. Women may be employed for their personal skills of listening, caring and sharing, but they have to struggle for more strategic positions. While some executives recruit women for their transforming skills, they do not understand that these decision-making roles are subject to hostility, or that their colleagues may not value women. They become disillusioned with their new director when she fails to deliver. Men fail to appreciate how difficult it is for isolated women to bring staff on board with new initiatives. Although some executives may support their besieged women directors, they remain uncertain about developing more sustaining work environments and most often leave the individual women to fight it out.

Innovators made scapegoats

Within traditional gender cultures those women who challenge management frameworks and efficiency continue to be vulnerable. Isolated women who challenge traditional practices, whether in management or in the professions, are often disliked by other women and can easily become scapegoats within local conflicts. One dramatic example of this dynamic is Dr Daly, who was sacked from a hospital after nurses decided that they did not like her or her ideas. She was Irish, single, attractive, childless and, more importantly, very committed to her work as a haematologist. The patients supported her unstintingly and she inspired confidence in the parents of children with leukaemia. In spite of her clinical expertise, she was subject to a barrage of complaints and rumours from nursing staff who were encouraged to write notes on her behaviour. She was active in meetings, questioned decisions and attempted to improve testing and other procedures in the department. After some time she was suspended and then dismissed – she won her case but lost the battle. She did not achieve reinstatement, in spite of patients lobbying their members of parliament. The gossip about her made national news and circulated around the medical profession across the country. She was made a scapegoat within the profession.

Men who question traditional practices may not be liked but they can also be praised for their bravery in speaking out. Women by contrast are not expected to speak out or be brave; they are ridiculed for being outspoken or critical. Men have noticed and been surprised at the level of animosity towards women who do not conform to the thinking and practices of their group.

The contradictions thrown up during the public sector reforms have mostly spiralled around the male gendered culture and have involved radical women who were recruited for their creativity and later punished for their deviation from traditional female gender roles. The turbulent times within health and local government resulted in those more imaginative chief executives headhunting women whom they had observed to be more capable of managing change within a difficult political climate. These women were not afraid to take risks, make mistakes, talk through strategies and more importantly could communicate with and inspire staff. The difficulty for both women directors and the men who appointed them was that many of their staff, including professionals and managers, were not ready for women leaders and remained very prejudiced against challenging women. The result was that many capable women in local government were handed a 'poisoned chalice' of difficult restructuring which few wanted to handle.

The friction was most acute between senior women and local politicians who attacked female directors for being 'middle-class feminists'. One woman chief officer recalled how she managed to survive only because the chief executive had supported her. But in spite of his public support she still had to endure constant references to her personal life in the press which were instigated by local Labour politicians. Hostility to senior women managers is often orchestrated in the press, aided and abetted by local politicians interested in personal kudos and votes. It is common for these politicians to advocate the same restructuring which a woman director is later criticized for: 'They like the fact you've got ideas during a time of crisis but they don't really want you to put them into practice.' Many said that they had been naive about party political groupings and thought that when a conflict occurred they would be supported.

The connections between innovation, challenge and scapegoating are real. The fears of challenging women, especially those in more senior and isolated positions, were and remain a reality. Those working within authoritarian organizations where the blame culture was prevalent were all vulnerable to attack, personal abuse, gagging clauses and being made scapegoats for other people's inactivity. The individuals who 'blow the whistle' on problems and abuse are in effect pointing the finger at entire work communities. The community then reacts out of inertia and a fear of activity to attack the messenger, the whistle-blower, and locate a scapegoat. Throughout the 1980s and 1990s whistle-blowing in the NHS increased as the blame culture intensified.

The blame culture

The women who felt most frustrated and least optimistic in management were those who worked in very authoritarian authorities where the blame culture made managers reluctant to take risks, engage in new initiatives or deviate in any way from tradition. All but the brave hide within a blame culture and avoid taking risks, however small. Extending relationships or working with other agencies and departments are especially difficult when you could be blamed for not sticking to traditional practices, not fulfilling all the existing obligations, or merely presenting as too confident. Within public administrations where formalities appeared as if set in stone, those breaking out would be criticized for any minor deviation from normal practices and for unsettling the work environment. In such an environment even letters and memos are standardized and those attempting to make changes, however small, are viewed as nonconformists and therefore threatening. Problems are ignored until they become crises for which someone has to be blamed. Even those in senior management behaved in this way, especially if they had only ever worked within one authority:

> We had a problem of litter, but instead of looking at how to improve the service the senior management team all sat around blaming each other. Every morning we'd have a meeting supposedly to go through significant issues. What really happened was that everyone attacked each other – it was a bruising experience and really a test to see if you were tough enough for management. Senior management can be very unpleasant. There is a lot of backbiting and bitchiness – when things go wrong they don't admit it. The old town clerk was very arrogant. He always blamed everyone but himself for poor services. Fortunately he's left now and life is better. What I really hate is the use of blame – so you never change the system, so something doesn't happen again, you merely catch the culprit or console the person who owns up – it's the 'woe is me' or 'it's not me guv' syndrome – who cares who's to blame as long as we can prevent it happening again. The blame culture was also seen as a very macho management style.

The blame culture encourages bullies, not necessarily physically to abuse staff but to intimidate them. Forms of bullying were reported by women who were isolated or had to work with difficult chief executives who would subject them to subtle forms of physical pressure:

> He would sit opposite me in meetings and disagree with everything I said. The last (woman) assistant director left because of his intimidation, he would withhold information from her, knowing that information is power.

Where managers were attempting to promote themselves rather than their work they made use of the punitive culture to get their own way. When their efforts turned to failures they blamed less powerful employees whom they made into scapegoats. Some work cultures were not aggressive but patronizing, formal and polite ('Gentleman's Club') in which women were congratulated for their female gender roles of 'mother', 'wife' or sometimes 'sex object' and mildly criticized if they did not appear to be caring enough about their partners or families:

> It's a very old fashioned environment of paper pushing and formality. You cannot get anything done by talking to people. It has to be minuted and passed around – being direct, I think, is sometimes seen as offensive by the older male officers, they don't expect to get much done and don't want to be shown up.

The 'Gentleman's Club' culture was common in many local authority education departments which were powerful as the largest budget holder. Education managers saw themselves as superior to other officers; they were and are very attached to the formalities of the bureaucratic traditions.

Education departments remain secretive and authoritarian, even after the reforms and the introduction of the Local Management of School (LMS). Women managers in education departments were particularly frustrated:

> They are obsessed with systems and never delegate, they treat people as machines. The director is a systems man, he likes everything and everyone tied down – they are scared of anything not pre-ordained and in the rule book. I think they do not know what is coming. Local government will be challenged in a way that no group of managers would ever have imagined. They see no reason to change, but the political changes towards budget holding and contracting are going to force everyone into a more reasoned perspective of how they are managing and what impact it's having.

Government expenditure cuts and contracting exacerbated this situation. Many education officers and departments became even more competitive and entrenched in their thinking about LMS. Several other women in education talked about colleagues not caring about education, schools or children:

> Many of the old guard are men who are underconfident and will never manage to cut through interdepartmental competition and hierarchies – and are not brave enough to speak out even if they disagreed with something.

The dominant culture within education departments bred inertia, very little sense of responsibility and a huge sense of fear tinged with a smug superiority. One woman working in community education reported:

> It is not too harsh to say that we have a management culture which has no collaboration, nor forum to discuss work, the culture deadens creativity and initiative. Long-standing officers who had been used to local government when services were the same year in year out were unprepared for change and did not know how to adjust.

Those men who were also irritated by bureaucracy saw new management techniques as a way of undermining the oceanliner tendency of some departments which drifted onwards and forwards no matter what was happening in the outside world. However, they did not challenge much for although they experienced the same organizational problems, they did not understand how change was possible. The men who were critical of red tape and bullish behaviour sometimes appeared to be more intimidated by smooth-talking bureaucrats than the women. They rarely spoke in meetings although they might back up women when they raised items in team meetings.

Unfortunately the internal market and management thinking have not rid local government of its blame culture or of the fear of change among many staff, men and women. Consultants working in London boroughs report the same fear of risk-taking, which if anything has increased (Macalpine and Marsh 1996). Although many senior managers are frustrated by this culture they are also under more pressure to deliver change and improve outcomes, but do not understand how to approach the problem. They assume that they can decree learning and changes in the same way that they can allocate budgets and planning proposals. They assume that the fear among staff is related to redundancy and sacking. As few in local government management have been made redundant they are unable to comprehend why staff are still so fearful. In fact the fear of making mistakes is not necessarily directly related to real risk or even redundancy, but to work cultures where individuals are criticized for any suggestion or comment. Staff at all levels become afraid to voice an opinion in case it is wrong. As the world changes and there is a need to analyse processes rather than facts and build relationships with other people, a blame culture can devastate a whole organization; for instance, some social services departments are frozen in fear which results in their being totally unable to adapt.

In a context which has been very controlled, a sudden lack of structure towards open-endedness is perceived as dangerous by staff; even training courses can be threatening because participants have to decide how to behave and fear being wrong and making mistakes. The lingering command–control culture is influencing the way in which public sector agencies are developing and undermining partnership and quality improvements. This 'do as I say' culture is prevalent in many British institutions and results in anyone who voices a dissenting view being named as a whistleblower. The culture has been reinforced by 'gagging clauses' which silence all employees from speaking outside the organization. Those most critical of practices either resign, change jobs or simply retire. Working collaboratively requires the time to talk and the confidence that managers are not going to react strongly at mistakes. New Public Management was supposed to have undermined these attitudes, but some would suggest that it has intensified them.

The impact of managerialism

The introduction of contracting intensified competition, not collaboration and reinforced the blame culture. What initially appeared as a liberation from red tape resulted in forms of performance management systems which rewarded cheap activities, fast results, macho and individualist behaviour. Associated evaluation systems tended to justify central measures and standard dimensions which ignored and rejected the judgement of specialists or professionals. What women managers desired from the dismantling of the bureaucracies was an openness to inclusive management, but what they got were tighter management systems which reduced the time for relationships with other staff and users. Contractual specifications were for the most part based on the traditional activities and easily quantifiable measures. The emphasis on value for money (VFM) efficiency measures resulted in huge increases in work activities for all staff, irrespective of their profession or grade. The time available for informal face-to-face communication plummeted. Almost all staff complained that they would like to develop new relationships but did not have the time. The efficiency measures increased output or productivity dramatically but reduced face-to-face contact:

> Community nurses are the least valued within the NHS, yet they whizz around their patients and can do ten diabetic injections before coffee – one worries that they have time to say 'hallo'. (HA officer 1997)

Practitioners reported that they lacked time for collaborative relationships with colleagues, staff and patients. Financial pressures and central performance targets had a domino effect on senior staff downwards. After the reforms senior managers spent inordinate amounts of time analysing whether their organization or department had met specified targets. More recently the focus is on risk assessment, possible mergers, litigation and new service configurations (mergers). While most practitioners were in agreement with national policies relating to community care, role extension and flexible team working, they were unenthusiastic about the new practices if they took them away from existing work responsibilities or if they felt exploited. Within the context of reduced budgets and increased activities, practitioners were attempting to improve service quality.

The impact on staff

By the 1990s many nurses were at breaking point; the levels of stress, sickness and turnover were high. They were expected to do more work and develop new protocols with reduced staff levels on the wards. Increased stress levels and work pressures were not only experienced by nurses, but also by managers who were demonized as the villains. Middle managers fared badly from 'downsizing' and those who did not lose their jobs, ended up doing their sacked colleagues' work. The merger of middle management posts and constant restructuring resulted in managers working excessively long hours in very hostile working environments. The pressure to increase performance made it extremely difficult for staff to develop new relationships. Many multi-professional teams and examples of integrated care were undermined by the increased activities and restrictive directives. New partnerships and relationships went unrewarded within the accountancy measurement framework. For example, a nurse manager who in 1995 developed new joint practice protocols involving consultants, midwives and managers was told the next year, after management cuts, that she would no longer have time for such activities as she was to be responsible for three other directorates. Improving performance by increasing activity levels reduces the time available for developing new relationships. As activities and the workloads grew with the introduction of new performance targets, staff numbers were reduced. The 'do it now and quick' culture intensified:

> The demands placed on people now due to restructuring are much greater, and there are now a lot of people in local government doing jobs they know nothing about. The culture does not encourage questioning, so they hide and pretend and fight to ward off criticism and comment. Those who do question get the blame and are abused.

The message that human face-to-face relationships are essential to networking and partnership appears not to have penetrated British institutions and managers find ever more ways of avoiding such contact with staff or customers. This bodes ill for those seeking to transform organizations by the involvement of staff and the creation of a collaborative culture.

After fifteen years of restructuring in the UK, public sector staff are completely mistrustful of managers and governments. An environment of mistrust has been created which cannot be dissipated merely by 'friendly words' or new rhetoric. The effects of the internal market and annual contracts have generated low morale and hostility among frustrated, disillusioned and insecure employees (Coote and Hunter 1996). Precise figures on the number of job losses in Britain due to public sector restructuring are difficult to establish, but they are considerable. Those in part-time and junior posts suffered the most; the demands for more flexible working patterns hit part-time women working on the front line. While the pace of change may have been unavoidable and flexible work patterns inevitable, frontline staff and junior practitioners suffered an unnecessary loss of control over their working lives and an increase in work activities for little return. Professionals and managers also work long hours and suffer from high levels of stress, but they have also increased their autonomy, status and pay levels far in excess of those of frontline staff. The Institute of Health Service Management estimated that 86% of managers suffered from stress and that 30 million working days were lost each year due to stress-related illnesses, costing the country around £5 billion (*IHSM* 23 November 1995). Public sector staff were overworked, mainly because of demands for increased productivity, staff shortages and high levels of turnover. Of nurses 75% found their jobs stressful and their suicide rate doubled between 1990 and 1992; doctors had a 72% greater risk of suicide than any other group in Britain (*IHMS* 2 November 1995). By the mid-1990s NHS managers had started to advertise for nurses from overseas because newly qualified nurses were not applying for jobs in the UK. Therapists such as psychologists, physiotherapists and occupational therapists were also in short supply. Nurses are experiencing a loss of role identity, job satisfaction and lack confidence in management. Nurses are also subject to conflicting messages from senior management teams and their professional bodies:

> Often nurses are being asked to conform to contradictory systems within the same organization. On the one hand they are asked to conform to national occupational standards and on the other to be flexible in their roles. For instance, inter-professional teams are encouraged to devise new roles and staff relationships by one director while another dictates orders. Those who were most active in the developmental working groups felt betrayed and demoralised by the autocratic directives. (Worsley 1996)

There has been dramatic haemorrhaging of nurses and doctors from the NHS. The medical profession is experiencing its biggest spillage from training ever. There were shortages of junior doctors, general practitioners and consultants in almost all major cities.

In local government staff morale is also low. The level of stress among teachers was so high in 1997 that the then minister refused to believe so many teachers wanted to retire and accused some of fraudulent claims of sickness (*Guardian* 8 January 1997). Ken Young (1996) reported that many local government managers had lost their interest in service development and that they were too demoralized to think it worth considering future services. Women managers had observed that few were interested in strategic change in the 1970s and 1980s and the reforms had exacerbated this situation.

The more innovative officers left local government altogether to work in consultancies:

> The overwhelming impression given by those findings was of a local government engulfed in a tidal wave of centrally inspired change, with officers wielding limited influence as the local mediators of the change process. (Young 1996: 364)

Local government social service staff reported a loss of status and direction in their work and felt deskilled. By the 1990s local government chief officers were no longer so convinced that contracting was going to assist service delivery or development and were aware of the effects on staff morale and motivation. This more sceptical approach led to a reluctance to extend Compulsory Competitive Tendering (CCT) to white-collar professional services in local government. Chief officers began to recognize that their staff were overburdened by paperwork (Young 1996). National auditors questioned the basis of internal charging costings which appeared to have little connection with real costs. While there was a greater awareness of user interest and the need to consider service quality as well as routine tasks, many are sceptical that managers or the government were really concerned about service quality; cost cutting was in any case essential given reduced government expenditure.

Those more confident senior managers did attempt to resist national directives which were in conflict with what they considered to be 'fair and good' practice. However, the majority of senior managers felt unable to do this; they were under no illusion that their jobs were at risk. The majority of chief officers felt as vulnerable as their employees – only a very few executives spoke out in defence of their staff under the Thatcher regime, even though most recognized the contradiction between development policies and tough restrictive practices. The impact of the internal market on staff was common knowledge and yet rarely recorded in policy documents. Yet managerialism and its tools has had a dramatic impact on professionals, staff and managers. The efficiency culture and managerialism have squeezed out the time available for personal relationships as these were a fault in the system.

Later research has shown that face-to-face relationships are the basis of joint practices; collaboration is dependent on the professionals' attitudes to each other and on time being available for them to communicate. The consequence of the efficiency culture has been that very few staff or practitioners have any spare time to develop relationships and those who do initiate change invariably do so in their own time. Managerial techniques and systems have not only removed the personal and the social from work, they have also resulted in measurement systems which do not value what matters. Innovative practitioners report that emergent relationships and collaborative work are not only unrecorded, they are also undervalued. Partnership, inter-agency working and multi-professional work all require development time. Finance is needed to develop processes. These activities cannot be an 'add-on' to mainstream tasks reinforced by management systems which work against relationships and people values. Unfortunately in Britain there are still too few commissioning bodies who are willing to pay for such development.

Persistent dynamics and tensions

The knowledge frameworks which separate policy and practice remain powerful because they are endorsed within managerial measurement systems. The tensions created by managerialism can still be observed in the current of context where policymakers call for partnership not competition. These include tensions caused by 'spin-doctoring' and hype, the rhetoric of devolved power in the context of increased centralization and the hostility of professional staff to generic systems and standardization. The gendered infrastructure fans these tensions rather than ameliorates them. Where there is an emphasis on speedy results and a climate of competition there is a tendency for managers to 'talk-up' their work and their part in delivering services and change. Impression management is not a new phenomenon – but one which has been greatly advanced by corporate hype and political 'spin-doctoring'. Those managers not involved or interested in the impact of management on staff frequently keep their distance from difficult situations and then proclaim their role in managing the 'difficult people'. Often it was women who had to negotiate between the various parties, either staff or members of the public, in order to untangle obstacles to change. Male colleagues were said to blow up problems in order to demonstrate their ability as crisis managers. Women tend to do the opposite and intervene before conflicts have time to develop. They also tend to underplay their role and activities and feel uncomfortable with the charade of formal meetings. Impression management was continually mentioned by women as the tactic used by poor managers in order to promote themselves as dynamic 'troubleshooters' when they were actually inadequate communicators.

> The other day I had to sort out a difficult problem to do with allocation and schools which the press would have been very interested in – but precisely because I did manage to sort it out it was assumed to have little importance or something anyone could have handled. By contrast one of the other managers, a man, is thought to be experiencing a very difficult management situation with staff. But it is difficult precisely because he hasn't talked to staff, won't negotiate with them, and cannot handle it. All the other managers think he is strong and has a vary hard job – they don't think he is being macho and incompetent. I'm not sure in this instance whether they would respect a woman for acting in this way or view her as a failure. The real problem is men like crisis, and women prefer to plan and negotiate.

This story was told to many women and the middle managers were unanimous in their agreement that such a scenario was common. Most senior managers said that they had personally experienced similar situations or knew other women who had. Talking up problems does tend to be a 'male' response, while the ability to manage is a quieter and more conciliatory manner remains invisible. Women continue to underplay their role in work projects or not to mention their involvement at all. Those who linger under the illusion that hiding and appearing humble are good tactics within a male world are mistaken. Those who solve problems before they have been identified as problems are rarely noticed as having senior manager potential; by contrast, crisis management continues to be applauded.

More responsibility, less power

The contracting environment created an 'Alice in Wonderland' scenario where those with least power are expected to be the most strategic, innovative and collaborative, while government and executives sit back, restructure, provide less finance and reduce local powers. Although the internal market and the purchaser–provider split did devolve responsibility, managers given local budgets were unsure how to respond to this new role and many discovered that although they had been given more responsibility, they had no power to change budgets, targets or perform- ance criteria. Some health and social care purchasing managers found that they had less power to decide who should receive what services and when than they had under the previous planning regimes. There was no real understanding of how to control budgets or of the social basis on which the budget was spent.

Senior managers inspired by the notion of devolved contracting and tighter performance management were frustrated when purchasing managers floundered and appeared unable to handle contracting; they did not grasp that there was a contradiction between their dictatorial style of management and the learning required of administrators if they were to become responsive managers. For example, social service purchasing managers were given greater responsibility without control over finances or strategic service development and they began to complain of the same frustrations as women managers when working within the traditional bureaucracies. One woman director who was aware of this problem attempted to increase devolved financial control:

> I made everyone's budget public, which resulted in some managers saying that I wasn't supporting them. They thought I was blaming them. They didn't realize we had to know what costs were to assess priorities. So I'd ask what their roles were. If they couldn't answer, I told them they'd better find a role because I didn't want pen pushers on £30,000 a year.

Generic and mechanical management

Public administrations in the UK continue to be systems driven and managers to be technocrats and tough-doers. Traditionally administrations relied on set rules and standards, procedures involved endless committees, reports and formal memos. What occurred between meetings appeared to be less important than getting the formalities of the minutes right. The tendency to think system not people remains strong in public admin- istrations (if weakened) and determines the attitude to change. Such a perspective is mechanical in its approach to implementing change, it focuses on the past, on classification and on making the systems work rather than on developing staff.

Those managers who commented on the inadequacy of management processes and the impact of restructuring on staff were likely to be labelled as 'wimps'. Energetic managers were often irritated by service or clinical detail and certainly by those staff who moaned; they relied heavily on textbook management. Many in the civil service and the NHS are 'fast-tracked' through the graduates schemes and lack experience of grass- roots problems. In the 1980s private sector executives were brought into public bodies to make them leaner and more efficient. This only further undermined those most committed to local services. One health executive said she could think of only one chief executive who understood the need for management to be anchored in service and user knowledge:

> Only one of the chief executives of purchasing authorities has any professional background and few are women. They cannot predict outcomes. This is frustrating because the NHS reforms could be made to work to the advantage of the disadvantaged, but this will not happen if managers are driven by a knowledge of social need and service. Those graduates who are fast-tracked on general management schemes and who grew up in the early 1980s do not have this knowledge nor in general commitment to social change – they are careerists. (Director of Priority Services 1996)

It is a lack of a synergy between these two knowledge frameworks which is at the root of boundary–management tensions, as well as being at the root of resolving the problem of sustaining individual learning and autonomy within formal systems. The combination of the civil servant's intellectual mindset and the British authoritarian culture rendered the spirit of many a cultural change programme redundant. It is not a coincidence that most continuous improvement and organization development programmes have been remoulded in public administrations to become technocratic systems. There is a constant search for the perfect system rather than effective and responsive services. This is reflected in the trend towards functional mapping, formal audit and logistic planning. A perfect management system is sought whereby the unpredictability of staff is eradicated, and where they are compelled to comply to blueprints often devised by those divorced from local realities. This tendency runs counter to learning and therefore to the development of more inclusive forms of management. The functional and systems approach to management tends to ignore individual experience, and undermine individual judgements and by its very nature matches staff to systems.

Within a contracting context, where finances are limited, the systems approach tends to reinforce the accountant's or treasury perspective, which undermines social capital and social relationships. Both the managerial and systems approach places financial priorities above those of users, service quality and staff (Gray and Jenkins 1993). Managers are reduced to pushing staff harder and harder to increase outputs and have to be confident to resist being driven by financial targets and standard performance measures:

> No one is good at presenting information on how to measure effectiveness, and the community sector is vulnerable in this respect – but the measure on the acute sector of 'final consultant episodes' tells us absolutely nothing about the quality or impact of the clinical care provided. (Health authority chair 1997)

The tensions between professionals and managers also reflect their very different approaches to individuals and to the organization of work.

Whereas previously in larger bureaucracies the two traditions of management and professional training could operate side by side, in smaller agencies this became impossible. Professionals are trained to concentrate on individual clients. Medics and other professionals dislike generic systems because they undermine their professional judgement and ability to make 'appropriate' as opposed to reflex decisions. The introduction of managerialism and the internal market was clearly intended to shift power from the professionals to the managers and to reduce professional autonomy. With hindsight, although the internal market did take power away from individual doctors, the medical establishment remains strong. Corporatism and generic management had an electrifying effect on medics but they also had unifying effect on previously warring colleagues. The introduction of managerialism and generic practices did lead to an increased tension between professionals and managers, but this is changing; the tensions now concern the type of management approach adopted by management and who decides performance indicators.

Unfortunately, many professionals have created a prison for themselves by reinforcing their establishment. Doctors are the gatekeepers of minimum standards but they are also frequently dinosaurs when it comes to changing roles and new practices. While they protect individual patients they can be the most intransigent parties in partnerships and in preventive and community care. While the male professions, such as medicine, are masterful at protecting existing services and individual rights, they are slow to recognize that there is a need to collaborate. Unfortunately, the contracting environment has shifted power but it has not removed doctors' power to block change and development, those initiatives which do not involve doctors are weak.

Gender and managerial cultures

Women reported that men appeared to have great faith in technical systems and very little confidence in learning and relationships. Often technical solutions appeared to be pursued simply because managers had a fear of personal interaction and lack of respect for people management. Within a diverse and changing world this preference is not just nonsensical it runs counter to business needs and to learning and change. The tendency towards perfect systems appears to be a rather male tendency and one certainly encouraged by male gender cultures. It is frequently observed how male managers appear to be pleased by systems, and satisfied by the pleasure of fitting together information in neat chunks within prescribed systems. This is unfortunate as there is a need for new less controlling frameworks in order that emergent relationships can breathe and new work realities can evolve.

The management approach put forward by more challenging women is open but firmly rooted in a social-value base which provides the confidence for change. Women managers were attempting to apply professional principles to management and to develop forms of inclusive and flexible structures which could cope with diversity while also underpinning general principles of fair practices and equity across the board. They realized that inclusive managements could not evolve within the contracting environment or through tight managerial control.

Unfortunately, the capacity of more radical women to transform management was undermined by the gendered nature of managerialism as much as it was within the bureaucratic public administrations. The colonization of managerialism has been so powerful that there is little public debate about its impact outside informal discussions. Yet, many women soon realized that 'transparency' alone did not make the criteria more appropriate or compensate for the central driving motor of financial control. Davies (1995) and Pollitt (1990) both suggest that the contracting environment had resulted in more macho cultures than those of the establishment bodies. In spite of this many policy-makers and managers remain doubtful about the value of 'softer' management practices. They remain unconvinced that the time taken for staff development is worth the cost. The systems people dominate. Those who tend to work in consultancies on change programmes are frequently disappointed when their work is never implemented. The fear of openness and risk taking remains in many public agencies. The trend of removing all risk through generic management does not result in greater sensitivity to local or user needs, but a greater control of staff at all levels, irrespective of experience and training.

> The new manager turns out to have many of the same characteristics as the old. He remains distant and controlled. He takes a critical stance towards the arguments and established practices of others, asking constantly for outcome data, cost information and performance measures. He follows his own convictions, is tough minded in that he must take hard decisions about 'what the market brings' without being swayed by the appeals of sympathy or particular cases. Above all he is a strong and active decision-maker who will not dodge controversy and confrontation, be it with staff or the public. (Davies 1995: 168–169)

Although various forms of contracting and purchasing have stimulated agencies to be innovative in niche markets, even after restructuring many habits acquired in the bureaucratic administrations lingered on. In some authorities the worst of both worlds dominated local agencies and relationships. The speed of change emphasized crisis and impression management. Women noticed that it was impossible to discuss difference and new practices within an organization where managers were reinforced for not talking, not thinking about consequences and being given kudos for their skills at crisis management. Most public sector managers had learnt their skills within the bureaucratic administrations and were in effect 'old managers' in 'new manager' clothes, most remained attached to masculine values and traditional practices (Davies 1995: 168–169).

Davies (1995) and Cox (1992) have both suggested that managerialism has created detached managers even more devoted to the rough, tough manager model and generic systems which can be applied in any type of organization anywhere in the world.

> New managerialism involves a challenging and questioning, the current aggressive style of interaction. . . . It assumes that money is the main motivational currency. The performance culture demands this, everyone is aware of that, individual appraisal and performance review are never far around the corner . . . some writers have begun to refer to a clutter of mistrust and have questioned the appropriateness of it for healthcare. Certainly it would seen that the very factors which often bring nurses into nursing – commitment, altruism, service ideals the same ideals that encourage them to come in early, go home late and work their breaks – are without a place in this model. (Davies 1995: 169)

The same frustrations of a lack of interest in service detail and process and a preoccupation with systems intensified after the introduction of managerialism. Women managers became more irritated by the pressure to reduce all information to sound bites and accountancy categories, rather than focus on users and effective outcomes. In the early 1990s the struggle over performance indicators began and specialists started to try to find ways of demonstrating the value of process and development, and of linking staff development with service quality. Yet the more contracting was driven by cost cutting the harder this became. The contracting environment, far from generating a synergy between learning, change and service improvements was working in the opposite direction. Where financial control dominated organizational restructuring as a priority, even the most innovative manager could alter the direction of changes towards public service improvements. Throughout the 1980s and early 1990s efficiency dominated over quality and effectiveness within the service sector where financial control rules and a social transformation is dependent on the value of the organization leading and driving not only operations but also staff.

The fragmentation of services and the narrowness of management thinking separates organization. A more holistic view and whole systems approach is needed if the management systems are to develop and service integrated care. Too often when staff voice their concerns they are penalized not rewarded. It is hardly surprising that each month new cases of abuse or neglect are highlighted in the press. Some of these cases take years to surface. This is not because the staff are terrible, they are humans trapped in blame cultures where anyone who speaks out is attacked. The culture within institutional settings and in established organizations determines how the majority of employees will act. A blind faith in technical systems does nothing to change the cultural nuances in organizations, which are often welded together by powerful male cultures. These act as glue to closed cultures inhibiting discussion and reinforcing silence. Silence and group loyalty are closely related. Most professions and groups reinforce loyalty. Too often, such loyalty to the group merely reinforces passivity, inertia and silence about events and information which is critical to complaints and service improvements. Moving beyond 'gang' mentality and from closed to more open cultures requires many changes. Apart from service reconfiguration and restructuring, staff need support and training if they are to open up. If employees are not rewarded for changing their behaviour they will remain firmly attached to their gang and firmly rooted in their boxes at work.

Partnerships and responsive services depend on people and agencies becoming more open and more responsive to diversity and new situations. Some have to learn the skill of juggling roles and being both generalist manager and focused specialist. Managers have to learn to value diversity and process as well as order and standards and risk taking the initiative in meetings and with colleagues. Those involved in change and inter-agency work have to be able to understand the alternative position and the thinking of people in very different contexts. This can be difficult for those who have pursued a single career route and have little experience outside their chosen profession. Many in public administrations are institutionalized and underconfident of breaking with traditional formalities. The inertia of many men is also connected to their gender role models and notions of masculinity. Many are reluctant to make fools of themselves, they are silent about anything they cannot predict or control. Consequently they have a lack of confidence in change and handle ambiguity badly. They are also hesitant about new relationships and new roles. This bodes ill for those desirous of joint working practices, and only further points to the significance of women who have moved professions and are not fearful of change. It is often women who fulfil these specifications.

Traditional, transactional management remains a problem in many public administrations. Attitudes have changed but closed cultures are still prevalent in central and local bodies. Many managers working in formerly industrial cities work within closed institutions which have roots in industrial and trade union histories. There remains a reluctance to shed this past and a powerful mismatch between the traditional cultures and visionary change agents. Many women would like to carve out more collaborative relationships were it not for these intransigent gender cultures.

10 Transformation: a gendered process: post command, post market and post postmodern

In spite of the jargon that 'employees are our main asset', efficiency drives and downsizing have undermined morale and employee relationships at a time when staff motivation is the key to the success or failure of organizations in western democracies. Companies have made great strides in the improvement of technical processes but they continue to treat employees as cogs in machines. Organizations have been restructured to become mean and lean, but brain dead. Employers are demanding far too much of employees and corporate ethics remain largely 'hot air' totally divorced from internal realities. Companies are people, organizations do not exist without staff. Yet in the boardroom the disjuncture between soft and hard management issues has reinforced a lack of internal commitment rather than inspired employees within change programmes. For many years the trade unions were cited as the cause of resistance, yet the demise of the trade unions has not resulted in a creative workforce. Creativity is not generated by a loss of autonomy but an increase in it.

Delusions are common in management; one is that financial (hard) management is more important than people (soft) management, another is that management is a rational and technical subject which can be decontextualized from internal realities and cultures. Managerialism has reinforced the notion that management systems are movable, unaffected by staff feelings, experiences and views. Expensive change programmes fail because employees and their views are disregarded. In fact the chasm between staff and corporate concerns is one of the reasons why the impact of poor morale and worsening work conditions on companies and management innovation continues to be ignored. Yet the evidence is there to see (Thackray 1998). Successful organizations require a synergy of interests between the corporate and the workforce, and a real shift in power relationships between managers and staff. This is especially true in public administrations which depend totally on the willingness and capacity of staff to collaborate. The question is what management approaches and frameworks are required to nudge demoralized staff who remain suspicious and hostile to change towards engagement in partnerships, networks and collaborative practices.

In Britain there is a desire to break down many of the barriers created by competition, institutions and cultural habits, but such good will is not aided by technical managerialism nor by corporate attitudes to change. Unfortunately, there remains a tendency to lurch from forms of structural determinism to overoptimistic ideas about individual employee potential and volition. There is a need to move beyond overdetermining frameworks which tip in favour of either structural determinism or unrealistic personal choice towards more balanced relationships and innovative approaches to change. The perspective which negates local empirical detail, draws on abstract theory and remains detached from daily reality does little to stop the swings of the marketplan pendulum between regulation and individualistic behaviour. Fresh thinking about the ways in which people and structures impact on one another is likely to emerge as much from innovative practice as from abstract modelling, largely because emergent relationships are unclear, unpredictable and locally determined. It is through a more 'process and people' perspective that reflexive relationships will develop. Management systems which work against this development process and focus on tightly controlling employees, whether through bureaucratic or managerial mechanisms, have a negative impact on employees and their relationships.

Within the public sector management there needs to be a reversal of the tightness of control at local and national level. Currently at the local level there is too much central control and standardization while at the central level there is little cohesion around the processes and values which underpin and encourage new partnerships. Local conditions need to be more open and flexible if they are to sustain learning and collaboration and develop new arrangements and partnerships which work. When such a shift occurs, employees will become more confident in partnership and change. The transformation process is also hampered by the fact that dynamic managers are rewarded for the wrong skills of, for instance, crisis and impression management or short-term gain, rather than transforming relationships, negotiating change, devising new work contracts and developing inclusive management practices.

There is clearly a connection between traditional male gender cultures and economic systems, management models and professional detached abstraction. Although the separation of 'private and personal' from the 'public' may have served societies well in the past, it is totally counterproductive to the development of a socially responsive global community and to ethical trading. Political decision-making is desperately in need of a social infrastructure which is inclusive rather than moralistic.

The paradigm shifts required and real changes in management are thwarted by male gendered cultures, but this is not to say that many women are not adept at impression management and deeply committed to their careers. However, women innovators do have a critical role to play in organizational transformation. The women managers interviewed wanted to kick-start change, but were met with bemused or blocking reactions when they put forward ideas and attempted to develop relationships. Some are now chief officers and represent a radical new breed of managers, politicized in the 1970s, seasoned in management in the 1980s and less intimidated than previous generations of senior women. These women persisted in demanding change because they were passionate about local government and confident that social transformation was possible, in spite of the fact that most worked with local authorities where authoritarian gender cultures were dominant. They were opposed to forms of restructuring that exaggerated social exclusion and marginalization. These exceptional women forged new agendas for management during the period of transition in local government between 1985 and 1995, at a time when many of their male colleagues left what they saw as a 'sinking ship' to join management consultancies. They wanted to incorporate emotions and new behaviours into management thinking. They said that those managers who persisted with a mechanical and systems approach to change and wanted to control staff were themselves obstacles. Challenging women managers had a passion for their organizations and wanted to change reality and incorporate people values into management performance criteria. In so doing they have proved to be exceptional managers, which is what made them threatening. These radical women who entered public administrations in the 1980s questioned the professional and managerial attitudes to organization and to staff and were in no doubt that the male culture within management influenced their colleagues' responses to them. Those who were most forceful in their desire to change management systems recognized that emergent relationships needed sustenance and endorsement, not just leadership. They also met with the most resistance, which they attributed to the gendered underpinning of local government evident in:

- a systems or structural approach to management and change and inadequate financial resources and accounting measures;
- internal market's values and frameworks which worked against partnership, as much as did the professional elites and the old bureaucracies;
- financial controls and efficiency measures which also mitigated against emergent relationships;
- performance measurement which did not value joint practice activities, even where they existed, and a tendency to assume that management systems were neutral;
- perpetuation of forms of control and supervision which reinforced blame cultures through gagging clauses in employment contracts;
- dominant narratives circulated through the media and press which contain and characterize specific realities, but which are divorced from social change and many other people's realities including a postfeminist discourse and postmodernist narrative, both of which undermine the confidence of change agents and the context of active participation social change.

Unfortunately those who were challenging middle managers were subject to various forms of marginalization such as gagging clauses and intimidation. Many were met by incredulity from those women and men who were more concerned with efficiency than social change. A critical mass of women will not of itself change the character of management and managers. Those who are motivated by social change rather than individual achievement are most likely to be criticized because they dare to contradict the dominant discourse. It would appear that radical women are no longer silenced by wizards as witches, but by popular narratives and managerialism. Social transformation is dependent on those who are willing to jettison the deterministic framework and male values; it is women who are the innovators precisely because they are driven by a passion for effectiveness and more democratic relationships.

A reversal of gender preferences and new relationships will not emerge merely by new definitions of feminism or politics, but requires the active negotiation of new relationships: the so-called paradigm shift from 'closed' to 'open' is dependent on the confidence and determination of active parties. Social transformation does not emerge only from argument and structural change, but also from struggle and negotiation. Fortunately those ignorant of or unimpressed by the chattering classes carry on struggling, often in the face of much ridicule and passivity, but the shifts that their activities signify, usually at the local and grassroots level, pass unnoticed. Change is registered by reference to major events or local leaders, yet these are merely pinnacles of a collective iceberg which has taken years to grow. The tendency to tidy up history in neat dates and key people obscures many of the realities involved in social change. Sheila Rowbotham (1973) described how women's struggles were 'hidden from history', but when they were unravelled were shown to have been highly influential in the way whole societies developed. This same silencing dynamic operates within management and is one explanation for why local partnerships and development work remain hidden from public view. Recording events is a gendered activity and one which affects the reality of change and transformation; it is not only leaders who hold the key to social change but also those in more lowly positions and those on the margins, but the significance of their efforts remains invisible. Emergent relationships require endless negotiation and preliminary work, often unrecorded and sustained by women who are the drivers of this backroom activity. Dominant male cultures affect the direction of change and the possibilities of social transformation and gender preferences influence which qualities and events are noticed in managers: what is defined and what is hidden, what matters enough to measure. Millions of women have no access to the media but their energies are the shifting sands of social change rather than eureka events, and those arguing for democratic organizations cannot impact on the mainstream if they are not given a voice.

A framework for engagement is needed; democratic change has never been achieved through autocratic central dictate. Restructuring which remains dependent on mechanical tools such as centralized and top-down measures undermines staff and increases their marginalization. A feminization process, by contrast, should start to open up communication channels and move in the direction of inclusiveness. This is not to dismantle management structures, nor to promote a strategy totally based on individual learning with no regard to power relationships or institutionalization (reminiscent of the human relations approach), but to develop strategic approaches to management which support staff in change and measure what matters. Social innovators and emergent relationships need endorsing in organizational thinking, practices and performance measurement. All employees need sustenance and support, but those who are challenging, especially also women, need their activities to be reflected in management mechanisms. Policymakers and managers have a choice: either organizations can move towards greater exclusiveness in management practices through central standards and generic systems or they can become even more inclusive of staff, users and the community. The latter strategy will benefit the company as much as the community, but is dependent on managers changing their attitudes to staff and their own confidence in democracy and change. Managers need to be confident in order to protect social transformation and new constellations. They have to have confidence in their own judgement when endorsed by experience, local needs and values. The docility of managers has bedevilled the NHS and continues to do so. Managers who do not tackle blame cultures and rely on transactional relationships do not have the ability to transform organizations and manage the complex change processes. They need the authority and confidence to criticize financial and management systems when they do not deliver quality services and inhibit emergent practices and relationships. Transforming managers have to be able to unite users and staff interests through management frameworks which reinforce those involved in emergent partnerships by:

- agreement on the social principles determining corporate management systems;
- collaborative cultures and a people approach among all employees;
- communication systems open to external and excluded voices;
- measurement of what matters including people, relationships, processes and social outcomes.

Unfortunately, there is a crisis of leadership among politicians and there is a growing tendency to see political decision-making as merely a managerial activity. This is dangerous – management systems are tools, not political agendas. The psychological impact of the New Right's thinking on the media, managerialism and postmodernist thought has been to create an air of defeatism. The interchange between politics and management could have been instructive but in the UK it is one-sided; politicians have been more influenced by managerial thinking rather than managers by politics and social values. The system's preference reinforces the notion of management as a neutral and sanitized activity. The management of politics has resulted in some national politicians appearing to be so overwhelmed by international financial systems that they feel capable only of managing existing economic frameworks; they no longer perceive that they have the power to endorse social change. The complexities of international realities appear to have a more overpowering effect in the UK than in other European countries, but what does appear to have been the result is a managerial attitude to politics rather than a more politicized view of management.

The passivity among politicians reflects a more general malaise; confidence in people and social relationships was shattered in the 1980s and the legacy of that period lingers on. The trading mentality of the 1980s resulted in an age of pessimism where the fundamentalists claimed the spiritual vacuum as their own and argued for a return to roots or religion. However, it is not a faith in god or in roots which is needed. In the 1980s whole communities were colonized and swamped by a trading mentality and there was a denial of society itself: 'There is no such thing as community' (Thatcher). Some were unable to resist the logic of market transactions and market values (Jameson 1991); their social lives and personal relationships were dominated by trading transactions which could only lead to alienation from their communities.

The New Right attacked feminism as it did Marxism in order to justify its unfettered market economy as the only rational economic and market system. Life in Britain was bleak in many cities and rural areas and the economic climate resulted in a desire for greater individual control, precisely because people felt so powerless. The psychological impact of extreme versions of alienation was to make learning less likely and to increase the desire for personal control. This tendency manifests itself when individuals become more detached or rootless; for example, during periods of unemployment or when individual social realities are denied, as is the experience of those who are marginalized or excluded from society.

The New Right generated forms of postmodern thinking that reinforced hype and alienation which undermined those struggling with social change; personal isolation was common and degenerated into a sense of hopelessness. Postmodern thinking captures this alienation, yet also perpetuates it, through a neglect of empirical and social realities and an unwillingness to refer to or acknowledge community, collectivity and fundamental human values. The adherents of postmodernism appear to doubt that there is a bedrock of human values and are incapable of making value judgements, fearful that when they do so they may be politically incorrect; their desire to wrap up reality in endings is not dissimilar from the desire of academics to trap processes in definition and pejorative classification.

Each generation of men and women had to grapple with their own realities and consequently they adopt the thinking and tactics which mirror their contemporary political perspective, including the particular gender culture. Managing in any gendered environment is a skill which requires exceptional mental agility, thus women have learnt to be strategic in their thinking and tactical in their behaviour. Although the postmodern perspective did undermine a confidence in social change the UK, this is now changing. The late 1990s appear to be opening up new agendas but Equality Feminism is not the answer. While single childless women may have the illusion of escaping the gendered landscape, those who are mothers will never be able to do this. Women in the 1990s are constantly cajoled to be successful at work and have to be economical with their time such that they are unlikely to engage in informal and creative relationships not endorsed by management. Yet almost all caring and sharing relationships are informal and unrecorded. Success in the modern world has come to mean adapting and adopting managerial thinking, which is narrowly economistic and going to undermine not only women but also their transforming style. Those ambitious in a competitive world are less likely to do babysitting. Women may have the transforming skills, but most do not necessarily use them: some lose them over time and others become disillusioned; many resign from executive posts because they 'have had enough' (Marshall 1986). As long as the twenty-four hour culture dominates organizations the less people will remain in organizations to challenge practices and undermine and transform the macho culture.

Social instability, a deterioration of community and the impermanence of personal relationships are blamed on feminism, which is an easy target when many men are confused about their personal relationships and male identities. There is no right way of changing gender relationships, it is a political process and involves tension, conflict and gender management. However, gender stereotypes can and do change. Change is also more likely when the silence on gender effects is lifted and there is a greater awareness of how male cultures influence decision-making, change and management. Such an awareness would liberate those who are struggling to transform practices by providing some explanation for why they encounter inexplicable resistance.

Social change is a complex process and one which will be all the slower if the difficult connection between masculinity and learning is avoided. Too often boys fail at school because their peer group encourages them 'not to make fools of themselves' and 'not to take risks'; when learning is a risk-taking process. A similar set of reactions can be observed in management. Masculinity plays a pivotal role in the dynamic between personal and organizational change, and is of interest not just to therapists, but also to politicians and managers. The narrowness and rigidity of popular masculinity frustrates learning and reinforces inertia, it usually reinforces speed, immediacy, toughness and being right first time. Such qualities may reflect those of the bullish leader or salesman but they oppress others and inhibit learning and communication. Managers must inspire and communicate, not bully. There is a need to blur the edges between young men and young women not towards tough young women but towards human beings who value and respect each other. Some men are changing roles and can be seen at the school gates, in health clinics and even buying toilet cleaner in the supermarket. There is a recognition of the value of more balanced gendered cultures.

However, the actions of a few individuals do not indicate a sea change. Neither is it merely a question of personal change and personal choice. The option to change roles is firmly anchored in the options presented by income, work and social milieu. Most women do care about society, do value friendships and their communities above the financial marketplace. Society should not assume that women's commitments are boundless, nor that women as a group will continue to be the carriers of warmth and the glue in social relationships. Social instability is not the result of feminism but due to a mismatch between modern life and traditional male cultures. What feminism has done is to give many women the opportunity to choose, have a confidence in alternatives and a voice. The genie cannot be put back in the bottle. Women are leaving marriages because they are fed up with carrying one-sided emotional partnerships. Understandably, many younger women are irritated by this confining caring role and many are rejecting it. But this does not indicate a lack of desire not to have partners or to throw away their values, they merely want a new deal. In some ways the new forms of feminism are based on a rejection of old gender roles, but this presents a conundrum for society as to who is to be socially responsible for public life? Who is to look after the children and develop community networks and services?

Women of different ages and social groups follow very different paths. But many are frustrated by the public expectation that they will continue to carry one-sided partnerships, whether they be within marriage or at work. Although women are expected to be emphatic, attentive and caring, they are ignored when they are insistent about the need for change. Women want partnership, not subservience, while their colleagues may want them to continue to be the coping, caring listener and negotiator within difficult relationships. Women are rebelling against these roles. Women managers have also realized adopting feminine roles in senior management renders them ineffective in many ways. Almost all women are becoming less willing to continue with impossible relationships where they are expected to drag unwilling partners into negotiation. They can see that those who expend more energy in the partnership process get hurt. The problem for women is that many are forced into battle because they have no willing partners in peace. War is easier because it can be initiated by one side whereas partnership requires two willing parties.

Partnerships are not the same as takeovers; successful partnerships depends on egalitarian relationships and trust. All new relationships can be difficult, but if each party is prepared for the process then both can accept a degree of pain. The same dynamics apply to organizations. Women will, if given the chance, attempt to transform organizational culture at their own expense. This attitude has perhaps changed, but the fact remains that many of those with visionary and transformational potential remain under-valued within macho, middle management cultures.

This challenging role is acceptable and well-established within policy-making and politics but rarely accepted in management. Yet, it is technical managerialism which dominates our lives and determines how policies are to be put into practice. The pressure on managers to refer to narrow targets within managerialism has reinforced the efficiency-driven culture where employees who are punished if they challenge the conventional wisdom of generic and controlling frameworks. Managerialism has led to reduction in critical thinking and appropriate responses at a time when they are most needed. It is only when a more inclusive or people-focused management approach is adopted that management practices will become more open to the visionary, the risk-takers and the unknown. At present mechanical processes and closed (blame) cultures are blocking social transformation. The passive acceptance of managerialism among politi-cians again suggests how dominant is the male preference for rational and technocratic management systems even when they are blatantly not fit for the purpose of delivering change or responsiveness. The dilemma for women innovators actually involved in new and emergent practices is whether to raise the issue of gender or keep quiet about it.

Organizations undergoing change need visionaries and challenging change agents as well as technicians. At present the traditionalists are not playing partnership because the institutions in which they work continue to reinforce combative rather than collaborative behaviours. Strategic management frameworks need to be inclusive of radical managers and of radical voices in the community. Management could be redirected away from narrow systems, blocking tactics and inertia as they are demonstrably not effective or efficient and thwart new practices. Challenging women have a role to play in loosening conventions but unfortunately as inno-vators they are frequently cast to the margins and scorned by politicians and executives alike. Innovative women are continuously maligned yet if they did not challenge traditional management practices organizations are more likely to fail and society be the poorer. It is radical and outspoken women who are socializing the market, developing networks and inclusive forms of management, yet within male cultures they are ridiculed for their transforming capacities.

Bibliography

Abramson, P.E., Goldberg, A., Greenberg, J.H. and Abramson, U.M. (1978) 'The talking platypus phenomenon: competency ratings as a function of sex and professional status', *Psychology of Women Quarterly*, 2: 114–124.

Acker, Joan (1987) 'Hierarchies, jobs and bodies: an outline for a theory of gendered organisations'. Paper to the American Sociological Association Annual General Meeting, Chicago, August.

Acker, J. (1989) 'The problem with patriarchy', *Sociology*, 23(2): 235–240.

Acker, J. (1992) 'Gendering organisational theory', in A.U. Mills and P. Tancred (eds) *Gendering Analysis*. London: Sage.

Acker, J. (1997) Gender and Organisation Conference, Manchester, January.

Adler, N.J. and Izraeli, D.N. (eds) (1994) *Women in Management Worldwide*. Armonk, NY: M.E. Sharpe Inc., pp. 141–156.

Ahlbrandt et al. (1992) 'Employee involvement programmes improve corporate performance', *Long Range Planning*, 25 (5): 91–98.

Alban Metcalfe, B. (1985) 'The effects of socialisation on women's management careers', *Management Bibliographies and Reviews*, 11(3).

Alban Metcalfe, B. (1987) 'Male and female managers: an analysis of biographical and self-concept data', *Work and Stress*, 1, July–September: 207–219.

Alban Metcalfe, B. (1989) 'What motivates managers? an investigation by gender and sectors of employment', *Public Administration*, 67: 95–108.

Alban Metcalfe, B. and Nicolson, N. (1984) *The Career Development of British Managers*. London: British Institute of Management.

Aldrich, H.C. (1979) *Organisations and Environments*. Englewood Cliffs, NJ: Prentice-Hall.

Aldrich, H.C. (1987) 'Organisation transformation and trends in US employee relations'. Paper to the Aston/Umist Labour Processes Conference.

Alexander, A. (1991) 'Managing fragmentation: democracy, accountability and the future of local government', *Local Government Studies*, 17(6): 63–76.

Alimo-Metcalfe, B. (1991) 'What a waste, women in the NHS', *Women in Management Review*, 6 (5).

Alimo-Metcalfe, B. (1992a) 'Gender and appraisal: findings from a national survey of managers in the British National Health Service'. Global Research Conference, Ottawa, Canada, October.

Alimo-Metcalfe, B. (1992b) 'Different gender–different rules: assessment of women in management', in P. Barrar and C.L. Cooper (eds) *Managing Organisations in 1992: Strategic Responses*. London: Routledge.

Alimo-Metcalfe, B. (1994) 'Performance related pay', *Health Service Journal*, 20 October.

Alimo-Metcalfe, B. (1995) 'Female and male constructs of leadership and empowerment', *Women in Management*, 10 (2): 3–8.

Allen, I. (1988) *Any Room at the Top?* London: Policy Studies Institute.

Alvesson, M. (1985) 'A critical framework for organisations analysis', *Organisation Studies*, 67 (2): 117–138.

Alvesson, M. and Billing, Y. (1992) 'Gender and organisation: towards a differentiated understanding', *Organisational Studies*, 13–14: 73–103.

Alvesson, M. and Willmott, H. (1992) *Critical Management Studies*, London: Sage.

Anatal, A.B. and Krebsbach-Gnath, C. (1988) 'Women in management: unused resources in the Republic of Germany', in N. Adler and D. Izraeli (eds) *Women in Management Worldwide*. Armonk, NY: M.E. Sharpe.

Anderson, T.D. (1992) *Transforming Leadership*. Amherst Massachusetts Human Resources Development Programme.

Andrews, J. (1994) 'You've got change in your pocket', *Nursing Management*, 1, 3 June.

Annandale, E. (1996) 'Working on the front-line: risk culture and nursing in the new NHS', *Sociological Review*, 44 (3): 416–451.

Argyris, C. (1964) *Integrating the Individual and the Organization*. New York: John Wiley.

Argyris, C. and Schon, D.A. (1978) *Organisational Learning: A Theory of Action Perspective*. Massachusetts: Addison Wesley.

Arroba, T. and James, K. (1987) 'Are politics palatable to women managers? How can women make wise moves at work?', *Women in Management Review*, 10 (3): 123–130.

Ascherson, N. (1996) 'Is it dead or only sleeping?', *Independent on Sunday*, 22 September.

Ascherson, N. (1996) 'Don't be fooled: multinationals do not rule the world', *Independent on Sunday*, December.

Ashburner, L. and Cairncross, L. (1993) 'Membership of the new style health authorities: continuity and change?', *Public Administration*, 71, Autumn.

Ashburner, L. and Fitzgerald, L. (1995) 'Beleaguered professionals: doctors and institutional change in the NHS', in H. Scarborough (ed.) *The Management of Experience*. London: Macmillan.

Ashburner, L. and Fitzgerald, L. (1995) 'Corporate governance in the public sector: some issues and evidence from the NHS', *Public Administration*.

Ashburner, L., Ferlie, E. and Fitzgerald, L. (1996) 'Organisational transformations and top down changes: the case of the NHS', *British Journal of Management*, 7 (1): 1–16.

Audit Commission (1993) *Taking Care, Health and Personal Services*, Bulletin, No. 1. London: HMSO.

Audit Commission (1994) *Taking Stock: Progress with Community Care*. London: HMSO.

Audit Commission (1996) *Fundholding Facts: A Digest of Information About Practices within the Scheme During the First Five Years*. London: HMSO.

Bacchi, Carol (1990) *Same Difference: Feminism and Sexual Difference*. Sydney: Allen and Unwin.

Balls, E. (1997) *Open Macroeconomics and the Open Economy*. London: Centre for Economic Performance.

Bannister, D. (1977) *New Perspectives in Personal Construct Theory*. London: Academic Press.

Bannister, D. (1985) *Issues and Approaches in Personal Construct Theory*. London: Academic Press.

Bannister, D. and Franscella, F. (1986) *Inquiry Man: The Psychology of Personal Constructs*. London: Croom Helm.

Barham, P. and Hayward, R. (1989) *From Mental Patient to Person*. London: Tavistock.

Barrett, M. (1987) 'The concept of difference', *Feminist Review*, 26: 29–40.

Barrett, M. (1991) *The Politics of Truth: From Marx to Foucault*. Cambridge: Polity.

Bartlett, W. and Le Grand, J. (1993) 'The theory of the quasi-markets', in J. Le Grand and W. Bartlett, *Quasi Markets and Social Policy*. London: Macmillan.

Bass, B.M. and Avolio, B.J. (1989) 'Potential bias in leadership measures', *Education and Psychological Measurement*, 49: 509–527.

Bass, B.M. and Avolio, B.J. (1993) *Shatter the Glass Ceiling.* Center for Leadership Studies: Binghamton University, Binghamton USA.

Bauman, Z. (1991) *Modernity and Ambivalence.* Cambridge: Polity.

Beck, W. (1992) *Risk Society Towards a New Modernity.* London: Sage.

Belenky, M., Clinchy, B., Goldberger, N. and Tarule, J. (1986) *Women's Ways of Knowing: The Development of Self, Voice and Mind.* New York: Basic Books.

Benn, M. (1998) *Madonna and Child: Towards a New Politics of Motherhood.* London: Cape.

Berger, P. and Luckman, T. (1967) *The Social Construction of Reality.* Garden City, NY: Anchor.

Berne, E. (1966) *The Games People Play.* London: Deutsch.

Bevan, S. and Thompson, M. (1992) *Merit Pay, Performance Appraisal and Attitudes to Women's Work.* Sussex: Institute of Manpower Studies.

Bewes, T. (1997) *Cynicism and Postmodernity.* London: Verso.

Bhaskar, Roy (1989) *Reclaiming Reality: A Critical Introduction to Contemporary Philosophy.* London: Verso.

Bion, W.R. (1961) 'Group dynamics' in *Expression in Groups.* London: Tavistock.

Blau, P.M. (1955) *Dynamics of Bureaucracy.* Chicago: University of Chicago Press.

Blau, P.M. and Scott, W.R. (1962) *Formal Organizations.* San Francisco: Chandler.

Blomquist, M. (1991) 'Work organisations in need of women'. Paper to the Ninth International Labour Processes Conference, Manchester.

Bloor, G. and Dawson, P. (1994) 'Understanding professional culture in organizations', *Organisational Studies*, 15 (2): 275–295.

Booth, C. (1995) *Equalities and Organizational Design.* Luton: LGMA.

Bordo, S. (1992) 'Feminism, postmodernism and gender scepticism' in L. Nicolson (ed.) *Feminism and Postmodernism.* London: Routledge.

Boviard, T. and Hughes, R. (1995) 'Re-engineering public sector organisations: a case study of radical change in a British local authority', *International Review of Administrative Sciences*, 61 (3): 355–372.

Boyd, H.W. and Westfall (1970) 'Interviewer bias once more revisited', *Journal of Marketing Research*, 7: 249–253.

Braverman, H. (1974) *Labour and Monopoly Capital.* New York: Monthly Review Press.

Breakwell, G.M. (1987) 'Identity', in H. Beloff and A.L. Colman, *Psychological Survey 1987*, Leicester: British Psychological Society.

Brenner, M. (1978) 'Interviewing' in M. Brenner and P. Marsh (eds) *The Social Context of Method.* London: Croom Helm.

Brenner, O.C., Tomkiezwicz, J. and Schein, V.E. (1989) 'The relationship between sex role stereotyping and requisite management characteristics revisited', *Academy of Management Journal*, 32.

Breugel, I. (1989) 'Sex and race in the labour market', *Feminist Review*, 32, Summer: 49–68.

Broverman, I.K. et al (1972) 'Sex role stereotypes: a current appraisal', *Journal of Social Issues*, 28: 59–78.

Broverman, I.K., Vogel, S.R., Broverman, D.M., Clarkson, F.E. and Rosenkrantz, P.S. (1975) 'Sex stereotypes: a current appraisal', in M.T. Schuch Mednick, S.S. Tangri and L.W. Hoffman (eds) *Women and Achievement: Social and Motivational Analyses.* New York: Hemisphere Publishing.

Brown, H. (1992) *Women Organising.* London: Routledge.

Brown, H. (1994) *Managing Beyond Gender Report.* London: The Office of Public Management.

Brown, H. and Goss, S. (1991) *Equal Opportunities for Women in the NHS.* London: NHS Management Executive.

Brown, H. and Goss, S. (1993) 'Can you hear the sound of breaking glass?', *Health Service Journal*, 23 September, 26–27.

Brownhill, E. and Marshall, P. (1994) 'Women in management', *Health Service Journal*, 17 March.

Brydon-Miller, M.L. (1984) 'Accessibility: self-advocacy at an independent living center: a participatory approach', PhD dissertation. Amherst: University of Massachusetts.

Bryman, A. (1984) 'Leadership and corporate culture: harmony and democracy', *Personnel Review*, 17 (2): 19–24.

Bryman, A. (1988) *Quantity and Quality in Social Research*. London: Routledge.

Bryman, A. and Howard, A. (1994) 'The empowering leader: change, job requirements and dimensions'. Paper given to Organisational Behaviour Congress, San Francisco.

Burns, J.M. (1978) *Leadership*. New York: Harper Row.

Burns, T. and Stalker, G.M. (1961) *The Management of Innovation*. London: Tavistock.

Burowoy, M. (1979) *Manufacturing Consent: Changes in the Labour Process Under Monopoly Capital*. Chicago: University of Chicago Press.

Burrell, Gibson (1984) 'Sex and organizational analysis', *Organization Studies*, 5.

Burrell, Gibson (1996) *Pandamonium*. London: Sage.

Burrell, Gibson and Morgan, Gareth (1979) *Sociological Paradigms and Organisational Analysis: Elements of the Sociology of Corporate Life*. London: Heinemann.

Cabinet Office (1987) *Working Patterns: A Study Document* (The Mueller report). London: Management and Personnel Office.

CAIPE Centre for the Advancement of Inter-Disciplinary Practices and Education Journal. Quarterly. London.

Calas, M.B. and Smircisch, L. (1989) 'Use of F word: feminist, theories and the social consequences of organisation research', in F. Hoy (ed.) *Academy of Management Proceedings*. Washington, DC: Academy of Management, pp. 335–359.

Calas, M.B. and Smircisch, L. (1991) 'Voicing seduction to silence leadership', *Organisation*, 12 (4): 567–602.

Cassells, C. and Walsh, S. (1991) 'Towards a woman friendly psychology of women: gender, power and organisation'. Paper to the Annual Occupational Psychology Conference, Cardiff.

Cassells, C. and Walsh, S. (1993) 'Being seen and not heard: barriers to women's equality in the workplace', *The Psychological Bulletin, The British Journal of Psychology*, 6: 110–114.

Castle, B. (1990) *The Castle Diaries 1964–76*. London: Macmillan.

Challis, L., Day, P., Klein, R. and Scrivens, E. (1998) *Joint Approaches to Social Policy: Rationality and Practice*. Cambridge: Cambridge University Press.

Chambers, R. (1995) *Whose Reality Counts?* London: ITP Publications.

Charlesworth, Clarke and Cochrane, A. (1996) 'Tangled webs? Managing local mixed economies of care', *Public Administration*, 74: 67–88.

Cheung Judge, M.Y. and Morrison, C. (1992) 'Whatever happened to equal opportunities?', *The Journal*, Newcastle.

Child, J. (1973) *Man and Organisation*. London: Allen and Unwin.

Chodorow, N. (1978) *The Reproduction of Mothering*. Berkeley: University of California Press.

Clarke, J. (1995) 'Doing the right thing? Managerialism and the social welfare'. Paper presented to the ERC Professions in Late Modernity seminar series, Imperial College, 26 June.

Clarke, J., Cochrane, A. and McLaughlin, E. (1995) *Managing Social Policy*. London: Sage.

Clarke, M. and Stewart, J. (1988) *The Enabling Council.* Luton: Local Government Training Board.

Clarke, M. and Stewart, J. (1992) 'Empowerment for the 1990s', *Local Government Study*, 11(2): 18–26.

Clegg, S. (1981) 'Organization and control', *Administrative Science Quarterly*, 26: 545–562.

Clegg, S. (1989) *Power.* London: Sage.

Clegg, S. and Dunkerley, D. (1986) *Organisation, Class and Control.* London: Routledge and Kegan Paul.

Clutterbuck, D. (ed.) (1985) *New Patterns of Work.* Aldershot: Gower.

CMPS (1992–94) Equality Audits by Corporate, Management and Policy Service.

Cochrane, A. (1991) 'The changing state of local government: restructuring for the 1990s', *Public Administration*, 69(3): 281–302.

Cockburn, C. (1983) *Brothers: Male Dominance and Technological Change.* London: Pluto Press.

Cockburn, C. (1985) *Machinery of Dominance: Women, Men and Technical Knowhow.* London: Pluto Press.

Cockburn, C. (1987) *Women, Trade Unions and Political Parties.* London: Fabian Society Research Series No. 349.

Cockburn, C. (1988) *Women's Progress: A Research Report.* Preston: Lancashire Polytechnic.

Cockburn, C. (1989) 'Equal opportunities: the long and short agendas', *Industrial Relations*, 20 (3): 213–225.

Cockburn, C. (1991) '*In the Way of Women': Men's Resistance to Sex Equality in Organisations.* London: Macmillan.

Coe, T. (1992) *The Key to the Gentleman's Club.* London: Institute of Management.

Cohen, L. (1980) *Research Methods in Education.* London: Croom Helm.

Cohen, S. and Taylor, L. (1978) *Escape Attempts: The Theory and Practice of Resistance in Everyday Life.* Harmondsworth: Paladin.

Coleman, G. (1991) *Investigating Organisations: A Feminist Approach.* Bristol: School of Advanced Urban Studies.

Collinson, D. and Hearn, J. (1994) 'Naming men as men: implications for work', *Gender, Work and Organisation*, 1 (1).

Community Care (1996) 'Blowing the whistle', 1–7 August.

Cooper, C. and Davidson, M. (1982) *High Pressure: The Working Life of Women Managers.* London: Fontana.

Cooper, C. and Davidson, M. (eds) (1984) *Women in Management.* Oxford: Heinemann.

Coote, A. and Hunter, D. (1996) *A New Agenda for Health.* London: PPR.

Corby, S. (1982) *Equal Opportunities for Women in the Civil Service.* London: HMSO.

Court, M. (1994) *Women Transforming Leadership: A Study of Shared Leadership and Career Development.* Palmerston North: Massey University, ERDC.

Cox, D. (1992) 'Crisis and opportunity in health service management', in Loveridge and Starkey (eds), *Continuity and Care in the NHS.* Buckingham: Open University Press.

Cox, C. and Cooper, C. (1988) *High Flyer.* Oxford: Oxford University Press.

Coyle, A. (1989a) 'Women in management: a suitable case for treatment?', *Feminist Review*, 31, Spring.

Coyle, A. (1989b) 'The limits of change: local government and equal opportunities for women', *Public Administration*, 67: 39–50.

Cronback, L.J. et al (1980) *Towards Reform of a Program Evaluation.* San Francisco: Jossey-Bass.

Crozier, M. (1962) *The Bureaucratic Phenomenon.* London: Tavistock.

Cuff, J. (1993) 'Dr Daly', *Independent on Sunday*, 24 July.

Cullen, D. (1992) 'Self actualisation and organisational structures: implications for women in management research'. Paper presented to the Global Research Conference on Women in Management, 23 October, Ottawa, Canada.

Cullen, D. (1994) 'Feminism, management and self-actualisation', *Gender, Work and Organisation*, 1, 127: 73.

Dahrendorf, R. (1959) *Class and Class Conflict in Industrial Society*. London: Routledge and Kegan Paul.

Dalton, M. (1959) *Men who Manage*. London: John Wiley.

Daly, M. (1994–97) Personal communication.

Davenport, E., Bengington, J. and Geddes, M. (1990) 'The future of the European motor industry regions: new local authority responses to industrial restructuring', *Local Economy*, 2: 129–146.

Davidson, M.J. (1989) 'Women in management – a personal research analogy', working papers no. NC 89–23. The University of Western Ontario, National Centre for Management Research Development, Ontario.

Davidson, M.J. and Cooper, C. (1987) 'Female managers in Britain: a comparative perspective', *Human Resource Managers*, 26, Summer: 217–242.

Davidson, M. and Cooper, C. (1992) *Shattering the Glass Ceiling: The Woman Manager*. London: Paul Chapman.

Davies, C. (1992) *Gender, History and Management Style in Nursing: Towards a Theoretical Synthesis*, in M. Savage and A. Witz (eds) *Gender and Bureaucracy*. Oxford: Blackwell.

Davies, C. (1995) *Gender and the Professional Predicament in Nursing*. London: Routledge.

Davies and Rosser (1986) *Processes of Discrimination*. A report of a study of women working in the NHS. London: HMSO.

Dawson, D. (1994) 'Costs and prices in the internal market: markets vs. the NHS management guidelines', discussion paper no. 115. Centre for Health Economics, University of York.

Deal, T. and Kennedy, A. (1984) *Corporate Cultures*. Reading, MA: Addison-Wesley.

De Lysa, Burnier (1994) 'Reinventing government from a feminist perspective: feminist theory, women's experience, and administrative reality', for Fourth Women's Policy Research Conference, Washington DC.

Deming, E. (1983) *Out of the Crisis*. Cambridge: Cambridge University Press.

De Stefano, C. (1990) 'Dilemmas of difference: feminism, modernity and post-modernity' in L. Nicholson (ed.), *Feminism and Postmodernism*. London: Routledge.

Deutscher, L. (1972) 'Public and private opinions: social situations and multiple realities', in S.Z. Nagi and R.G. Corwin (eds), *The Social Contexts of Research*. London: Wiley.

Devine, F. (1994) 'Segregation and supply: preferences and plans among "self-made" women', *Gender, Work and Organization*, 1 (2): 94–110.

Dewey, J. (1934) *Logic: The Theory of Critical Enquiry*. New York: Minton, Balch.

DHSS (1987) *Promoting Better Health – the Government's Programme for Improving Primary Health Care*. London: HMSO.

DHSS (1994) *Medical Audit in the Hospital and Community Health Services*. London: HMSO.

DiMaggio, P. and Powell, W.W. (1991) *The New Institutionalisation in Organizational Analysis*. Chicago: Chicago University Press.

Dinnerstein, D. (1977) *The Mermaid and the Minotaur: Sexual Arrogance and Human Malaise*. New York: Harper Row.

Djilas, M. (1957) *The New Class*. New York: Praeger.

DoH (1990) *Community Act Reforms*. London: HMSO.

DoH (1993) Community Care, EL(93) 119/C1(93) 35. London.

DoH (1997) *The New NHS*. London: HMSO.

Dorward, Smythe and Lambert (1992) *The Power of the Open Company*. London: Dorward, Smythe and Lambert (client owned).

Dowling, C. (1982) *The Cinderella Complex: Women's Inner Fear of Independence*. New York: Fontana.

Drucker, P.F. (1955) *The Problems of Management*. New York: Harper Row.

Drucker, P.F. (1988) 'The coming of the new organisation', *Harvard Business Review*, 66 (1): 45–53.

Drucker, P.F. (1989) *The New Realities*. London: Mandarin.

Drummond, H. (1992) *The Quality Movement: What Total Quality Management is Really all About!* London: Kogan Page.

du Gay, D. (1993) 'Entrepreneurial management in the public sector', *Work, Employment and Society*, 7 (4): 643–648.

Dunleavy, P. (1995) 'Policy disaster: explaining the UKs record', *Public Policy and Administration*, 10(2): 52–70.

Durkheim, E. (1934) *The Division of Labour in Society*. London: Macmillan.

Easterby-Smith, M. (1995) 'Organisational learning: less than meets the eye'? Paper to British Academy of Management Conference, September.

Edlund, C. (1993) 'Learning from women's leadership styles: female public managers'. Paper to ASP/CASU National Training Conference, San Francisco.

Ehrenreich, B. (1983) *The Hearts of Men: American Dreams and the Flight From Commitment*. London: Pluto Press.

Elliott, L. (1997) 'Proof of trickle pudding is not in the eating', *The Guardian*, 15 September.

Epstein, B. (1996) 'Why post-structuralism is a dead end for progressive thought', *Socialist Review*, Autumn: 82–117.

Eraut, M. (1985) 'Knowledge creation and knowledge use in the professional contexts', *Studies in Higher Education*, 10 (2): 117–133.

Eraut, M. (1988) 'Developing the knowledge base: a process perspective on professional education' in Ronald Barnett (ed.) *Learning to Effect*. Milton Keynes: Open University Press.

Erikson, E. (1958) 'The nature of clinical evidence' in David Learner (ed.) *Evidence and Inference*. Glencoe Free Press.

Etzioni, A. (1964) *Modern Organizations*. Englewood Cliffs: Prentice-Hall.

Fanon, F. (1965) *The Wretched on the Earth*. New York: Grove Press.

Fay, B. (1987) *Social Theory and Political Practice*. London: Allen and Unwin.

Fayol, H. (1949) *General and Industrial Management*. London: Pitman.

Feldberg and Glenn (1979) 'Men and women: job versus gender moulds in the world of work', *Social Problems*, 26 (5): 524–538.

Ferguson, C. (1984) *The Feminist Case Against Bureaucracy*. Phil Temple University Press.

Ferlie, E. and Pettigrew, A. (1996) 'Managing through networks: some issues and implications for the NHS', *British Academy of Management*, special issue, 7, S81.S99 March.

Ferlie, E. and Fitzgerald, L (1996) 'Transformation and its impact on the public sector'. Paper to Public Services Unit Conference, Warwick.

Feyerbend, P. (1987) *Farewell to Reason*. London: Verso.

Figes, O. (1996) *A People's Tragedy*. London: Pimlico.

Flynn, N. (1990) *Public Sector Management*. Hemel Hempstead: Harvester Wheatsheaf.

Foucault, M. (1972) *The Archaeology of Knowledge*. London: Tavistock Publications.

Foucault, M. (1979) *Disciple and Punishment: The Birth of the Prison*. New York: Vintage.

Foucault, M. (1984) *The Foucault Reader*. London: Penguin.

Franzway, S., Connell, R.W. and Court, D. (1989) *Staking a Claim: Feminism, Bureaucracy and the State.* Cambridge: Polity.

Fraser, N. (1989) *Unruly Practices.* Minneapolis: MN Press.

Fraser, N. and Nicolson, L. (1990) 'Postmodernism and gender relations in feminist theory', in Linda Nicholson (ed.) *Feminism and Post Modernism.* New York: Routledge.

Freeman, Jo (1978) 'The tyranny of structurelessness'. Paper to the National Women's Conference in the UK, Oxford.

Freeman, S.J.M. (1992) *Changing Lives: Corporate Women and Social Change.* Massachusetts: University of Massachusetts Press.

Friedman, B. (1986) *The Second Stage.* New York: Summit Books.

Fuchs, E. (1991) 'The ways men and women lead: a discussion', *Harvard Business Review*, January–February.

Fukuyama, F. (1995) *Trust: The Social Virtues and the Creation of Prosperity.* London: Hamish Hamilton.

Fukuyama, F. (1997) *The End of Order, Social Market Foundation.* London.

Galbraith, J.R. (1974) 'Organisation design: an information process view', *Interfaces*, 4: 28–36.

Galbraith, J.R. (1982) 'Designing the innovation organization', *Organisation Dynamics*, 10: 5–25.

Garrett, B. (ed.) (1987) *The Learning Organization: The Successful Strategist Series.* London: Harper Collins.

Garson, B. (1973) 'Women's work', *Working Papers for a New Society*, 1: 5–14.

Gergen, K.J. (1971) *The Concept of Self.* New York: Holt, Reinhart and Winston.

Gergen, K.J. (1973) 'Social psychology as history', *Journal of Personality and Social Psychology*, 26: 309–320.

Gherardi, S. (1996) 'Gendered organisational cultures: narratives of women travellers in a male world', *Gender Organisation and Work*, 3 (4): 187–197.

Ghoshal, S. and Bartlett, A. (1995) 'The changing role of top managers: beyond the structures to processes', *Harvard Business Review*, 86.

Giddens, A. (1974) *Positivism and Sociology.* London: Macmillan.

Giddens, A. (1976) *New Rules of Sociological Method.* London: Macmillan.

Giddens, A. (1979) *Central Problems in Social Theory.* London: Macmillan.

Giddens, A. (1991) *Modernity and Self-Identity.* Oxford: Polity Press.

Giddens, A. (1995) *A Contemporary Critique of Historical Materialism.* Basingstoke: Macmillan.

Gilligan, Carol (1982) *In a Different Voice: Psychological Theory and Women's Development.* Cambridge, MA: Harvard University Press.

Glaser, B. (1978) *Theoretical Sensitivity.* Mill Valley, CA: Sociology Press.

Glaser, B. and Strauss, A.L. (1967) *The Discovery of Grounded Theory.* Chicago: Aldine.

Glazer, P. and Slater, M. (1991) 'Between a rock and a hard place: a woman's professional organisations in nursing and class, racial and ethnic inequalities', *Gender and Society*, 5 (3): 351–372.

Glendinning, C. et al. (1997) *From Collaboration to Commissioning Developing Relationships between GP and Social Services Departments.* Manchester: NPCRDC.

Glenn, E.N. and Feldman, R.L. (1979) 'Male and female: job versus gender in the sociology of work', *Social Problems*, 26 (5): 524.

Gloubermaid and Mintzberg (1995) 'Managing care and the cure of discare'. Conference Paper.

Goffman, E. (1959) *Presentation of Self in Everyday Life.* Garden City, NY: Doubleday.

Goldberger, N.R., Clinchly, M., Belenky, M.F. and Tarule, J.M. (1987) 'Women's ways of knowing' in B. Shaver and C. Hendrick (eds) *Sex and Gender*. Newbury Park: Sage.

Goldsmith, W. and Clutterbuck, D. (1985) *The Winning Steak*. London: Guild.

Gordon, S. (1991) *Prisoners of Men's Dreams: Striking out for a New Feminine Future*. Boston: Little Brown and Company.

Goss, S. and Brown, H. (1991) *Equal Opportunities for Women in the National Health Service*. London: Office of Public Management.

Goss, S. and Parston, G. (1989) *Public Management for New Times*. London: Labour Coordinating Committee.

Gowler, A.W. and Legge, K. (1983) 'The meaning of management and the management of meaning: a view from social anthropology', in M.J. Earl (ed.) *Perspectives on Management: A Multidisciplinary Analysis*. Oxford: Oxford University Press.

Graham, P. (1991) In debate: 'Is it time to stop talking about gender differences?' in 'The ways men and women lead', *Harvard Business Review*, January–February.

Gray, H. (1983) 'Men and women bosses: some gender issues in management education', *Management Education and Development*, 1, 16: 2.

Le Grand, J. and Bartlett, W. (eds) (1993) *Quasi-Markets and Social Policy*. London: Macmillan.

Grant, J. and Tancred, P. (1992) 'A feminist perspective on state bureaucracy', in A.J. Mills and P. Tancred (eds), *Gendering Organisational Analysis*. London: Sage.

Gray, A. and Jenkins, B. (1993) 'Markets, management and the public service: the changing role of a culture', in P. Taylor-Gooby and R. Lawson (eds), *Markets and Managers: New Issues in the Delivery of Welfare*. Buckingham: Open University Press.

Gray, A. and Jenkins, B. (1995) 'From public administration to public management: reassessing a revolution?', *Public Administration*, 73, Spring: 75–99.

Green, E. and Cassells, S. (1994) 'Women managers: gendered cultural processes and organisational change'. A paper to Labour Processes Conference, Birmingham UK.

Griffiths, D. (1992) 'Strategic and service management: the Kirklees experiment', *Local Government Studies*, 18 (3): 2240–2248.

The Guardian (1956) '8th Name The Final Agenda', Mori Poll.

Gutek, B.A. (1989) 'Sexuality in the workplace: key issues in social research and organisation practice', in Jeff Hearn et al. (eds), *The Sexuality of Organisation*. Newbury Park, CA: Sage.

Gutek, B.A. and Larwood, L. (1987) *Women's Career Development*. Newbury Park, CA: Sage.

Gutek, B.A. and Stevens, D.A. (1979) 'Differential responses of males and females to work situations which evoke sex-role stereotypes', *Journal of Vocational Behaviour*, 14: 23–32.

Guy, M. (1992) 'The Feminisation of public administration: today's reality and tomorrow's promise', in Timney, Bailey and Mayer (eds), *Public Management in an Interconnected World*. New York: Greenwood Press.

Halford, A. (1993) *No Way up the Greasy Pole*. London: Constable.

Halford, S., Savage, M. and Witz, A. (1997) *Gender Careers and Organisations*. London: Macmillan.

Hall, E.T. (1976) *Beyond Culture*. New York: Anchor Press.

Hall, R.H. (1977) *Organisations, Structures and Process* (2nd edition). Englewood Cliffs, NJ: Prentice-Hall.

Hammond, Valerie (1988) *Women in Management*. Kent: Ashridge Management College.

Hammond, V. and Holton, V. (1991) *A Balanced Workforce: Achieving Cultural Change for Women*. Berkhamsted: Ashridge Management Centre.

Hancock, C. (1997) Standby for Super-Nurse, *Health Services Journal*, 9 January: 17.

Handy, C. (1976) *Understanding Organisations*. Middlesex: Penguin.

Handy, C. (1978) *Gods of Management*. London: Pan Books.

Handy, C. (1984) *The Future of Work*. Oxford: Blackwell.

Handy, C. (1989) *The Age of Unreason*. London: Hutchinson.

Handy, C. (1991) in personal communication.

Handy, C. (1994) *The Empty Raincoat: Making Sense of the Future*. London: Hutchinson.

Hansard (1990) *The Report to the Hansard Society Commission on Women at the Top*. London: HMSO.

Harding, S. (1986) *The Science Question in Feminism*. Ithaca, NY: Cornell University Press.

Harding, S. and Hintikka, M.B. (eds) (1983) *Discovering Reality: Feminist Perspectives on Epistemology, Metaphysics, Methodology and Philosophy of Science*. London: D. Reidel Publishing Company.

Harragan, K.R. (1977) *Games Mother Never Taught You: Corporate Gamesmanship for Women*. New York: Warner Books.

Harre, R. (1978) 'Accounts, actions and meaning – the practice of participatory psychology', in M. Brenner, P. Marsh and M. Brenner (eds) *The Social Context of Method*. London: Croom Helm.

Harre, R. and Secord, P.F. (1972) *The Explanation of Social Behaviour*. Oxford: Blackwell.

Harris, R. (1987) *Power and Powerlessness in Industry: An Analysis of the Social Relations of Production*. London: Tavistock.

Harris (1992) 'The politics of evidence based medicine in the UK', *Policy and Politics*, 26 (1).

Hartmann, Heidi (1979) 'The unhappy marriage of Marxism and feminism: towards a more progressive union', *Capital and Class*, 8: 1–33.

HAY Consultants (1994) 'Differentiating management styles' used in training materials for client use only. London.

Hazen, M.A. (1994) Multiplicity and change in persons and organisations', *Journal of Organisational Change Management*, 7 (6): 72–81.

Hearn, J. (1992) 'Changing men and changing management: a review of issues and activities', *Women in Management Review*, 7 (1): 3–8.

Hearn, J. and Parkin, W. (1983) 'Gender and organisations: a selective review and critique of a neglected area', *Organization Studies*, 4 (3): 219–242.

Hearn, Jeff and Parkin, Wendy (1987) *'Sex at Work': The Power and the Paradox of Organisation Sexuality*. Brighton: Wheatsheaf Books.

Hearn, J., Sheppard, D.L., Tancred-Sheriff, P. and Burrell, G. (eds) (1989) *The Sexuality of Organization*. London: Sage.

Henderson, H. (1993) *Paradigms in Progress: Life beyond Economics*. London: Adamantine Press.

Hendricks, J.J. (1992) 'Women centred reality and rational legalism', *Administration and Society*, 23: 455–467.

Hennessey, P. (1996) *Muddling Through: Power, Politics and the Quality of Government in Postwar Britain*. London: Victor Gollanz.

Hennig, M. and Jardim, A. (1978) *The Managerial Woman*. London: Marion Boyars.

Herlin, H. (1984) 'Chef pa deltid – gar det? en interjuundersokning paper for FOA, FOA Report, May. Reported in Ressner, *Hidden From Hierarchies*.

Hirsh, W. and Jackson, C. (1990) 'Women into management: issues influencing the entry of women into management jobs', IMS Report, 158, University of Sussex: Institute of Manpower Studies.

Hiscock, J. and Pearson, M. (1996) 'Professional costs and invisible value in the community nursing market', *Journal of Interprofessional Care*, 10 (1): 23–31.

Hochschilds, A. (1983) *The Second Shift*. New York: Avon.

Hofstede, G. (1980) *Cultures Consequences*. London: Sage.

Hofstede, G. (1994) *Cultures and Organizations: The Successful Strategist Series*. London: Harper Collins.

Hoggett, P. (1990) *Modernisation, Political Strategy and the Welfare State: An Organisational Perspective*. Bristol: School of Advanced Urban Studies.

Hoggett, P. (1991) 'A new management with public sector', *Policy and Politics*, 19 (4): 247–256.

Hoggett, P. (1992) *Partisans in an Uncertain World: The Psychoanalysis of Engagement*. London: Free Association Books.

Hoggett, P. (1994) *The Future of Civic Forms of Organization*. Demos Paper no. 4: London: Demos.

Holden, B. (1997) Personal communication.

Hollis, P. (1997) *Jenny Lee: A Life*. Oxford: Oxford University Press.

Hollway, W. (1982) 'Identity and gender difference in adult social relations'. Unpublished PhD thesis, University of London.

Hollway, W. (1984) 'Gender differences and the production of subjectivity', in J. Henriques, W. Hollway, C. Urwin, C. Venn and V. Walkerdine, *Changing the Subject: Psychology, Social Relations and Subjectivity*. London: Methuen.

Hollway, W. (1989) *Subjectivity and Method in Psychology: Gender, Meaning and Science*. London: Sage.

Hollway, W. (1991) *Work, Psychology and Organisation*. London: Sage.

Hollway, W. and Mukuras, L. (1994) 'Women managers in the Tanzanian Civil Service', in N.J. Adler and D.N. Izraeli (eds) *Competitive Frontiers: Women Managers and Global Economies*. London: Blackwell.

Holter, H. (1984) *The Reorganised Patriarchy: Some Sociological Characteristics*. Stencil.

Holter Ingham, M. (1985) *Men*. London: Century Publishing.

Hood, C. (1991) 'A public management for all seasons?', *Public Administration*, 69: 3–19.

hooks, bell (1987) *Ain't I a Woman?* London: Pluto.

hooks, bell (1989) *Talking Back: Thinking Feminist, Thinking Black*. London: Sheba Feminist Publishing.

Humphries, D. and Littlejohns, P. (1995) 'The development of multi-professional audit and clinical guidelines: their contribution to quality assurance and effectiveness in the NHS', *Journal of Inter-Professional Care*, 9 (3).

Hunter, D. (1991) 'Beware the New Hierarchies: From Hierarchies to Partnership'. Proceedings IHSM Conference November.

Hutt, R. (1985) *Chief Officer Profiles: Regional and District Nursing Officers*, IMS Report No. 105. Brighton: Institute of Manpower Studies.

Hutton, W. (1994) *The State We're In*. Jonathan Cape: London.

Huws, U. (1997) 'New dimension', *Red Pepper*, October: 26.

Iannello, K. (1992) *Decisions Without Hierarchy: Feminist Interventions in Organisational Theory and Practice*. New York: Routledge.

Institute of Personnel Management (1992) *Performance Management in the UK: An Analysis of the Issues*. London: IPM.

James, A. (1994) *Public Sector Organisation*. London: Pitman.

James, G. (1991) *Quality of Working Life and Total Quality Management*. Occasional Paper 50, November, ACAS Work Research Unit.

Jameson, F. (1991) *Postmodernism, or The Logic of Late Capitalism*. Durham, NC: Duke University Press.

Janeway, E. (1974) *Between Myth and Morning*. New York: William Morrow.

Jenkins, Kate, Caines, Karen and Jackson, Andrew (1988) *Improving Management in Government: The Next Steps* (The Ibbs Report). London: HMSO.

Jenson, J., Hagan, E. and Reddy, Ceallaigh (eds) (1988) *Feminisation of the Labour Force: Paradoxes*. Oxford: Polity Press.

Jewson, Nick and Mason, David (1986) 'The theory and practice of equal opportunities policies: liberal and radical approaches', *Sociological Review*, 34 (2), March.

Jones, K.B. (1993) *Compassionate Authority: Democracy and the Representation of Women*. London: Routledge.

Kahn, R.L. (1964) *Organisational Stress: Studies in Role Conflict and Ambiguity*. New York: Wiley.

Kalabadse, A.K. (1986) *The Politics of Management*. London: Gower.

Kandol, R. and Fullerton, J. (1994) *Managing the Mosaic: Diversity in Action*. London: IPD.

Kanter, R.M. (1977) *Men and Women of the Corporation*. New York: Basic Books.

Kanter, R.M. (1988) 'When a 1000 flowers bloom: structural, social and conditions for innovation in organisations', *Research in Organisation Behaviour*, 10.

Kanter, R.M. (1989) *When Giants Learn to Dance: Mastering the Challenge of Strategy, Management and Careers in the 1990s*. New York: Unwin.

Kanter, R.M. (1991) 'Championing change', *Harvard Business Review*, January–February: 119–130.

Kanter, R.M. (1995) 'Thriving locally in a global economy', *Harvard Business Review*, September–October: 151–163.

Kanter, R.M. and Eccles, R. (1992) 'Conclusion: Making network research relevant to practice', in N. Nohria and R. Eccles (eds) *Networks and Organisations: Structures, Forms and Actions*. Boston: Harvard Business School.

Katz, D. and Kahn, R.L. (1966) *The Social Psychology of Organisations*. New York: Wiley.

Katz, D. and Kahn, R.L. (1970) 'Open systems theory', in O. Grusky and G.A. Miller (eds) *The Sociology of Organisations: the Limits of Social Control*. New York: Random Books.

Kelly, A. (1996) 'The concept of specialist community nurse', *Journal of Advanced Nursing*, C4: 42–52.

Kelly, A. (1991) 'The enterprise culture and the welfare state: restructuring the management of health and social services', in G. Burrows (ed.) *Deciphering Enterprise Culture*. London: Routledge.

Kelly, G.A. (1955) *The Theory of Personality: The Psychology of Personal Constructs*. New York: Norton.

Kingston, W. (1995) 'Innovation or bureaucracy?', *Creativity and Innovation Management*, 4 (3): September.

Kirkpatrick, I. and Martinez Lucas, M. (1995) Introduction: The contract state and the future of public management, *Public Administration*, 74: 1–8.

Knights, D. and Willmott, H. (1985) 'Power and identity in theory and practice', *Sociological Review*, 33 (1): 22–46.

Knights, D. and Willmott, H. (1986) *Gender and the Labour Process*. Aldershot: Gower.

Konrad, A. (1990) 'Welcome to the women-friendly company', *Business Week*, 6 August: 48–55.

Korbik, K. and Rosin, H.M. (1991) 'Corporate Flight of Women Managers: Moving from Fiction to Fact'. Paper presented at the Western Academy of Management. Santa Barbara, California, USA. March.

Kotter, J.P. (1988) *The Leadership Factor*. New York: Free Press.

Kotter, J.P. (1990) *How Leadership Differs from Management*. New York: Free Press.

Kotter, J.P. (1995) 'Leading change: why transformation efforts fail', *Harvard Business Review*, March/April: 59–68.

Kuhn, T.S. (1970) *The Structure of Scientific Revolution* (2nd edition). Chicago, IL: University of Chicago Press.

Lacy, W.B., Bokemeier, J.L. and Shepard, J.M. (1983) 'Job attributes preferences and work commitment for men and women in the United States', *Personnel Psychology*, 36: 315–329.

Landry, C. et al. (1985) *What a Way to Run a Railroad: An Analysis of Radical Failure*. London: Comedia.

Larkin, T.J. and Larkin, S. (1996) 'Reaching and changing frontline employees', *Harvard Business Review*, May/June.

Larrabee, M.J. (1993) *An Ethic of Care*. New York: Routledge.

Lauer, R.H. and Handel, W.H. (1977) *Social Psychology: The Theory and Application of Symbolic Interactionism*. Boston, MA: Houghton Mifflin.

Lawrence, E. (1993) *Developing Feminist Perspectives on the Study of Women's Trade Unionism*. Women's Studies Conference (UK), Northampton, July.

Lees, S. and Scott, M. (1990) 'Equal opportunities rhetoric or action?' *Gender and Education*, 2 (3): Autumn.

Lefton, R. (1989) 'US and Britain differ in view of managers', *The Independent*, 4 July.

Lenin, V.I. (1961) *Collected Works Vol VIII*. London: Lawrence and Wishart, 335–356.

Leonard, P. (1984) *Personality and Ideology: Towards a Materialist Understanding of the Individual*. London: Macmillan.

Liff, S. and Dale, K. (1994) 'Formal opportunity, informal barriers, black women managers within local government', *Work, Employment and Society*, 8 (2): 177–198.

Light, D. (1995) 'Homoeconomicus: Escaping the traps of managed competition', *European Journal of Public Health*, 5 (3): 145–154.

Likert, R. (1961) *New Patterns of Management*. New York: McGraw Hill.

Likert, R. (1976) *New Ways of Managing Conflict*. New York: McGraw Hill.

Lipsky, M. (1980) *Street Level Bureaucracy: Dilemmas of the Individual in Public Services*. New York: Russell Sage.

Local Government Chronicle (1993) 'Survey of Women in Local Government', *Local Government Chronicle*: London.

Local Government Management Board (1997) *Local Government Best Value Partnership*. Luton: LGMB.

Local Government Management Board (1993) *Equal Opportunities in Local Government*. Luton: LGMB.

Local Government Operational Research Unit (1982) *Women in Local Government: The Neglected Resource*. London: LGORU.

Loden, M. (1985) *Feminine Qualities of Leadership and How to Succeed in Business Without Being One of the Boys*. New York: Time Books.

Lunt, N., Mannion, R. and Smith, P. (1996) 'Economic discourse and the market: the case for community care', *Public Administration*, 74, Autumn: 370–391.

Lyall, J. (1995) 'Stress in the health service', *Health Service Journal*, 18 May.

Macalpine, M. and Marsh, S. (1995) *Our Own Capabilities: Clinical Nurse Managers Thinking: A Strategic View*. London: Kings Fund.

Macalpine, M. and Marsh, S. (1996) 'Negotiating a "borderland": nursing, gender and management'. Paper to Conference, Nottingham. marion.macalpine@posnet.co.uk

McCall and Symons (1969) *Issues in Participant Observation: A Textbook Reader*. Reading, MA: Addison-Wesley.

Maccoby, M. (1978) *The Gamesmen: The New Corporate Leaders*. New York: Simon Schuster.

Maccoby, E.E. and Jacklin, C.M. (1974) *The Psychology of Sex Differences.* Stanford, CA: Stanford University Press.

McCormack, I. (1992) 'A pattern for the future'. Paper to British Council Women's Conference, Managing Gender. Manchester.

McGregor, D. (1968) *Leadership and Motivation.* Cambridge, MA: MIT Press.

McGuire, S. (1998) 'Women who dare to break the mould', *The Guardian*, 21 January.

Machnzeck, A. and Wang, Q. (1996) 'Breaking the functional mind-set in process organisation', *Harvard Business Review*, September–October: 93–99.

Mackintosh, M. (1992) 'Partnership: issues of policy and negotiation', *Local Economy*, 7 (3): 210–224.

Mackintosh, M. (1997) 'Social Exclusion'. Paper to IDPM Conference, Manchester.

Maddock, S. (1993a) 'Women's frustration with, and influence on local government management in the UK', *Women in Management Review*, 8 (1): 3–9.

Maddock, S. (1993b) 'Barriers to women are barriers to local government', *Local Government Studies*, 19 (3).

Maddock, S. (1995) 'Is macho management back?', *Health Service Journal*, 105.

Maddock, S. (1995) 'Rhetoric and reality: the business case for equality and why it continues to be resisted', *Women in Management Review*, 10 (1): 14–20.

Maddock, S. and Morgan, G. (1998) 'Barriers to bureaucracy: beyond the market', *International Journal of Public Sector Management*. Autumn.

Maddock, S. and Neilson, E. (forthcoming) 'Community care, purchasing and management'.

Maddock, S. and Parkin, D. (1993) 'Gender cultures: women's choices and strategies at work', *Women in Management Review*, 8 (2): 3–10.

Maddock, S. and Parkin, D. (1994) 'Gender cultures: how they affect men and women at work', in M. Davidson and R. Burke (eds), *Women in Management: Current Research Issues.* London: Paul Chapman.

Maddock, S. and Parkin, D. (1994) *Barriers to Women Hospital Doctors.* Manchester: North West Regional Health Authority.

Magretta, J. (1997) 'Growth through global sustainability: an interview with Monsanto's CEO, Robert Shapiro', *Harvard Business Review*, January–February: 79–88.

Maguire, P. (1984) *Women in Development: An Alternative Analysis.* Amherst, MA: Center for International Education.

Maguire, P. (1987) *Doing Feminist Research.* Amherst, MA: Center for International Education.

Mainguy, W. (1988) 'Leadership qualities: Europe's CEOs are surveyed by Management Centre Europe', *European Management Journal*, 6 (3).

Majchrzak, A. and Quanwei Wang (1996) *Harvard Business Review*, September–October.

Management and Personnel Office (1984) *Equal Opportunities for Women in the Civil Service: Programme for Action.* London: HMSO.

Mangham, I.L. (1990) 'Managing as a performing art', *British Journal of Management*, 1: 105–155.

Marshall, J. (1984) *Women Managers: Travellers in a Male World.* Chichester: Wiley.

Marshall, J. (1986) 'The experiences of women managers', in S. Wilkinson (ed.) *Feminist Social Psychology.* Milton Keynes: Open University Press.

Marshall, J. (1991a) 'Senior women managers who leave employment', *Women in Management Review*, 6 (3): 4–9.

Marshall, J. (1991b) 'Patterns of occupational awareness as coping strategies for women managers', in S.E. Kahn and B.C. Long (eds) *Coping and Working Women: An Integration.* Montreal: McGill-Queen's University Press.

Marshall, J. (1992) 'Organisational cultures: attempting change often means more of the same', *Women in Organisation and Management* 3: 4–7.

Marshall, J. (1993) 'Viewing organisational communication from a feminist perspective', in S.A. Deetz (ed.), *Communication Yearbook*, 16. Newbury Park, CA: Sage, pp. 122–143.

Marshall, J. (1994a) 'Why women leave senior management jobs: my research approach and some initial findings', in M. Tantum (ed.), *Women in Management: The Second Wave*. London: Routledge.

Marshall, J. (1994b) 'Working as a broad member: some of the issues for women'. Paper to the Women's Careers Research Forum, European Women's Management Development Network, Sundridge Park Management Centre, Kent.

Maruta (1995) 'The changing role of top managers', *Harvard Business Review*, February–March: 86.

Maslow, A.H. (1970) *Motivation and Personality* (2nd edition). New York: Harper and Row.

Matheson, D. and Matheson, J. (1998) *The Smart Organisation*. Cambridge, MA: Harvard Business School Press.

Mayer, C.S. (1964) 'The interviewer and his environment', *Journal of Marketing Research*, 1: 24–31.

Mbigi, A. (1991) *Managing Diversity: The Spirit of African Management*. Berkhamstead: Ashridge Management College.

Merton, R.K. (1957) *Social Theory and Social Structure*. New York: Free Press of Glencoe.

Miles, R. and Snow, C. (1995) 'The new network firm: a spherical structure built on a human investment philosophy', *Organisational Dynamics*, 23 (4): 4–18.

Milkman, R. (1986) 'Women's history and the Sear's case', *Feminist Studies*, 12 (2): 375–400.

Mill, J.S. (1869) (reprinted 1929) *On the Subjection of Women*. London: Dent.

Millar, B. (1997) 'Human interest', *Health Services Journal*, 2 October.

Miller, E.J. (1976) *Task and Organisation*. London: Wiley.

Miller, E.J. (1989) 'Organising development and industrial democracy', in Roy McLennan (ed.) *Managing Organizational Change*. Englewood Cliffs, NJ: Prentice-Hall.

Miller, E.J. and Rice, A.K. (1967) *Systems of Organisation: Control of Task and Sentient Boundaries*. London: Tavistock.

Miller, J.B. (1974) *Towards a New Psychology of Women*. Boston: Beacon Press.

Miller, J.G. and Wheeler, K.G. (1992) 'Unravelling the mysteries of gender differences in intentions to leave the organisation', *Journal of Organisational Behaviour*, 13: 465–478.

Mills, A.J. (1988) 'Organization, gender and culture', *Organizational Studies*, 9 (3): 351–369.

Mills, A.J. (1989) 'Gender, sexuality and organization theory', in J. Hearn et al. *The Sexuality of Organization*. London: Sage.

Mills, C.W. (1961) *The Sociological Imagination*. New York: Grove Press.

Mintzberg, H. (1983) *Power in and around Organisations*. Englewood Cliffs, NJ: Prentice-Hall.

Mintzberg, H. (1979) *Mintzberg on Management*. New York: Macmillan.

Mintzberg, H. (1987) 'Crafting strategy', *Harvard Business Review*, July–August.

Mobley, W.H. (1982) *Employee Turnover: Causes, Consequences and Control*. Philippines: Addison-Wesley Publishing Company Inc.

Moir, A. and Jessell (1986) *Brain Sex*. London: Michael Joseph.

Moore, H. (1994) 'Feminist production of knowledge', *Feminist Review*, 47, Summer.

Moore, W.E. (1962) *The Conduct of the Corporation*. Random House Vintage.

Morgan, G. (1984) 'Opportunities arising from paradigm diversity', *Administration and Society*, 16: 306–327.

Morgan, G. (1986) *The Images of Organization*. London: Sage.

Morgan, G. and Sturdy, A. (1992) 'Organisational change and management discourse'. Modes of Organising Conference, University of Warwick.

Morgan, P. (1986) 'Marketable women', *Prospect*, May: 16–17.

Morley, L. (1993) 'Glass ceiling or iron cage'. Women in Academia. Unpublished.

Morrison, A.M. and Glinow, M.A. (1990) 'Women and minorities in management', *American Psychologist*, 45: 200–208.

Morrison, T. (1971) 'What black women think of women's lib', *New York Times*, 22 August.

NEDO/RIBA (1990) *Women Managers: The Untapped Resource*. London: Kogan Page.

Newman, J. (1993) 'Women, management and change', *Local Government Policy Making*, 20 (2): 38–43.

NHS Executive (1994) 'Developing NHS purchasing and GP fundholding: towards primary care led NH, EL(194) 79. Department of Health.

NHS Executive, South Thames (1995) 'Evaluation of Nurse Practitioners' pilot projects'.

NHSME (1992) 'Implementing caring for people, EL(92) 13.

NHSME (1994) 'NHS Women's Unit Report on women managers in the National Health Service'.

NHSE Primary Care (1996) *The Future*. London: HMSO.

Nicholson, L. (ed.) (1992) *Feminism and Post-modernism*. London: Routledge.

Nieva, V.F. and Gutek, B.A. (1980) 'Sex effects on evaluation', *Academy of Management Review*, 5: 267–276.

Nohria, N. (1992) 'Is a network perspective a useful way of studying organisations?', in N. Nohria and R. Eccles (eds) *Networks and Organisations: Structures, Forms and Action*. Boston: Harvard Business School.

Nohria, N. and Eccles, R. (eds) (1992) *Networks and Organisations: Structures, Form and Action*, Boston: Harvard Business School.

Oakley, A. (1974) *The Sociology of Housework*. Oxford: Martin Robertson.

Oakley, A. (1983) 'Interviewing women: a contradiction in terms', in H. Roberts (ed.) *Doing Feminist Research*. London: Routledge.

Office of the Minister for the Civil Service (1988) *Equal Opportunities for Women in the Civil Service: A Progress Report*. Cabinet Office. London: HMSO.

Office of Public Management (1994) *Managing Beyond Gender*. Report. London: Office of Public Management.

O'Leary, V.E. (1974) 'Some attitudinal barriers to occupational aspirations in women', *Psychological Bulletin*, 81: 809–26.

Oliver, C. (1992) 'The antecents of the institutionalisation', *Organisation Studies*, 63 (4): 563–558.

Osborne, D. and Gaebler, T. (1992) *Reinventing Government: How the Entrepreneurial Spirit is Transforming the Public Sector*. New York: Addison Wesley.

Ouchi, W. (1980) 'Markets, bureaucracies and clans', *Admin. Science Quarterly*, 25: 129–141.

Ouchi, W.A. (1981) *Theory Z, How American Business Can Meet the Japanese Challenge*. Reading, MA: Addison Wesley.

Parkin, D. (1992) *Women's Units at a Time of Change*. Work and Gender Research Unit, Occasional Papers No. 5, University of Bradford.

Parkin, D. (1994) Personal communication.

Parsons, T. (1951) *The Social System*. New York: Free Press.

Pateman, Carole (1988) *The Sexual Contract*. Policy Press: Oxford.

Pedler, M., Burgoyne, J. and Boydell, T. (1991) *The Learning Company*. London: McGraw-Hill.

Peters, T.J. (1988) *Thriving on Chaos*. New York: Alfred A. Knopf.

Peters, Thomas J. and Waterman Jr, Robert H. (1982) *In Search of Excellence*. New York: Harper and Row.

Peters, T.J. and Austin, N. (1985) *A Passion for Excellence*. New York: Random House.

Pettigrew, A.M. (1979) 'Study of organisational cultures', *Admin. Science Quarterly*, 24.

Pettigrew, A.M. (1990) 'Corporate culture management', in D. Wilson and R. Rosenfeld *Managing Organisations*. London: McGraw-Hill.

Pettigrew. A. and Whipp, R. (1991) *Managing Change for Competitive Success*. Oxford: Blackwell.

Pettigrew, A.M. and Whipp, R. (1993) *Managing Change for Competitive Levels*. Oxford: Basil Blackwell.

Phillips, A. (1979) 'The new feminism', *The Guardian*, 20 January.

Philllips, A. (1998) 'Been there, done that', *The Guardian*, 20 Janaury.

Policy Studies Institute (1984) *Black and White in Britain*. London: PSI.

Pollert, A. (1981) *Girls, Wives, Factory Blues*. London: Macmillan.

Pollert, A. (1988) *The Flexible Firm: A Model in Search of Reality and a Policy in Search of Practice*. Warwick Working Papers in Industrial Relations no. 19, Coventry.

Pollitt, C. (1990) *Managerialism and the Public Services: The Anglo American Experience*. Oxford: Blackwell.

Poplewitz (1984) *Paradigm and Ideology in Educational Research*. New York: Falmer Press.

Popper, K. (1959) *The Logic of Scientific Discovery*. New York: Basic Books.

Potter, C. (1989) 'What is culture and can it be useful for organisational change agents?', *Leadership and Organisational Development Journal*, 10 (3): 17–25.

Powell, G.N. (1988) *Women and Men in Management*. Newbury Park, LA: Sage.

Powell, W. (1991) 'Neither markets nor hierarchy, network forms of organisation', in G. Thompson et al. (eds) *Markets, Hierarchies and Networks*. London: Sage, pp. 265–276.

Poxton, R. (1995) *Joint Commissioning*. London: Kings Fund.

Pringle, Rosemary (1983) *Gender at Work*. Sydney: George Allen and Unwin.

Pringle, Rosemary (1988) *Secretaries Talk: Sexuality, Power and Work*. London: Verso.

Procter, J. and Jackson, C. (1992) *Women Managers in the NHS: A Celebration of Success*. London: National Health Service Executive.

Procter, J. and Jackson, C. (1993) 'Senior women managers: a process of change in the NHS'. Unpublished.

Quinn, J.B. (1980) *Strategies for Change: Logical Incrementalism*. Homewood, IL: Irwin.

Rakow, L.F. (1986) 'Rethinking gender research in communications', *Journal of Communication*, 365: 11–21.

Reason, P. and Marshall, J. (1987) 'Research is a personal process', in D. Bond and V. Griffin (eds) *Appreciating Adult Learning*. London: Kogan Page.

Reason, P. and Rowan, J. (eds) (1981) *Human Inquiry: A Sourcebook and New Paradigm Research*. New York: John Wiley.

Reed, M.I. (1988) 'The problem of human agency in organisational analysis', *Organisation Studies*, 9 (1): 33–46.

Reed, M. (1997) 'In praise of dualists and dualism: methodology agency and studies in organisation analysis', *Org. Studies*, 18 (1): 21–24.

Reger, R.K., Gustafson, C.T., Demasie, S.M. and Mullare, J. (1994) 'Reforming the organisation: why implementing role quality is easier said than done', *Academy of Management Review*, 19 (3): 565–584.

Ressner, U. (1979) *Hidden from Hierarchy: A Study of Women in Management.* Aldershot: Gower.

Ressner, U. (1987) *Hidden from Hierarchy: A Study of Women in Management.* Aldershot: Gower.

Rhodes, D. (1990) 'Theoretical perspectives of sexual difference', in D. Rhodes, *Theoretical Perspectives on Sexual Difference.* London: Wiley.

Rice, A.K. (1965) *Learning for Leadership.* London: Tavistock Publications.

Riley, P. (1983) 'A structuralist account of political context', *Admin. Science Quarterly*, 28: 414–437.

Roberts, H. (1981) *Doing Feminist Research.* London: Routledge.

Roethlisberger, F.J.H. and Dickson, W.J. (1939) *Management and the Worker.* Boston: Harvard University Press.

Roffey Park Management Agenda (1998) Roffey Park College: UK.

Roper, M. (1993) *Masculinity and the British Organisation: 1945 to the Present.* Milton Keynes: Open University Press.

Rosen, M. (1988) 'You asked for it', *Journal of Management Studies.*

Rosen, M. and Jerdee (1974) 'The influence of sex role stereotypes on evaluation of male and female supervisors', *Journal of Applied Psychology*, 57.

Rosenau, P.M. (1992) *Post-modernism and the Social Sciences: Insights, Inroads and Intrusion.* Princeton, NJ: Princeton University Press.

Rosener, J.B. (1990) 'Ways women lead', *Harvard Business Review*, November–December: 119–125.

Rosin, H.M. and Korabik, K. (1990) 'Corporate flight of women managers: moving from fiction to fact'. Santa Barbara Paper to the Western Academy of Management, March.

Ross, R. and Schneider, R. (1992) *From Equality to Diversity: A Business Case for Equal Opportunity.* London: Pitman.

Rotter, J.B. (1972) 'Generalised expectancies for internal versus external control of reinforcement', in J.B. Rotter et al. (eds), *Applications of a Social Learning Theory of Personality.* New York: Holt, Reinhart and Winston.

Rowbotham, S. (1973) *Women's Consciousness, Man's World.* Harmondsworth: Penguin.

Rowbotham, S. (1980) 'The trouble with patriarchy', *New Statesman*, 1 February.

Rowbotham, S. (1990) 'Working women's untold story', *Z Mag*, 2 April.

Royden, A.M. (1917) 'The future of the women's movement', in V. Gollanz (ed.), *The Making of the Women.* Oxford: G. Allen and Unwin.

Rubery, J. and Humphries, J. (1992) 'Women's employment in the 1980s'. Paper to European Network for Women's Employment.

Rukeyser, M. (1997) Publication in *The Face*: London.

Ryan, A. (1996) 'Doctor–nurse relations: a review of the literature', *Social Services in Health*, 2 (2): 93–106.

Ryle, G. (1949) *The Concept of Mind.* London: Hutchinson.

Sahdev, K. and Vinnicombe, S. (1997) 'Downsizing and survivor syndrome: a study of human resource directors' views on survivors'. Paper to the 13th European Group on Organization Conference, organizational responses to radical environmental changes. Budapest, 3–5 July.

Salaman, C.F. (1979) *Work Organisations: Resistance and Control.* New York: Longman.

Salaman, C.F. (1986) *Working.* London: Tavistock.

Salvage, J. (1991) 'Making the best use of nursing skills: managers and clinicians in partnership', *Journal of Management in Medicine*, 5: 54–59.

Sauser, W.I. and York, C.M. (1978) 'Sex differences in job satisfaction: a re-examination', *Psychology*, 31: 537–547.

Savage, W. (1986) *A Savage Enquiry: Who Controls Childbirth.* London: Virago.

Scase, R. and Gofee, R. (1989) *Reluctant Managers: Their Work and Lifestyles*. London: Unwin Hyman.

Schein, E.H. (1973) *Professional Education*. New York: McGraw Hill.

Schein, E.H. (1985) *Organisational Culture and Leadership: A Dynamic View*. San Francisco: Jossey-Bass.

Schein, E.H. (1988) 'Organisational socialisation and the profession of management', *Sloan Management Review*, 53 (classic reprint from 1969).

Schein, E.H. (1996) 'The culture of management: the key to its learning; *Sloan Management Review*, Autumn.

Schein, V.E. (1973) 'One relationship between sex-role stereotypes and requisite management characteristics', *Journal of Applied Psychology*, 57 (2): 95–100.

Schein, V.E. (1975) 'Relationships between sex-role stereotypes and requisite management characteristics among female managers', *Journal of Applied Psychology*, 60: 340–344.

Schein, V.E. (1978) 'Sex role stereotyping, ability and performance', *Personnel*, 4 (31): 259–268.

Schein, V.E. (1989) 'Sex role stereotyping and requisite management characteristics'. Paper on current research to Women in Management conference, Ontario, Canada.

Schein, V.E. (1993) 'The work/family interface', *Women in Management Review*, 8: 4.

Schein, V.E. and Mueller, R. (1992) 'Sex role stereotyping and requisite management characteristics: A cross cultural look', *Journal of Organisational Behaviour* 13: 439–447.

Schnoder, A. (1989) 'A model of managerial effectiveness', *Competence and Assessment*, May.

Schon, D.A. (1983) *The Reflective Practitioner: How Professionals Think in Action*. New York: Basic Books.

Schor (1996) *New Ways To Work Bulletin*. November. London.

Schumpeter, J.A. (1947) 'The creative impulse in economic history', *Journal of Economic History*.

Schutz, A. (1967) *The Phenomenology of the Social World*. Evanston: North Western University Press.

Schwartz, F.N. (1989) 'Management women and the new facts of life', *Harvard Business Review*.

Schwartz, F.N. (1991) In debate: 'Isn't it time we stopped talking about gender differences?', *Harvard Business Review*, January–February.

Segal, L. (1990) *Slow Motion: Changing Masculinities, Changing Men*. London: Virago.

Seivers, B. (1986) 'Beyond the surrogate of motivation', *Organisation Studies*, 7 (4).

Sekaran, V. (1990) 'Frontiers and new vistas', *Journal of Business Ethics*, 9: 3–4.

Seligman, M.E.P. (1975) *Helplessness*. San Francisco: Freeman.

Selznick, P. (1957) *Leadership in Administration*. New York: Harper Row.

Selznick, P. (1961) 'Critical decisions in organisation design', in A. Etziono (ed.), *Complex Organisations*. New York: Holt Reinhart.

Senge, P.M. (1990) *The Fifth Discipline*. London: Random House.

Senge, P.M., Keiser, Robert P., Ross, A. and Smith, C. (1994) *The Fifth Disciple Handbook*. London: Doubleday.

Shapiro, G. (1994) *Equality Driven Total Quality* for The European Union, Equal Opportunities Unit DG-V. CENTRIM: Brighton.

Sheppard, D. (1989) 'Organisations, power and sexuality: the image and self-image of women managers', in J. Hearn, D. Sheppard, P. Tancred-Sheriff and G. Burrell *The Sexuality of Organisation*. London: Sage.

Shiva, V. (1989) *Staying Alive: Women, Ecology and Development*. London: Zed Books.

Silver, J. (1987) 'The ideology of excellence: management and neo-Conservatism', *Studies in Political Economy*, 24, Autumn.

Silverman, D. (1970) *The Theory of Organisations*. London: Heinemann.

Slater, P. and Bennis, W. (1990) 'Democracy is inevitable', *Harvard Business Review*, September–October: 167–171.

Smircisch, L. (1983) 'Concepts of culture and organisation analysis', *Admin. Science Quarterly*, 28: 339–358.

Soros, G. (1997) 'Capital crimes', *The Guardian*.

Spencer, E. and Welchman, R. (1991) 'Twice as good to go half as far: experiences and aspirations of women managers in local government', *Social and Community Planning*.

Spender, D. (1980) *Man Made Language*. London: Routledge and Kegan Paul.

Spender, Dale (1982) *Women of Ideas: And What Men Have Done to Them*. London: Routledge and Kegan Paul.

Stacey, M. (1988) *The Sociology of Health and Healing*. London: Unwin Hyman.

Stacey, M. (1992) *Regulating British Medicine*. London: The General Medical Council.

Stein, L., Watts, D. and Howell, T. (1990) 'The doctor–nurse game revisited', *New England Journal of Medicine*, 322: 546–49.

Stewart, J. (1992) *The Rebuilding of Public Accountability*, in J. Stewart et al. (eds), *Accountability to the Public*. London: European Policy Forum.

Stewart, J., Greer, A. and Hoggett, P. (1995) *The Quango State: An Alternative Approach*. London: Commission for Local Democracy.

Stewart, J. and Ranson, S. (1988) 'Management in the public domain', *Public Money and Management*, 8 (2): 13–18.

Stocking, B. (1995) *Initiative and Interia in the NHS*. London: Nuffield Provincial Hospital Trust.

Stone, Isabella (1988) *Equal Opportunities in Local Authorities: Developing Effective Strategies for the Implementation of Policies for Women*. Equal Opportunities Commission. London: HMSO.

Strauss, A. (1987) *Qualitative Research for Social Scientists*. New York: Cambridge University Press.

Strauss, A. and Corbin, J. (1990) *Basics in Qualitative Research: Grounded Theory Procedures and Techniques*. London: Sage.

Stumpt, S.A. and Dawley, P.K. (1981) 'Predicting voluntary and involuntary turnover', *Academy of Management Journal*, 24 (1): 148–163.

Tallis, R. (1997) *Enemies of Hope: A Critique of Contemporary Pessimism*. London: Macmillan.

Tannen, D. (1992) *You Just Don't Understand*. London: Virago.

Taylor, F. (1947) *Scientific Management*. New York: Harper and Row.

Taylor, K.E. and Weiss, D.J. (1972) 'Prediction of individual job termination from measurements and biographical data', *Journal of Vocational Behaviour*, 2: 123–132.

Taylor, L. (1993) 'Developing an organisational strategy for equal opportunities', *Women in Management Review*, 8: (2).

Taylor, L., Steven, J. and Bogdan, R. (1984) *Introduction to Qualitative Research Methods: The Search for Meanings*. Chichester: John Wiley and Sons.

Thackray, R. (1998) 'It's staff who square the circle', *Independent on Sunday*, 2 August.

Thomas, M. (1994) 'What you need to know about: business process re-engineering', *Personnel Management*, 26 (1): 28–31.

Thompson, M. (1992) *Pay and Performance: The Employer Experience*. IMS Report no. 281, Sussex: Institute of Manpower Studies.

Thompson, P. and Ackroyd, S. (1995) 'All quiet on the workplay front', *Sociology*, 29 (4): 615–633.

Thompson, P. and McHugh, D. (1990) *Work Organisations: A Critical Introduction*. London: Macmillan.

Tichy, N.M. (1973) 'An analysis of clique formation and structures in organisations', *Admin. Science Quarterly*, 18: 194–208.

Tichy, N.M. and Devanna, M.A. (1986) *The Transformational Leader*. Chichester: John Wiley.

Tichy, N.M. and Ulrich, D. (1984) 'The leadership challenge: a call for the transformational leader', *Sloane Management Review*, 26: 59–68.

Tiefenbrun, I. (1993) ET Parker Lecture, Royal Society of the Arts, London, 27 March.

Tolson, Andrew (1977) *The Limits of Masculinity*. London: Tavistock.

Townley, B. (1994) *Reframing Human Resource Management: Power, Ethics and the Subject at Work*. London: Sage.

Toynbee, P. (1997) 'Yes, the old option is dead – and it is women you should be thanking', *The Independent*, 25 September.

Traynor, M. (1995) 'Job satisfaction and nurse morale in NHS', *Nursing Times*, 91 (26): 42–45.

Trompenaars, F. (1993) *Riding the Waves of Culture: Understanding Cultural Diversity in Business*. London: Nicholas Brealey.

Van De Ven, A.H. and Ashley, G. (1983) 'Mapping the field to create a dynamic perspective on organisation design and behaviour', in A.H. Van De Ven and W.F. Joyce (eds) *Perspectives on Organisation Design and Behaviour*. New York: John Wiley.

Van Mannen, J. and Barley, S.R. (1984) 'Occupational community: culture and control in organisations', *Research in Organisational Behaviour*, 6.

Van Strien, P.J. (1982) 'In search of an emancipatory social psychology' in P. Stringer (ed.) *Confronting Social Issues: Applications of Social Psychology*, Vol 2. London: Academic Press.

Vince, R. (1994) 'Everyday process for avoiding equality in local government'. SCEPSTA Conference, Bristol.

Vince, R. and Booth, C. (1996) 'Equality and organisational design'. Bristol: LGMB/Department of the Environment.

Vinnicombe, S. (1987) 'What exactly are the differences in male and female working styles?', *Women in Management Review*, 3 (1).

Viscusi, W.K. (1980) *Sex Differences in Worker Quitting: A Review of Economics and Statistics*, 62: 388–395.

Wainwright, H. and Elliot, D. (1982) *The Lucas Plan: A New Trade Unionism in the Making*. London: Allison and Busby.

Wajcman, Judy (1983) *Women in Control: Dilemmas of a Workers' Co-operative*. Milton Keynes: Open University Press.

Wajcman, Judy (1993) 'The management of gender relations'. Paper from the Industrial Relations Unit, University of Warwick.

Walby, S. (1986) *Patriarchy at Work*. Oxford: Polity.

Walby, S. (1990) *Theorizing Patriarchy*. Oxford: Basil Blackwell.

Walby, S., Greenwell, L., Mackay, L. and Soothill (1994) *Medicine and Nursing: Professions in a Changing Health Service*. London: Sage.

Walsh, K. (1995) *Public Services and Market Mechanisms: Competition, Contracting and the New Public Sector Management*. London: Macmillan.

Walters, N. (1997) *The New Feminism*. New York: Little Brown.

Webb, Jannette and Liff, Sonia (1988) 'Play the white man: the social construction of fairness and competition in equal opportunities policies', *Sociological Review*, 36 (3).

Weber, M. (1947) *The Theory of Social and Economic Organisation*. New York: Free Press.

Webster, B. (1985) 'A woman's issue, the impact of local authority cuts', *Local Government Studies*, March/April.

Weigert, A.J., Smith Teitge, J. and Teitge, D.W. (1986) *Society and Identity: Towards a Sociological Psychology*. New York: Cambridge University Press.

Weistein, N. (1997) 'Power, resources and science', *New Politics*, Winter.

West Midlands County Council (1985) 'Survey of women representatives in local government'. Unpublished report.

Wexler, P. (1983) *Critical Social Psychology*. Boston: Routledge and Kegan Paul.

Wheatley, M. (1992) *Leadership and the New Science*. San Francisco: Barrett-Koehler Publishers.

Wheedon, C. (1987) *Feminist Practice and Postmodernist Theory*. Oxford: Blackwell.

Wheeler, K.G. (1983) 'Comparison of self-efficacy and expectations on models of occupational preferences for college males and females', *Journal of Occupational Psychology*, 56 (1): 21–24.

White, B., Cox, C. and Cooper, C. (1993) *Women's Career Development: A Study of High flyers*. London: Blackwell.

Whyte, M.K. (1973) 'Bureaucracy and modernisation in China: the Maoist critique', *American Sociological Review*, April.

Wilkinson, H. (1994) *No Turning Back: Generations and Genderquake*. London: DEMOS.

Williams, A., Robins, T. and Sibbald, B. (1997) *Culture Differences Between Medicine and Nursing: Implications for Primary Care*. Manchester: NPCRDC.

Willmott, H. (1993) 'Strength is ignorance – slaving is freedom', *Journal of Management Quarterly*, 30 (4): 515–552.

Willmott, H. (1995) '"The odd couple": re-engineering processes: management union related new technology', *Work and Employment*, 10 (2): 89–99.

Wistow, G. (1982) 'Collaboration between health and local authorities: why is it necessary?', *Social Policy and Administration*, 16: 62.

Wistow, G. (1990) *Community Care Planning: A Review of Past Experiences and Future Imperatives*. London: Department of Health.

Wistow, G. (1994) *Social Care in the Mixed Economy*. Buckingham: Open University Press.

Wistow, G. (1994) 'Community care future: inter-agency relationships: stability or continuing change?', in Titterton (ed.) *Caring for People in the Community: The New Welfare*. London: Jessica Kingsley.

Wistow, G. (1995) *Local Government and the NHS: The New Agenda*. Luton: Local Government Management Board.

Wistow, G., Knapp, M., Hardy and Allen, C. (1992) 'From providing to enabling: local authorities and the mixed economy of social care', *Public Admin.*, 70 (1): 25–45.

Witz, A. and Savage, M. (1992) 'The gender of organisations', in A. Witz and M. Savage (eds) *Gender and Bureaucracy*. Oxford: Blackwell.

Wolffe, J. (1977) 'Women in organizations', in S. Clegg and D. Dunkerley (eds) *Critical Issues in Organizations*. London: Routledge and Kegan Paul.

Wollstonecraft, M. (1792) (reprinted 1953) *The Vindication of the Rights of Women*. Harmondsworth: Penguin.

Wood, D. and Spacey, B. (1991) 'Towards a comprehensive theory of collaboration', *Journal of Applied Behavioural Science*, 27 (2): 139–162.

Wood, Stephen (ed.) (1989) *The Transformation of Work*. London: Unwin Hyman.

Worsley, M. (1996) Personal communication for ERSC study report on management innovation, NHS.

Young, K. (1996) 'Reinventing local government? Some evidence reassessed', *Public Administration*, 74: 347–367.

Index